Writing
DOS Device Drivers
in
C

Phillip M. Adams
Chairman
Department of Computer Science
Nova University, Ft. Lauderdale, Florida

Clovis L. Tondo
International Business Machines Corporation

Department of Computer Science
Nova University, Ft. Lauderdale, Florida

PRENTICE HALL, Englewood Cliffs, New Jersey 07632

This book was typeset by the authors using LATEX and PCTEX and it was printed with the Chelgraph IBX typesetter by TYPE 2000, 16 Madrona Avenue, Mill Valley, CA 94941.

Cover illustration provided courtesy of Image Bank.
Cover design by Wanda Lubelska.

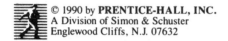 © 1990 by **PRENTICE-HALL, INC.**
A Division of Simon & Schuster
Englewood Cliffs, N.J. 07632

The publisher offers discounts on this book when ordered in bulk quantities. For more information, write:
    Special Sales/College Marketing
    Prentice-Hall, Inc.
    College Technical and Reference Division
    Englewood Cliffs, NJ 07632

Printed in the United States of America

10 9 8 7 6 5 4 3

For information about our audio products, write us at:
Newbridge Book Clubs, 3000 Cindel Drive, Delran, NJ 08370

ISBN 0-13-970864-2

Prentice-Hall International (UK) Limited, *London*
Prentice-Hall of Australia Pty. Limited, *Sydney*
Prentice-Hall Canada Inc., *Toronto*
Prentice-Hall Hispanoamericana, S.A., *Mexico*
Prentice-Hall of India Private Limited, *New Delhi*
Prentice-Hall of Japan, Inc., *Tokyo*
Simon & Schuster Asia Pte. Ltd., *Singapore*
Editora Prentice-Hall do Brasil, Ltda., *Rio de Janeiro*

Contents

Foreword

DOS is the most widely used operating system in the world, running on tens of millions of personal computers. The key to the success of DOS is the availability of tens of thousands of applications and the ability to run DOS on many different IBM and IBM compatible systems with thousands of types of I/O adapters and peripherals.

The mechanism in DOS that supports these thousands of I/O adapters and peripherals is the DOS device driver. The DOS device driver provides the insulating layer that allows the application developer to produce applications independent of specific adapter or peripheral characteristics. So, in addition to providing support for hardware, the device driver concept has enabled more rapid development of applications.

Dr. Adams and Dr. Tondo, using their experience working with DOS as part of the IBM Entry Systems Division team, have produced a book that greatly simplifies the designing, developing and testing of DOS device drivers.

I know that DOS device driver developers will welcome this book.

Mel Hallerman
Senior Technical Staff Member
IBM Entry Systems Division

Preface

This is a DOS device driver workbook. It contains the information necessary for you to perform your own experiments on DOS device drivers or to design and build your own special-purpose DOS device drivers.

The first part of the book introduces you to the vocabulary and tools used throughout the rest of the book. The second part develops the concept, architecture, and operational characteristics of a DOS device driver. This part provides a methodical, hands-on approach to developing DOS device drivers using a general DOS device driver template written in the C language. The third part of the book walks you through the design, implementation, and debug of a full-function write-once-read-many (WORM) device driver.

The current information on DOS device drivers requires a level of unnecessary complication; i.e., development in Intel 8086/88 assembler language. You will find the examples, programs, and DOS device drivers we provide here are written entirely in the C language. This high-level language approach to DOS device drivers allows you to focus on the problem the device driver is designed to solve rather than on the minute details of the hardware environment supporting the execution of DOS.

Device drivers provide an excellent means of realizing a user-defined abstraction (interface) in the DOS environment. This is a much more general statement than saying DOS device drivers provide a means of attaching both low- and high-speed devices to your computer system. We discuss the device driver interface in the third part of the book, which culminates with the development of a complete DOS device driver.

We think we have contributed something to your understanding of this fascinating topic. We have also attempted to make your life a little easier by providing all of the programs in this book on diskette for twenty dollars. To order, mail a check to:

Phillip M. Adams, D.Sc., Ph.D.
Nova University
3301 College Avenue
Ft. Lauderdale, Florida 33314

We thank the friends that helped us produce this book: Suann Adams, Anne Aldous, Lynn Christensen, Joe Dalezman, Greg Doench, Larry Holmstrom, Chris King, Phil Korn, Bruce Leung, Joan Magrabi, Steve Mackey, Darren Miclette, Sophie Papanikolaou, Freeman Rawson, Ed Simco, Carlos Tondo, John Wait, Yin Wong, and Eden Yount. Your assistance and unselfish donation of your time to this project made it possible. We sincerely thank you.

PMA
CLT

Part I

Introduction

Chapter 1

Introduction

Device drivers are an essential part of any modern-day operating system. They implement a standard interface to all devices attached to the computer system. In other words, device drivers provide a common mechanism for accessing hardware devices no matter how dissimilar the devices may be.

Personal computers that execute DOS (whether PC-DOS or MS-DOS) benefit from DOS device drivers. For example, DOS device drivers allow you to use the same DOS commands and utilities to access your files on a variety of devices such as diskettes, hard disks, CD-ROMs, and WORMs.

Without DOS device drivers each DOS application would need to support every device that is not supported by your standard DOS. Therefore, as every new device appears, each of us would have to buy a new version of our favorite DOS applications to obtain support for the new device!

As DOS has evolved over the years, significant change has occurred in the area of device drivers. Prior to DOS Version 2.0, the concept of a user-installed device driver did not exist — a situation that forced many devices to go unsupported in the early days of the personal computer.

DOS Version 2.0 provided many enhancements over previous versions. To people versed in UNIX, DOS Version 2.0 came as welcome relief, supporting many of the features found in UNIX. One of the most striking resemblances came in the area of device drivers. DOS Version 2.0 adopted the UNIX input/output philosophy of having both character and block devices. Each device class supports a small number of device class commands, such as READ and WRITE.

DOS Version 2.0 also adopted the concept of a device-specific control mechanism, referred to as the I/O ConTroL (IOCTL) interface. The IOCTL interface, or device command, allows applications to provide more specific control information to devices than is normally available through the standard READ and WRITE commands.

3

DOS device drivers seem to be able to do almost anything. Obviously, that is not the case. DOS device drivers perform a very specific function in a personal computer and are required to conform to a very rigorous structure and format. Details about the function, structure, and format of DOS device drivers are provided in the *DOS Technical Reference Manual.* We have provided a condensed version of it in the Appendix B.

1.1   Background

Writing device drivers is exciting and challenging. This book will teach you how to design and implement your own DOS device drivers. You will be provided with the knowledge and tools (programs) to properly analyze existing DOS device drivers as well as those of your own design.

As you go along, you will learn the details of the DOS device driver interface. And you will probably learn more about all aspects of your personal computer than by reading any other book. This is because device drivers reside between the DOS kernel and your personal computer's hardware. Therefore, the more you learn about the DOS device driver interface, the more functional your device driver will become. Likewise, the more you learn about the interface between your personal computer hardware and device driver, the more powerful your device driver will become.

With the knowledge and understanding you gain from reading this book, running the programs, and using the tools provided, you can begin to analyze, design, implement, and debug DOS device drivers of your choice.

1.2   Intended Audience

This book is intended for programmers who need to develop an understanding of DOS device drivers. The book is written more as a laboratory manual than a reference document. You should be able to read this book and work through the examples that we provide.

The examples in this book are written in the C programming language so a good understanding of the C programming language is necessary. Furthermore, to experiment with the examples presented in this book you will need access to a C compiler and an assembler for the personal computer. We have used TURBO C Version 2.0 and TURBO Assembler to create the examples.

Because DOS device drivers deal primarily with the characteristics of hardware devices attached to your personal computer, it will be helpful for you to have a working knowledge of your personal computer's hardware, including peripheral devices. Typically you will have a hardware technical reference manual that comes with your computer and describes it in great detail. You do not need to memorize the information in your manual or even understand all of it. But your understanding of DOS device drivers will come easily if you have been introduced to the topic.

Because we are going to discuss the interface between DOS and the hardware for your personal computer it will be helpful for you to have a working knowledge of DOS as well as your personal computer. The best source of information about DOS is the *DOS Technical Reference Manual.* Just as the hardware technical reference manual provides detailed information about your computer, the *DOS Technical Reference Manual* discusses DOS at a very detailed level. Once again, you do not need to commit the contents of the manual to memory, but you will have an easier time understanding sections of this book if you have been introduced to DOS concepts.

Be assured, though, that even if you have never read the hardware technical reference manual for you personal computer or the *DOS Technical Reference Manual,* you will develop a better understanding of your hardware and DOS by reading on! As you read each part of this book and experiment with the examples we provide, you will develop a better understanding of DOS and device drivers.

1.3 Intended Benefits

You will derive numerous benefits from reading and thinking about the contents of this book. For one, you will learn detailed information about DOS that is difficult to discover by yourself. In addition, the book presents the concepts of the hardware interface architecture in a way that is simple and easy to understand.

The most beneficial aspect of this book is that you can investigate the DOS device driver architecture and interface in a step-by-step manner by working through the examples presented. You can begin reading and experimenting right from the start. By the time you complete the book, you will have developed an understanding of device drivers as well as a complete set of operational tools designed to assist you in your future investigations of DOS device drivers.

1.4 Conventions Used

All the programs in this book are written in C. More specifically, all the programs in this book are written in TURBO C Version 2.0. Although TURBO C provides enhancements to the American National Standards Institute (ANSI) standard for the C programming language, we have attempted to conform to the ANSI standard in the programs presented. However, due to the nature of systems programs, specifically DOS device drivers, the direct register access feature of

TURBO C must be used.

The direct register access feature of TURBO C allows every register of the Intel processor to be accessed directly. Direct access is accomplished by using a set of pre-defined names that consist of an underscore followed by the capitalized form of the name of the register; i.e., _AX, _BX, etc.

This programming language feature can be very dangerous (error-prone). For this reason, we have limited direct register access to the sections of code that absolutely require its use, such as in the case of servicing interrupts.

Note that although we use this feature of TURBO C, you can achieve the same effect with any C compiler by writing assembler language programs to accomplish the functions performed through the direct register access feature of TURBO C. For example, the following TURBO C program statements:

```
_AX = 0xFFFF;
_BX = _CX;
```

can be written in assembler language as in the following code fragment:

```
mov     ax,0FFFFh
mov     bx,cx
```

which yields the same results.

In short, we selected the TURBO C programming language to reduce the complexity of the examples presented in this book while at the same time minimizing the cost of materials required to experiment with the examples you find here.

1.5   Overview of Contents

This book is organized in three parts. The first part, the one that you are reading now, is devoted to introductory information intended to steer you through the rest of this book.

Part II presents information about DOS device drivers. It attempts to present the information contained in the *DOS Technical Reference Manual*. The information is presented in terms of C programs and program segments that ultimately are combined into the DOS device driver template that you can use to develop your own DOS device drivers.

Part III expands your horizons. It attempts to solve a real-world problem by developing, from start to finish, a DOS device driver. We implement a WORM device driver.

Each chapter within each part summarizes the learning activities presented in the chapter. Each chapter also includes a number of important questions that you should be able to answer after reading the chapter.

Chapter 2

Fundamentals

The most difficult aspect of developing a DOS device driver in C is understanding how the compiler handles the segmented architecture of the Intel series of processors. This chapter describes the basics of the segmented architecture.

2.1 Intel 8086/8088 Architecture

The Intel 8086/8088 architecture is based on a segmented memory model and supports thirteen 16-bit registers: four segment registers, four general-purpose accumulators, two index registers, two pointer registers, and a flags register.

2.1.1 Memory Addressing

Each of the four 16-bit segment registers, which function somewhat like base registers, is designated for a specific segment: one for a code segment (CS), one for a data segment (DS), and one for a stack segment (SS) with an extra segment (ES) register designated for data movement.

The processor uses two steps to calculate a memory address. First, it selects the appropriate segment register and shifts the contents of the register four positions to the left. The criteria for selecting the segment register are simple. If the memory access is due to an instruction reference, as in the case of a jump to a specified program location, then the processor selects the CS register. If the memory access is due to an instruction's request for a memory operand, then the processor selects the DS register. And if the memory reference is a result of a stack operation, then it selects the SS register.

Second, the processor adds a segment offset to the left-shifted value of the selected segment register. This operation yields a 20-bit address, which can access up to one megabyte of memory.

2.1.2   General-Purpose and Index Registers

Each of the four 16-bit general-purpose accumulators AX, BX, CX, and DX can function as two 8-bit accumulators. This is done by designating the high portion (AH of AX) or the low portion (AL of AX) of the 16-bit accumulator.

The two 16-bit index registers are designated SI and DI. These registers are useful in developing indexed addresses in the manipulation of data tables.

Two additional 16-bit registers are designated as pointer registers. The base-pointer (BP) register is useful in implementing high-level languages that require activation records and recursive variable frame pointers. The stack-pointer (SP) register functions as both a hardware and a software stack pointer.

Finally, the Intel architecture supports a 16-bit FLAGS register, which maintains the condition codes from the previous instructions.

Note that by employing a high-level language approach to implement DOS device drivers much of this lower-level processor architecture detail is masked from you. This is very important because you will be able to spend more time contemplating the details of your algorithm and less time attempting to remember which register or instruction must be used to accomplish the task at hand.

Suffice it to say that if you conform to the philosophy presented in this book, you will not need to focus on the lower-level details of the processor's architecture. By following the examples presented throughout this book you will be able to develop your DOS device driver algorithms in C as if you were developing any other C program.

2.2   Segmentation and C Compiler Models

You will find a number of terms associated with a segmented memory model that you do not typically find when discussing a processor that supports a flat memory model. Because the personal computer architecture is based on a segmented memory model, we must define these terms and describe how they affect the compilers of high-level languages that generate code for the personal computer.

The first concept to grasp is that the entire address space of the personal computer — one million bytes — is not directly addressable without modifying one or more of the segment registers: CS, DS, SS, and ES. The processor is designed to address only 64 kilobytes of memory at a time. Each 64-kilobyte block of memory is referred to as one segment, from which we get the term segmented memory architecture. Consequently, it is important that compilers of high-level languages develop a uniform methodology for addressing memory.

Intel proposed the concept of various memory models that the compiler could use to generate code. In other words, Intel proposed a number of different ways in which memory addressing could be achieved on their processors, leaving you to instruct the compiler which form of memory addressing you would like your program to use.

Intel designated these various memory models as *small model*, *medium model*, *large model*, and *huge model*. Borland International introduced two other models in their TURBO C compiler; these are called *tiny model* and *compact model*. We will briefly discuss each of these memory models.

2.2.1   Tiny Model

Tiny model is the smallest of the memory models that the compiler can generate. All four segment registers (CS, DS, SS, and ES) are initialized to the same value. Therefore, you have an address space of only 64 kilobytes for your entire program including code, data, and local stack variables. This model uses near pointers — 16-bit values. Near pointers are also called offsets.

2.2.2   Small Model

Small model programs allow twice the addressable memory of *tiny model* programs. This is accomplished by having one segment allocated to the code and one segment allocated to the data. Therefore, the maximum size a *small model* program can be is 128 kilobytes of memory. This model uses near pointers for code references and near pointers for data references.

2.2.3   Medium Model

Medium model programs allow the code space of the program to be up to one megabyte of memory. The compiler accomplishes this by generating far pointers — 32-bit values — consisting of a 16-bit segment value and a 16-bit offset value for all instruction references. The data space in a *medium model* program is limited to one segment (64 kilobytes) as in the *small model*. This model uses far pointers for code references and near pointers for data references.

2.2.4   Compact Model

Compact model programs are the opposite of *medium model* programs. In other words, the code space is limited to one segment (64 kilobytes) of memory and the data is allowed to occupy up to one megabyte of memory. This model uses near pointers for code references and far pointers for data references.

2.2.5   Large Model

Large model programs use far pointers for both data and code references. This allows both the code and data to occupy up to the one-megabyte addressing limit of the processor.

2.2.6   Huge Model

Huge model is an extension of *large model*. *Huge model* allows more than one segment of statically allocated data to be present in the program. As with the *large model* programs, *huge model* programs employ far pointers in all cases.

2.3   A Closer Look at Tiny Model

A DOS device driver must conform to the structural architecture defined in the *DOS Technical Reference Manual*. You will learn more about this topic in the next section, but a couple of items must be discussed before we can proceed in this section.

A DOS device driver must be a .COM file. A .COM file is a *tiny model* program that does not declare a specific stack segment. Because TURBO C includes the stack segment within the data segment of the program, it is possible to transform a *tiny model* program's .EXE into a .COM file by using the EXE2BIN utility of DOS.

A DOS device driver must have a special device driver header located at address zero. This device driver header contains various data values and pointers.

The initialization routine of a DOS device driver is usually placed at the end of the device driver code. This allows the device driver to release the space required for the routine after the initialization process has completed.

The developer of a device driver must control the physical location and the order of various components of the DOS device driver. Obviously, this is an easy task in assembler language but not quite so easy in a high-level language such as C.

Finally, when you use a C compiler, it is important that you understand the assumptions the compiler makes when it compiles your code. For example, TURBO C assumes that when you link your compiled program, you will include the start-up module in the linking process. The start-up module is responsible for initializing the processor registers to a specified value and establishing the C run-time environment prior to calling the function that you have named `main`.

DOS device drivers have their own set of initialization criteria, criteria that in many ways violate that of the start-up routine in TURBO C. Therefore, during the development of the DOS device drivers in this book, we will not include the start-up routine, and you do not need to name any of your routines `main`.

2.4 Our First Tiny Model Program

The best way to understand what a *tiny model* program means is to create one, then inspect the output of the compiler. The following program, `first.c`, uses a number of features of the C programming language that we will use later in the DOS device driver examples.

```
/* - - - - - - - - - - - - - - - - - - - - - - - - - - - - - - -*/
/*                                                               */
/*   PROGRAM :         F i r s t                                 */
/*                                                               */
/*   REMARKS :         First is a program that is designed to be */
/*          compiled in TINY model by the TURBO C Version 2.0    */
/*          compiler.  Once compiled the assembler output is     */
/*          reviewed to identify the structure and problems that */
/*          will be encountered when developing a DOS device     */
/*          driver in this language.                             */
/*                                                               */
/* - - - - - - - - - - - - - - - - - - - - - - - - - - - - - - -*/

#include    <stdio.h>


/* - - - - - - - - - - - - - - - - - - - - - - - - - - - - - - -*/
/*                                                               */
/*      Global Data Required For This Program                    */
/*                                                               */
/* - - - - - - - - - - - - - - - - - - - - - - - - - - - - - - -*/

unsigned int    global_int;
unsigned char   global_byte;
```

```
/* - - - - - - - - - - - - - - - - - - - - - - - - - - - - - -*/
/*                                                             */
/* FUNCTION:        F u n c t i o n                            */
/*                                                             */
/* REMARKS :        Function is a function responsible for     */
/*        accessing the supplied parameters and assigning the  */
/*        global data variables to the current values of the   */
/*        parameters.                                          */
/*                                                             */
/* - - - - - - - - - - - - - - - - - - - - - - - - - - - - - -*/

Function (int param_int, char param_byte)
{
    global_int  = param_int;
    global_byte = param_byte;
}




/* - - - - - - - - - - - - - - - - - - - - - - - - - - - - - -*/
/*                                                             */
/* FUNCTION:        m a i n                                    */
/*                                                             */
/* REMARKS :   main is the main program function that is       */
/*      responsible for initializing its local data variables  */
/*      and then calling Function with them as parameters.     */
/*                                                             */
/* - - - - - - - - - - - - - - - - - - - - - - - - - - - - - -*/

void main (void)
{
    int     local_func_int;
    char    local_func_byte;

    local_func_int = 0;
    local_func_byte = 0;

    Function (local_func_int, local_func_byte);
}
```

The program `first.c` declares two global variables that are visible to the entire program. It contains a function `main` and another function `Function`, which has two formal parameters.

You will notice that even though `first.c` is a very small and simple C program, it performs the following types of operations:

- Global variable access

- Local (stack) variable access

- Parameter passing to a function

- Function parameter access

- Function invocation.

Each of the above operations is critical to the operation of a C program. Therefore, an understanding of these items is important in the development of DOS device drivers written in the C programming language.

`first.c` was compiled with TURBO C version 2.0. We used the following command to compile the program:

```
tcc -mt -y -M first.c
```

This command requests the TURBO C compiler to generate a *tiny model* program (`-mt`) that includes line number information (`-y`) and a link/load map (`-M`). The following is the link/load map created from this compilation:

```
Start   Stop    Length Name        Class

00000H  00659H  0065AH _TEXT       CODE
00660H  007E7H  00188H _DATA       DATA
007E8H  007EBH  00004H _EMUSEG     DATA
007ECH  007EDH  00002H _CRTSEG     DATA
007EEH  007EEH  00000H _CVTSEG     DATA
007EEH  007EEH  00000H _SCNSEG     DATA
007EEH  00837H  0004AH _BSS        BSS
00838H  00838H  00000H _BSSEND     STACK
```

Address	Publics by Name
0000:02D6	DGROUP@
0000:07CF	emws_adjust
0000:07D3	emws_BPsafe
0000:07CB	emws_control
0000:07D1	emws_fixSeg
0000:07B5	emws_initialSP
0000:06F5	emws_limitSP
0000:07C5	emws_nmiVector
0000:07C1	emws_saveVector
0000:07D5	emws_stamp
0000:07C9	emws_status
0000:07CD	emws_TOS
0000:07D9	emws_version
0000:02C0	_abort
0000:046F	_atexit
0000:063A	_brk
0000:06CF	_environ
0000:06DB	_errno
0000:0305	_exit
0000:02D8	_Function
0000:07EE	_global_byte
0000:07EF	_global_int
0000:02E9	_main
0000:0574	_malloc
0000:0648	_sbrk
0000:06DD	__8087
0000:06CB	__argc
0000:06CD	__argv
0000:07E6	__atexitcnt
0000:07F2	__atexittbl
0000:06ED	__brklvl
0000:06D1	__envLng
0000:06D3	__envseg
0000:06D5	__envSize
0000:0220	__exit
0000:07DC	__exitbuf
0000:07DE	__exitfopen
0000:07E0	__exitopen
0000:06E9	__heapbase
0000:07E2	__heaplen

```
0000:06F1    __heaptop
0000:06BB    __Int0Vector
0000:06BF    __Int4Vector
0000:06C3    __Int5Vector
0000:06C7    __Int6Vector
0000:06D9    __osmajor
0000:06DA    __osminor
0000:06D7    __psp
0000:07EE    __RealCvtVector
0000:0283    __restorezero
0000:07EE    __ScanTodVector
0000:033A    __setargv
0000:0425    __setenvp
0000:06DF    __StartTime
0000:07E4    __stklen
0000:06D9    __version
0000:05E2    ___brk
0000:06E5    ___brklvl
0000:0836    ___first
0000:06E3    ___heapbase
0000:06E7    ___heaptop
0000:0832    ___last
0000:0495    ___pull_free_block
0000:0834    ___rover
0000:0606    ___sbrk
```

Address	Publics by Value
0000:0220	__exit
0000:0283	__restorezero
0000:02C0	_abort
0000:02D6	DGROUP@
0000:02D8	_Function
0000:02E9	_main
0000:0305	_exit
0000:033A	__setargv
0000:0425	__setenvp
0000:046F	_atexit
0000:0495	___pull_free_block
0000:0574	_malloc
0000:05E2	___brk
0000:0606	___sbrk
0000:063A	_brk
0000:0648	_sbrk
0000:06BB	__Int0Vector
0000:06BF	__Int4Vector
0000:06C3	__Int5Vector
0000:06C7	__Int6Vector
0000:06CB	__argc
0000:06CD	__argv
0000:06CF	_environ
0000:06D1	__envLng
0000:06D3	__envseg
0000:06D5	__envSize
0000:06D7	__psp
0000:06D9	__version
0000:06D9	__osmajor
0000:06DA	__osminor
0000:06DB	_errno
0000:06DD	__8087
0000:06DF	__StartTime
0000:06E3	___heapbase
0000:06E5	___brklvl
0000:06E7	___heaptop
0000:06E9	__heapbase
0000:06ED	__brklvl
0000:06F1	__heaptop
0000:06F5	emws_limitSP

```
0000:07B5    emws_initialSP
0000:07C1    emws_saveVector
0000:07C5    emws_nmiVector
0000:07C9    emws_status
0000:07CB    emws_control
0000:07CD    emws_TOS
0000:07CF    emws_adjust
0000:07D1    emws_fixSeg
0000:07D3    emws_BPsafe
0000:07D5    emws_stamp
0000:07D9    emws_version
0000:07DC    __exitbuf
0000:07DE    __exitfopen
0000:07E0    __exitopen
0000:07E2    __heaplen
0000:07E4    __stklen
0000:07E6    __atexitcnt
0000:07EE    __ScanTodVector
0000:07EE    __RealCvtVector
0000:07EE    _global_byte
0000:07EF    _global_int
0000:07F2    __atexittbl
0000:0832    ___last
0000:0834    ___rover
0000:0836    ___first
```

```
Line numbers for first.obj(first.c) segment _TEXT

    41 0000:02D8    44 0000:02DB    45 0000:02E1    46 0000:02E7
    59 0000:02E9    64 0000:02F0    65 0000:02F2    67 0000:02F6
    68 0000:02FF
Program entry point at 0000:0100
Warning: no stack
```

You can see from this link/load map that the compiler includes a number
of functions and variables that are not present in the original source code. The
majority of these inclusions come directly from the start-up module that the
compiler links to your C programs.

The linker produces the message **Warning: no stack**. This is a normal
message for a *tiny model* program.

Now, let's analyze the structure of this simple C program. The following
lines from the link/load map indicate that the output from the compiler begins
with the code segment, **_TEXT**, which starts at hex location 0000 and continues
until hex location 0659 with a length of hex 065A.

```
Start    Stop    Length  Name       Class

00000H  00659H  0065AH  _TEXT      CODE
00660H  007E7H  00188H  _DATA      DATA
007E8H  007EBH  00004H  _EMUSEG    DATA
007ECH  007EDH  00002H  _CRTSEG    DATA
007EEH  007EEH  00000H  _CVTSEG    DATA
007EEH  007EEH  00000H  _SCNSEG    DATA
007EEH  00837H  0004AH  _BSS       BSS
00838H  00838H  00000H  _BSSEND    STACK
```

The code segment is followed by the data segment, _DATA. _DATA contains the
initialized data values for the program. `first.c` does not contain any initialized
global variables, but you will find that the C start-up module does.

The segment named _BSS is the segment containing the uninitialized global
variables. This is where the two global variables from `first.c` can be found.
Following the _BSS segment, you will find the _BSSEND segment, which identifies
where the stack can be placed without declaring a specific **STACK** segment.

From this brief analysis, you can see that a problem exists in the ordering
of the segments produced by the compiler. Specifically, the data must precede
the code in a DOS device driver. This particular topic is left for discussion in
Section 2.5.

A structural problem with the output from the compiler indicates the
likelihood of a number of problems with the more detailed aspects of the code and

data generated by the compiler as well. The only way to determine whether this statement is true is to have the compiler produce assembler language output, then inspect that output for instances that might conflict with the guidelines specified for DOS device drivers.

first.c must be recompiled with the options required to produce assembler language output. The following command is sufficient to accomplish this task:

```
tcc -mt -y -c -S first.c
```

This command requests TURBO C to generate a *tiny model* program (-mt) that includes line number information (-y), compile it only (-c), and produce an assembler language listing (-S). The assembler language listing will be in first.asm.

We edited first.asm to remove various debugging statements produced by the compiler, and we have reformatted portions of the assembler language program for readability.

```
_TEXT     segment byte public 'CODE'
DGROUP    group   _DATA,_BSS
          assume  cs:_TEXT,ds:DGROUP,ss:DGROUP
_TEXT     ends
_DATA     segment word public 'DATA'
d@        label   byte
d@w       label   word
_DATA     ends
_BSS      segment word public 'BSS'
b@        label   byte
b@w       label   word
_BSS      ends
_TEXT     segment byte public 'CODE'

;         Line #  41
_Function         proc    near
          push    bp
          mov     bp,sp
;         Line #  44
          mov     ax,word ptr [bp+4]
          mov     word ptr DGROUP:_global_int,ax
;         Line #  45
          mov     al,byte ptr [bp+6]
          mov     byte ptr DGROUP:_global_byte,al
@1:
;         Line #  46
          pop     bp
          ret
_Function         endp

;         Line #  59
_main     proc    near
          push    bp
          mov     bp,sp
          sub     sp,2
          push    si
;         Line #  64
          xor     si,si
;         Line #  65
          mov     byte ptr [bp-1],0
;         Line #  67
          push    word ptr [bp-1]
```

```
            push     si
            call     near ptr _Function
            pop      cx
            pop      cx
@2:
;           Line #   68
            pop      si
            mov      sp,bp
            pop      bp
            ret
_main       endp
_TEXT       ends


_BSS        segment  word public 'BSS'
_global_byte         label    byte
            db       1 dup (?)
_global_int          label    word
            db       2 dup (?)
_BSS        ends
_DATA       segment  word public 'DATA'
s@          label    byte
_DATA       ends
_TEXT       segment  byte public 'CODE'
_TEXT       ends
            public   _global_int
            public   _global_byte
            public   _Function
            public   _main
            end
```

You will notice that a group named DGROUP is defined as being the data segment, _DATA, followed by the uninitialized data segment _BSS. However, the code segment _TEXT is not contained in this group even though the program can grow only to a maximum size of one segment (64 kilobytes). Furthermore, you will see that all named variable references are preceded with the name of the group (DGROUP) to calculate correctly the offset of the variable within the program. However, this is not the case when references are made to locations within the code segment (_TEXT) as indicated by the call to _Function.

Although this might seem like a lot of double-talk, it really is important that you understand some basic concepts concerning just how the compiler is generating code from your C program. The main reason for taking you through this exercise is to demonstrate that the data segment must be relocated to the

beginning of the object file, as we will explain in the next section. Once this
has been accomplished, the references to the code segment will be incorrect
because the compiler assumes the code segment will always begin at location
zero. Therefore, we must take corrective action to resolve this problem as well.

2.5   Data First, Please

If we are to conform to the specification of a DOS device driver, we must change
the order of the segments generated by the compiler. In other words, the data
segment must be relocated to the beginning of the output file, and the code must
be moved to the end of the output file.

The following changes to the assembler output are sufficient to accomplish
the desired results:

```
DGROUP   group    _DATA,_BSS,_TEXT
         assume   ds:DGROUP,ss:DGROUP,cs:DGROUP
```

The changes are simple. First, the code segment (_TEXT) was included in the
data group (DGROUP). Second, the assembler is instructed that the code segment
register (CS) is assumed to be relative to the data group (DGROUP).

You can make these changes with your favorite editor. However, this type of
operation is prone to errors. That's why we developed a utility called arrange,
which performs these modifications.

arrange also modifies the code references to include the DGROUP prefix rather
than maintaining the compiler's assumption that the code segment always begins
at location zero. The source code for the arrange utility appears in Appendix C.

2.6   C Stack and Data

The stack a C program uses during execution is established by the start-up
module that is linked with the program's object module. Because the DOS
device driver is not linked with the C start-up module, some provision must be
made to support a stack during program execution. One of the best ways to
address this problem is to view it as an Interrupt Service Routine (ISR) that
must save all registers on entry and establish its own operating environment
every time it is executed.

We will establish a stack for program execution each time the DOS device
driver is executed. The stack size will be determined by the setup code contained
within the DOS device driver. Typically, a DOS device driver attempts to
minimize the usage of resident memory. Therefore, the amount of stack space
allocated from within a DOS device driver varies from a few hundred bytes to
as much as one kilobyte.

The stack size can be thought of as a very limited resource. It would be nice to understand just what type of operations require space on this stack. In C any time we make a function call, we use stack space to record the return address and the parameters being passed to the function. The stack is also used when a function declares any local variables. These variables are allocated on the stack unless we use the `static` keyword to promote them to a global allocation level.

Clearly, you do not want to attempt to allocate a local array of two thousand elements! The stack should be used for local variables, such as loop control variables, and any large allocations should be declared as global to the entire program. Remember, if you run out of stack space within a DOS device driver anything can happen!

2.7   The C Run-Time Libraries

DOS device drivers are not allowed to use DOS functions or services. The reason for this is that when a DOS device driver is executing, an application has already requested a specific DOS function or service to be performed. DOS is attempting to accomplish the specified DOS operation by invoking the appropriate DOS device driver. If that device driver were to request a DOS function or service to be performed, then DOS would have to be reentrant, which it is not. Therefore, DOS device drivers are not allowed to use any DOS functions or services.

Later in this book (Section 8.4) you will find that specific DOS functions can be used within a DOS device driver, but it is in your best interest right now to simply remember not to use any DOS services!

The C run-time libraries are comprised of many functions that perform a variety of useful and common operations. In general, C programmers attempt to use as many of these functions as possible to reduce development time and to improve standardization of their C code. There is one small problem with this philosophy when developing DOS device drivers in C.

The problem encountered in DOS device drivers written in C that use the supplied C run-time routines is that those routines might attempt to issue a DOS request. As mentioned above, this is not allowed because DOS is not a reentrant operating system. Therefore, the use of C run-time routines must be limited to those functions that do not require DOS intervention. Here is a short list of some of these routines:

- String functions (`strcpy`, ...)

- Memory movement (`memmove`, ...)

- Direct console I/O (`cprintf`, `cput`, ...)

As a general rule, the list of C run-time routines that you can use safely is provided with the documentation for your C compiler. You should be aware that this list will change from compiler to compiler. Our examples attempt to reduce any dependencies on the C run-time routines. However, the run-time routines that we use are safe routines that most compilers have available in their libraries.

2.8   Summary

Intel Architecture

- segment registers: CS, DS, SS, ES

- general-purpose registers: AX, BX, CX, DX

- index registers: SI, DI

C Compiler Models

- *tiny model*: it has one address space of 64 kilobytes and uses near pointers.

- *small model*: it has one segment for code and one segment for data. It uses near pointers.

- *medium model*: it has one segment for data and more than one segment for code. It uses near pointers for data and far pointers for code.

- *compact model*: it has more than one segment for data and one segment for code. It uses far pointers for data and near pointers for code.

- *large model*: it has more than one segment for code and more than one segment for data. It uses far pointers for both data and code references.

- *huge model*: it is an extension of *large model*. It uses far pointers for both data and code references.

Tiny Model Programs

- To compile a *tiny model* program and generate assembler language output use:

```
tcc -mt -y -c -S filename.c
```

- To relocate the data segment to the beginning of the output file, use:

```
arrange  cmds  input.asm  output.asm
```

where the utility takes `input.asm`, arranges it according to `cmds`, and produces `output.asm`

- The linker produces the message `Warning: no stack`. This is a normal message for a *tiny model* program.

C Run-Time Libraries

- DOS is not reentrant

- Use C run-time routines that do not require DOS intervention

2.9 Exercises

Exercise 2.1 List the registers available on the Intel 8086/8088 architecture.

Exercise 2.2 Explain segmented memory model. List and explain the different models.

Exercise 2.3 Explain the difference between near and far pointers.

Exercise 2.4 Compile `first.c` and generate assembler output.

Exercise 2.5 Use the `arrange` utility to move the data segment in front of the code segment. Compare the two `.asm` files.

Exercise 2.6 Find the list of library routines that are safe — i.e., that do not require DOS intervention — available with your C compiler.

Part II

DOS Device Drivers

Chapter 3

DOS Device Driver Fundamentals

It is difficult to develop DOS device drivers without an understanding of the operational characteristics of DOS. This chapter presents the most salient features of DOS as they relate to DOS device drivers.

DOS is an operating system that has a set of layered interfaces. Each of these interfaces has a specific function as well as a calling convention. The following is a list of the major functional interfaces in DOS:

- Application programming interface

- Device driver interface

- Basic input/output system (BIOS) interface

- Hardware device interface.

DOS device drivers interact with each of these functional interfaces in DOS. Therefore, it is important that you understand the functional capability as well as the calling convention of each of these interfaces. But before we discuss these interfaces in detail, it is worthwhile to spend a little time addressing the more abstract notion of software classification and how it relates to architected software interfaces.

3.1 Architected Software Interfaces

An interface represents the implementation of some abstract function or set of functions. An architected software interface has two major components. The first component is the set of functional abstractions accessible via the interface. For example, the notions concerning file management are abstractions. However, when implemented, these abstractions become the file management interface that allows us to create, access, and delete files.

The second component of an architected software interface is the standardized calling convention used to access the underlying functional abstractions. Although there is an infinite number of ways to invoke a function in a programming environment, architected software interfaces represent a single (standardized) method of invoking the underlying function.

The DOS interfaces that we discuss in subsequent sections represent both a select number of functions as well as a standardized method of invoking those functions.

You might be wondering what the advantages of an architected software interface really are. The following list represents a few of the more significant advantages derived from such an interface:

- Software layers

- Information hiding

- Reduction of complexity

- Functional flexibility.

3.1.1   Software Layers

The definition of an interface implies a layer of software functionality. Each layer, or interface, in DOS has a specific purpose. As we mentioned previously, there are four major functional interfaces in DOS.

The first of these interfaces deals with the services DOS provides to the application programs that execute in a DOS environment. These services, or operating system functions, are very abstract or hardware-independent. For example, an application can request that DOS create a file named `myfile`. There is nothing hardware-dependent about this type of operating system service. This service simply indicates the high level of abstraction associated with this particular layer of the operating system.

This is not meant to imply that an application program's request to open `myfile` will not cause some detailed hardware-dependent operations to occur. However, those hardware-dependent operations will occur only on the basis of a request from the application programming interface layer to hardware-dependent interface layers.

The number and content of the layers depend on the system architecture. But is it possible to determine the appropriateness of the selected system architecture? The answer is "Yes," and the factor used to determine the appropriateness is referred to as the "fan-out" of the interfaces.

In other words, we can view the system architecture as a triangle with the application program request for a DOS service located at the peak of the triangle (Figure 3.1). The DOS services manager receives and processes the DOS service request. Each DOS service issues subsequent requests to the DOS device drivers. The DOS device drivers, in turn, issue requests to the BIOS layer. Finally, the BIOS layer issues requests to the hardware itself.

The number of requests issued to subsequent layers in the system architecture as a result of a request from a higher layer's request is termed the "fan-out." The fan-out is visually depicted by the width of the base of the request triangle, as indicated in Figure 3.1.

Note that as the fan-out of the request triangle decreases, the overhead in the system increases. This is because when a layer makes a request to a subsequent layer in the system architecture, the request has to be encoded to conform to the calling convention of the subsequent layer. The subsequent layer must then decode the request in order to perform the operation. As the fan-out approaches one, the system approaches the state where it is doing nothing more than encoding and decoding interface requests.

Therefore, by obtaining the fan-out of each DOS interface, it is possible to determine the success of the system architecture relative to the application programs being executed.

3.1.2 Information Hiding

In the discussion of software layers in the previous section, it is easy to see that the application program making a request to open a file does not have to control the hard disk adapter that controls the disk drive that contains the file. The software layering approach allows each layer to "hide" specific details, or information, concerning its operation from other layers in the system.

3.1.3 Complexity Reduction

The ability to functionally decompose a complex software system into software layers or interfaces reduces the complexity of the overall system. This means that the system can be analyzed, component by component, without attempting to analyze the entire system at one time.

3.1.4 Functional Flexibility

In a complex system, the ability to change the implementation of a layer without altering the architected software interface provides a great deal of functional

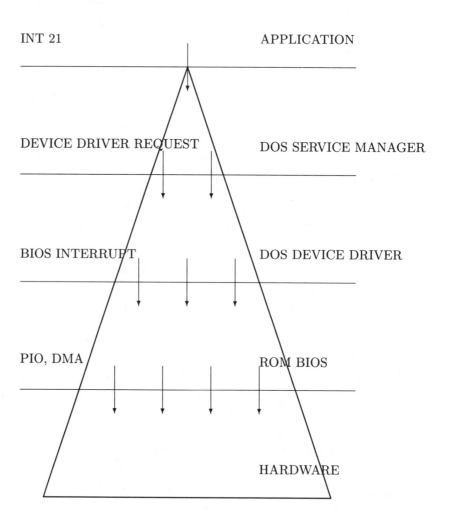

Figure 3.1: System Request Triangle

flexibility. For example, it is possible to completely rewrite a layer in the system without affecting application programs. Furthermore, it is possible to replace hardware components without affecting any software layers.

3.2 Application Programming Interface

The application programming interface (API) is the common name for DOS services or functions. In particular, API refers to the INT 21 services. The term INT 21 is used because that is the calling convention used to invoke the appropriate DOS service or function.

The Intel 808X class of processors provides a software interrupt capability. This capability is in the form of an interrupt instruction (INT) followed by the interrupt number desired. Therefore, an INT 21 is simply a software interrupt instruction that will cause the interrupt vector location to be accessed. By the way, the 21 in this discussion is hexadecimal 21, or 33 decimal.

The DOS API provides the application programmer with a host of useful services that would require untold hours to develop if the programmer were to reproduce them in the application. Even if the application programmer could reproduce these services in the application, many of the services would have to be continually updated to reflect the changes in DOS releases. For this reason, application programmers should attempt to use whatever features DOS provides, and then let the company that supplies them DOS worry about making the changes to those features!

As we mentioned above, the DOS API provides a host of useful features that are accessible through the INT 21 interface. This interface, or calling convention, requires the AH register of the CPU to indicate the DOS service you are requesting. Any additional information is provided via the other CPU registers.

The following program excerpt demonstrates how you can use one of the services available through the DOS API.

```
struct DOS_struct far *dos_ptr;

_AX = 0x5200;
geninterrupt (0x21);
dos_ptr = MK_FP (_ES, _BX);
```

Let's analyze what this program excerpt accomplishes.

First, the code declares dos_ptr to be a far pointer (a 32-bit pointer). This pointer will point to a structure of type DOS_struct. For this discussion it is not necessary to worry about the exact contents of the DOS_struct structure.

Second, the `AH` register (the high portion of `AX`) is loaded with hexadecimal 52 and the `AL` register (the low portion of `AX`) is loaded with zero. The hexadecimal 52 in `AH` tells DOS that we are requesting the DOS service that returns the far address of the DOS variables section.

Third, a software interrupt 21 instruction is executed. This is the instruction that causes DOS to receive control, and it is the avenue applications take when requesting services from the DOS API or service manager.

Finally, the DOS service is performed and DOS returns the desired address: register `ES` contains the segment and register `BX` contains the offset. The macro `MK_FP` takes the contents of these registers and builds a far pointer that is usable by C programs.

A complete list of services available through the DOS API is provided in Appendix D.

3.3   Device Driver Interface

The DOS device driver interface is similar to the application programming interface. However, a number of significant differences exist; we will discuss them in this section.

The DOS API is an interface between the application program and the DOS service manager. The device driver interface, on the other hand, is an interface between the DOS service manager and the BIOS or the hardware itself. This difference is not of great significance until you realize that DOS is not a reentrant operating system. Therefore, as the application's request progresses through the system, from DOS API to device driver interface to BIOS and finally to the hardware, there is less flexibility in what types of operations can be performed.

Another way to look at this is that when a request reaches the device driver interface, it is not possible for the device driver to make a request through the DOS API. In short, the closer the request comes to the hardware level, the less abstraction is available to the operating software servicing the request.

The device driver interface represents, in general, the entire set of DOS device drivers in the system. The best way to understand the device driver interface is to dissect it.

DOS device drivers have two major characteristics: first, their structure and, second, the device driver requests (commands) they respond to. The following sections address these characteristics.

3.3.1   DOS Device Driver Structure

A DOS device driver is a memory-image file, .COM, that contains all the logic required to realize the device attachment or implementation. Although the device driver file is a standard type of file, it does have one main difference. Typically, .COM files are required to start at hexadecimal location 100. This requirement allows DOS to create a 256-byte Program Segment Prefix (PSP) in memory prior to loading the .COM file itself. If the .COM file were to start at location zero, then when DOS loaded the file it would write over the PSP and the program would not be able to operate.

DOS device drivers do not start at location 0x100. Instead, DOS device drivers start at location zero. You might be wondering why DOS allows device drivers, but not for .COM files in general, to start at location zero. The answer is quite simple. DOS device drivers represent an extension to the DOS kernel. Therefore, DOS has allocated memory and specific internal data structures to manage the location and operation of each device driver in the system. Furthermore, once DOS device drivers are loaded, their memory addresses do not change. However, .COM files are constantly being loaded into memory, executed, and then removed from memory. There is no guarantee they will occupy the same memory locations if they are executed repeatedly.

For this reason .COM files require a more sophisticated program management facility than do DOS device drivers. This program management facility requires the construction and management of the PSP for each .COM file loaded in the system. But how does DOS manage the DOS device drivers? The following list indicates the topics we must discuss in order to answer this question.

- DOS device management

- DOS device driver headers

- DOS device driver classification

DOS Device Management

All DOS device drivers must have a DOS device driver header located at location zero. This should sound familiar after the discussion concerning the creation of PSPs at location zero for .COM files. The DOS device driver header is analogous to the PSP for .COM files. DOS uses the device driver header to link all device drivers into a singly-linked list of device drivers. Therefore, if we were to find the head of the list of DOS device drivers we should be able to see all of the devices in our system. More about this idea in a moment.

The DOS device driver header has a specific format. The following C structure describes that format.

```
struct  DDH_struct
{
        struct  DDH_struct  far *next_DDH;
        unsigned int        ddh_attribute;
        unsigned int        ddh_strategy;
        unsigned int        ddh_interrupt;
        unsigned char       ddh_name [8];
};
```

As you can see, the DOS device driver header contains five fields.

- The first field has the address of the next device driver.

- The second field has the attribute word.

- The third field has the offset for the **Strategy** function.

- The fourth field has the offset for the **Interrupt** function.

- The fifth field has the name field (character device driver) or the number of units (block device driver).

We will discuss each of these fields is more detail in the following paragraphs.

DOS uses the first field to link to the next device driver. Because DOS device drivers can be located anywhere in physical memory, this field must be a far pointer (segment:offset). The first field typically is set to the value of 0xFFFFFFFF to indicate it is the only DOS device driver present in this file. If this is not the case, then it is important that each device driver present be statically linked together with the final device driver header containing 0xFFFFFFFF in the first field.

The second field in the DOS device driver header is the control field, or the attribute word. This word informs DOS of the attributes, or capabilities, of this particular DOS device driver. Table 3.1 defines the bits in the attribute word.

The attribute word of the device driver header is a critical element of the device driver header. If this word is not properly initialized, your device driver may be unable to respond to the DOS device driver requests.

The most important bit in the attribute word is bit 15. This bit informs DOS that this particular device driver is either a character device driver or a block device driver. We will discuss the distinction in "DOS Device Driver Classification" on page 43. Suffice it to say that the distinction between these two types of DOS device drivers is a critical factor in their operation.

The lower nibble of the attribute word identifies whether this device driver will replace one of the internal device drivers that control the console or the clock. This feature of DOS device drivers allows users to replace an internal or

Bit #	Bit Value Description
Bit 0 (LSB)	0 - Not current standard input device 1 - Current standard input device
Bit 1	0 - Not current standard output device 1 - Current standard output device
Bit 2	0 - Not current NUL device 1 - Current NUL device
Bit 3	0 - Not current clock (CLOCK$) device 1 - Current clock (CLOCK$) device
Bit 4	0 - 1 - Reserved
Bit 5	0 - 1 - Reserved
Bit 6	0 - 1 - generic I/O ConTroL
Bit 7	0 - 1 - Reserved
Bit 8	0 - 1 - Reserved
Bit 9	0 - 1 - Reserved
Bit 10	0 - 1 - Reserved
Bit 11	0 - Does not support removable media 1 - Supports removable media
Bit 12	0 - 1 - Reserved
Bit 13	0 - IBM format block device 1 - Non-IBM format block device
Bit 14	0 - Does not support I/O ConTroL 1 - Supports I/O ConTroL
Bit 15 (MSB)	0 - Block device 1 - Character device

Table 3.1: Attribute Word

existing DOS device driver with one of their own choice. There is one exception. The NUL device cannot be reassigned even though the attribute word provides a NUL device bit.

Note that the I/O control string bit in the attribute word determines whether the device driver can process device driver-specific control strings. These strings, or commands, are referred to as IOCTL calls and are specific to the device driver.

The third and fourth fields in the DOS device driver header are simply offsets into the device driver. DOS uses these offsets whenever a request is sent to the device driver. The procedure for issuing a request to the device driver is described in the following paragraphs.

First, DOS initializes the ES and BX registers to the address of the request that is to be sent to the device driver. Next, DOS performs a far call to the Strategy function of the device driver. The Strategy function entry point (address) is built by taking the segment of the device driver header and combining it with the value of the strategy offset contained in the device driver header.

The device driver Strategy function is responsible for saving/queueing the request address found in the ES and BX registers. After completing this task, the Strategy function performs a far return to DOS. DOS immediately performs a far call to the Interrupt function of the device driver.

The device driver Interrupt function is responsible for obtaining the request address (queued up by the Strategy function), decoding the request, and performing the requested operation. On completion of the task, the Interrupt function performs a far return to DOS.

The fifth field in the device driver header is referred to as the name or unit field. If the device driver is a character device driver, then this field contains the eight-character name of the device. If, however, the device driver is a block device driver, then the first byte of the name field is set to the number of units the block device driver supports and the remaining bytes of the field are not used.

DOS Device Driver Headers

We have spent a considerable amount of time discussing the importance of the DOS device driver headers and their contents. Wouldn't it be nice if we had a program that could show us the real thing? Well, that is exactly what the next program will do.

Remember the example we used to discuss the INT 21 interface? We left undefined the type struct DOS_struct. It is now time to revisit that program fragment and provide the required data structure definitions.

We encounter one problem in implementing a program that will display the list of device driver headers: we don't know where the list of device driver headers begins. The program fragment on page 33 returns a far pointer to the following structure:

```
struct  DOS_struct
{
        unsigned char        reserved [34];
        struct    DDH_struct    far *ddh_ptr;
};
```

As you can see from the definition of DOS_struct, we have a far pointer to the beginning of the list of device driver headers, ddh_ptr. Therefore, all we have to do is obtain the pointer to the DOS_struct from DOS, then traverse the linked list and visit each device driver header, printing them along the way.

The following program implements this algorithm. The program is simple, but provides a lot of information.

```
/* - - - - - - - - - - - - - - - - - - - - - - - - - - - - - - -*/
/*                                                               */
/*  PROGRAM :    S h o w _ D D H                                 */
/*                                                               */
/*  REMARKS :    Show_DDH obtains the pointer to the beginning   */
/*        of the DOS device driver headers and then walks the    */
/*        list, printing the contents of each header.            */
/*                                                               */
/*  NOTES   :    tcc -M -mt -y show_ddh.c                        */
/*                                                               */
/* - - - - - - - - - - - - - - - - - - - - - - - - - - - - - -*/

#include    <dos.h>
#include    <conio.h>
#include    <stdio.h>
```

```c
/* - - - - - - - - - - - - - - - - - - - - - - - - - - - - - -*/
/*                                                             */
/*      DOS Device Driver Header Structure                     */
/*                                                             */
/* - - - - - - - - - - - - - - - - - - - - - - - - - - - - - -*/

struct  DDH_struct
{
    struct  DDH_struct  far *next_DDH;
    unsigned int        ddh_attribute;
    unsigned int        ddh_strategy;
    unsigned int        ddh_interrupt;
    unsigned char       ddh_name [8];
};


/* - - - - - - - - - - - - - - - - - - - - - - - - - - - - - -*/
/*                                                             */
/*      DOS Internal Variables Block Structure                 */
/*                                                             */
/* - - - - - - - - - - - - - - - - - - - - - - - - - - - - - -*/

struct  DOS_struct
{
    unsigned char       reserved [34];
    struct  DDH_struct  far *ddh_ptr;
};
```

```
/* - - - - - - - - - - - - - - - - - - - - - - - - - - - - - -*/
/*                                                             */
/*  FUNCTION:    P r i n t _ D D H                             */
/*                                                             */
/*  REMARKS :   Print_DDH displays the DOS Device Driver       */
/*        Headers (DDHs).  These are the headers               */
/*        described in the DOS Technical Reference             */
/*        Manual.  They contain such items as the type of      */
/*        device and the location of both the Strategy and the */
/*        Interrupt functions of the device driver.            */
/*                                                             */
/* - - - - - - - - - - - - - - - - - - - - - - - - - - - - - -*/

void Print_DDH (struct DDH_struct far *ddh_ptr)
{
    unsigned int        i;
    struct  DDH_struct  far *z;

    z = ddh_ptr;
    while (FP_OFF (z) != 0xFFFF)
    {
        clrscr ();
        printf ("\n\n\t\tDevice Driver Entry (%Fp)\n\n", z);
        printf ("\tNext Device Driver    : %Fp\n", z->next_DDH);
        printf ("\tDevice Attributes     : %04X\n",
                                        z->ddh_attribute);
        printf ("\tDevice Strategy Offset : %04X\n",
                                        z->ddh_strategy);
        printf ("\tDevice Interrupt Offset: %04X\n",
                                        z->ddh_interrupt);
        printf ("\tDevice Driver Name    : ");

        for (i = 0; i < 8; i++)
        {
            putchar (z->ddh_name [i]);
        }
        printf ("\n");
        z = z->next_DDH;
        getch ();
    }
}
```

```
/* - - - - - - - - - - - - - - - - - - - - - - - - - - - - - -*/
/*                                                              */
/*  FUNCTION:    m a i n                                        */
/*                                                              */
/*  REMARKS :   Main is the driver routine for the Show_DDH     */
/*         code.  It performs a DOS function 0x52 in order to   */
/*         obtain the pointer to the DOS variables structure.   */
/*         It then calls Print_DDH to display the DOS           */
/*         device driver headers.                               */
/*                                                              */
/* - - - - - - - - - - - - - - - - - - - - - - - - - - - - - -*/

void main (void)
{
    unsigned int        es_reg;
    unsigned int        bx_reg;
    struct  DOS_struct  far *dos_ptr;
    struct  DDH_struct  far *ddh_ptr;

    clrscr ();

    _AX = 0x5200;
    geninterrupt (0x21);
    bx_reg = _BX;
    es_reg = _ES;

    dos_ptr = MK_FP (es_reg, bx_reg);
    ddh_ptr = (struct DDH_struct far *) &dos_ptr->ddh_ptr;

    Print_DDH (ddh_ptr);
}
```

This program locates all device drivers in a DOS environment. It also identifies the characteristics and capabilities of each device driver.

It becomes a simple task for you to write the strategy and interrupt addresses on a piece of paper, execute the debug program of DOS, then set a break point at the addresses you have just written down. This simple technique allows you to analyze the exact sequence of operations and data flows associated with any, or all, the DOS device drivers installed in your system.

DOS Device Driver Classification

The previous two sections have given you a detailed look at the DOS device driver environment. You have been able to compile and execute the show_DDH program, which displays all the DOS device driver headers in your system. You are now ready to ask, and answer, some questions concerning the output of the show_DDH program.

The first question is "Why does the system have so many device drivers?" We can now answer that question. No device in DOS can be accessed unless it has a device driver associated with it. Therefore, all the communication devices (COM1, COM2, COM3, AUX, ...), as well as the print devices (LPT1, LPT2, LPT3, PRN, ...), must have an associated device driver header.

The next question is "Which of these device driver headers is the disk device driver header?" The answer to this question is a little more difficult because we must now understand the differences between character devices and block devices.

Character devices are designed to perform variable length I/O operations. What this means is that a character device may be able to operate on a single character or any number of characters. Character device drivers typically support devices such as printers, video displays, keyboards, local area networks, and communication devices.

Each character device in DOS has a name. This name is assigned by the device driver implementer and can be found in the device driver header. Each character device has one device driver header and one name. It is possible to load a character device driver that has the same name as a previously loaded character device driver. In this case, the character device driver loaded last becomes the operational device driver and the others will not be called by DOS.

Block devices are designed to perform fixed length I/O operations. Block devices drivers typically support disk and diskette drives. Unlike character device drivers, a block device driver in DOS does not have a name. The block device driver is identified by a drive letter (A, B, C, ...). Block device drivers can have units within them. In this way, a single block device driver can be responsible for, or control, more than one disk or diskette drive.

For example, a device driver named DRIVER1 can be responsible for four drives or units. Therefore, DRIVER1 will be assigned four drive letters and the user will access these physical drives through the assigned drive letters. But how are the drive letters and the physical drives or units associated?

The association between the drive units and the drive letters is determined by the position of the driver in the chain of device drivers. For example, if device driver DRIVER1 is the first block device driver in the list of device drivers, then drive letters A, B, C, and D are used to access the physical drives that DRIVER1 controls. If DRIVER2 is the second driver in the chain and it controls two physical drives, then drive letters E and F would be assigned to DRIVER2's physical drives or units. DOS allows 26 separate drive letters (A-Z) to be assigned in this manner.

3.3.2   DOS Device Driver Requests

In the latest version of DOS, the interface between DOS and the device driver supports nineteen commands. The following is a list of these DOS device driver requests (with command codes).

1. (00) Initialize

2. (01) Check Media

3. (02) Build BIOS Parameter Block (BPB)

4. (03) IOCTL Input

5. (04) Input From Device

6. (05) Input Without Waiting

7. (06) Obtain Input Status

8. (07) Flush Input Buffer

9. (08) Output To Device

10. (09) Output And Verify Data

11. (10) Obtain Output Status

12. (11) Flush Output Buffer

13. (12) IOCTL Output

14. (13) Open Device

15. (14) Close Device

16. (15) Check If Media Is Removable

17. (19) IOCTL To Device

18. (23) Get Logical Device Map

19. (24) Set Logical Device Map

Each of these DOS device driver requests or commands has a specific request format associated with it. However, a portion of the DOS device driver request is common to all nineteen. This common portion is referred to as the DOS device driver request header. The following C structure describes the contents of the common portion of the DOS device driver request header.

```
struct  REQ_struct
{
        unsigned char length;
        unsigned char unit;
        unsigned char command;
        unsigned int  status;
        unsigned char reserved [8];
};
```

The DOS device driver request header, `REQ_struct`, contains five fields. The first field is the length, in bytes, of the request. The common portion of the request is always 13 bytes in length: three `unsigned char` (three bytes), one `unsigned int` (two bytes), and eight `unsigned char` (eight bytes).

The second field in `REQ_struct` is the unit. This field is used for accessing specific units of a block device driver. Clearly, a character device driver does not require this field because there is only one character device driver per device driver header. However, a block device driver must use the unit field to select the appropriate portion of code to execute in order to control the specified physical device (unit).

The third field in `REQ_struct` is the DOS device driver command. The list on page 44 identifies (in parentheses) the value used in this field for the current DOS device driver command. The device driver decodes this field and performs the appropriate action.

The fourth field in `REQ_struct` is the return status word. This field indicates the result of the requested DOS command. The high-order bit of the status word indicates whether an error occurred. If an error occurred, then the low-order byte of the status word contains one of the following error codes. (See `dos_dd.h` in Appendix F.)

```
#define  WRITE_PROTECT 0x00  /* Write Protect Violation  */
#define  UNKNOWN_UNIT  0x01  /* Unit Not Known By Driver */
#define  NOT_READY     0x02  /* Device Is Not Ready      */
#define  UNKNOWN_CMD   0x03  /* Unknown Device Command   */
#define  CRC_ERROR     0x04  /* Device CRC Error         */
#define  BAD_REQ_LEN   0x05  /* Bad Drive Req Struct Len */
#define  SEEK_ERROR    0x06  /* Device Seek Error        */
#define  UNKNOWN_MEDIA 0x07  /* Unknown Media In Drive   */
```

```
#define  NOT_FOUND     0x08  /* Sector Not Found        */
#define  OUT_OF_PAPER  0x09  /* Printer Out Of Paper    */
#define  WRITE_FAULT   0x0A  /* Device Write Fault      */
#define  READ_FAULT    0x0B  /* Device Read Fault       */
#define  GENERAL_FAIL  0x0C  /* General Device Failure  */
```

Bit 7 of the status word indicates the operation is complete, and bit 8 indicates the device is still busy.

The fifth field is the reserved portion of REQ_struct. Following the reserved portion of REQ_struct is the variable portion of the data that is required for each of the commands. For more information about the format and content of the variable portion of the DOS device driver commands, refer to Appendix B and dos_dd.h in Appendix F.

3.3.3   Tracing An Application Request

We are now ready to complete our discussion concerning the DOS device driver interface. It is only appropriate that we develop a program to display the commands issued by DOS that constitute this interface. As you might have already guessed, this program is a further refinement of the show_DDH program we presented earlier.

This utility is named visual because it allows you to visually inspect the DOS device driver interface. Before we implement visual we must interpose logic between DOS and the device drivers in the system. This is easily accomplished by altering the device driver headers.

We developed visual to exploit some of the flexibility provided by a standardized interface. The implementation of visual is by no means an optimal one, but it is sufficient to illustrate the DOS device driver interface.

The algorithm embodied in visual is simple. First, visual obtains the pointer to the list of DOS device drivers. The method employed is the same as the one used in show_DDH.

Next, a set of internally defined DOS device driver headers is initialized to the contents of the original device driver headers. The LPT3 device driver header is used to provide the internal DOS block device driver with a strategy and interrupt offset that is within the same segment as the internal DOS block device driver.

Finally, visual terminates and stays resident in the system. After that, visual will be invoked anytime a DOS request is made through the DOS device driver interface. visual intercepts the request, displays the contents of the request, invokes the original device driver with the request, displays the result of the request, and then returns to DOS. Because visual is a terminate and stay resident (TSR) program, you will have to reboot your machine following its use.

The source for `visual` is included in Appendix E. You will find that studying the source for `visual` is informative as well as thought-provoking. The power you now have, being able to interpose your programs between DOS and the DOS device driver interface, is considerable.

3.4 BIOS Interface

The Basic Input/Output System (BIOS) interface is the software that resides in ROM on the system board and the associated adapter boards. BIOS provides device level control for major I/O devices in the system. ROM modules may be located on add-in adapter boards to provide device level control for that particular option board.

BIOS routines enable applications to perform block or character-level I/O operations without concern for device addressing or device operational characteristics. Similarly, physical hardware devices may be replaced by radically different ones without affecting the operational characteristics of the system so long as the BIOS interface is maintained.

The goal of BIOS is to provide an operational interface to the system and to relieve the programmer of the concerns relating to the specific characteristics of the hardware devices. The BIOS interface insulates application programs from the hardware and vice versa. Thus, new devices can be added to the system without consequence as long as they conform to the BIOS interface. In this way, the hardware devices are merely logical devices to the application programs, and the application programs become immune to hardware modifications and enhancements.

The calling convention for BIOS is developed using the Intel 808X software interrupt instructions. Each BIOS routine is accessible through its own software interrupt. The following list provides the major BIOS entry points or routines and their associated software interrupt value. (See Appendix H.)

1. (10) Video

2. (11) Equipment Check

3. (12) Memory

4. (13) Disk/Diskette

5. (14) Communications

6. (15) Cassette

7. (16) Keyboard

8. (17) Printer

9. (18) Resident BASIC

10. (19) Bootstrap

11. (1A) Time Of Day

12. (1B) Keyboard Break

13. (1C) Timer Tick

14. (1D) Video Initialization

15. (1E) Diskette Parameters

16. (1F) Video Graphics Characters.

The BIOS routines implement a register-based parameter passing scheme. In other words, all parameters required by the BIOS routine are stored in specific CPU registers before the appropriate software interrupt is executed. If the BIOS routine can perform several different operations, then the specific operation is provided in the AH register. For example, the following code fragment sets the time of day.

```
_AH = 1;
_CX = Count_MSW;
_DX = Count_LSW;
geninterrupt (0x1A);
```

where the variables `Count_MSW` and `Count_LSW` contain the values that define the current time of the day. (See Appendix H.)

Another BIOS call reads the time of day. It happens to use the same BIOS routine. Therefore, the value of AH should change. The code to perform the read is illustrated below.

```
_AH = 0;
geninterrupt (0x1A);
```

In general, BIOS routines raise the level of abstraction of a physical device. Often you will find this level of interface integral in the more intelligent hardware adapters and devices. Therefore, the application program may view these more as abstract devices than physical ones.

The BIOS interface provides the DOS device driver implementer with a viable alternative to directly controlling the physical hardware. Yes, the DOS device driver can use the BIOS routines and reduce the task of implementing a device driver that must directly control the hardware. This is, however, the choice of the DOS device driver implementer as we will see in the next section.

3.5   Hardware Device Interface

The hardware device interface is the lowest-level interface in the system. This interface allows software to directly control the hardware adapter or device attached to the system. Direct control of hardware is typically accomplished through one of two techniques.

The first of these hardware control techniques is programmed I/O. Programmed I/O uses the IN and OUT instructions of the Intel 808X series to transfer data to and from the I/O adapter or device. Because an instruction, IN or OUT, is required to communicate with the device, the CPU must be programmed to execute these instructions at the proper time. Thus we have the term "programmed I/O."

The second control technique for hardware control is memory-mapped I/O. This interface technique requires the hardware device to decode specific memory addresses. Whenever these specific memory addresses are present on the address bus, the hardware device will read from or write to the data bus and the I/O operation is performed.

Although direct control of the hardware appears simple, it should be noted that each hardware device has a different architecture and control structure. Therefore, two different hardware devices can be designed to interface to the system in the same way (programmed I/O or memory-mapped I/O) and yet have drastically different control requirements.

The architecture of each hardware device is so different that without the hardware technical manual for the hardware device, it is impossible to present any further generalizations about their operation.

3.6   Summary

Architected Software Interfaces

An interface represents the implementation of some abstract function or set of functions. An architected software interface has two major components:

- A set of functional abstractions accessible via the interface

- A standard calling convention.

Application Programming Interface

The application programming interface (API) is the common name for DOS services or functions. It refers to INT 21 services. INT 21 is a software interrupt instruction that accesses an interrupt vector location.

Device Driver Interface

The device driver interface is an interface between the DOS service manager and BIOS or the hardware itself.

DOS device drivers have two major characteristics:

- Device driver structure

  - Device management
  - Device driver headers (see `show_DDH` program)
  - Device driver classification: character and block

- Device driver requests (see `visual` utility).

BIOS Interface

The BIOS interface is the software that resides in ROM and provides device level control for major I/O devices in the system. It insulates application programs from the hardware and vice versa. See Section 3.4 for a list of the major routines (entry points).

Hardware Device Interface

The hardware device interface is the lowest-level interface in the system. You can control the hardware either with programmed I/O or memory-mapped I/O.

3.7 Exercises

Exercise 3.1 What is an architected software interface? List some advantages.

Exercise 3.2 Describe the system request triangle.

Exercise 3.3 Explain Application Programming Interface.

Exercise 3.4 Explain the characteristics of DOS device drivers.

Exercise 3.5 Find the details about the attribute word in your *DOS Technical Reference Manual.*

Exercise 3.6 Explain device driver headers. How can you find the address of this linked list?

Exercise 3.7 What is the BIOS interface? List its major routines (entry points).

Exercise 3.8 Explain how you can pass parameters to a BIOS routine.

Exercise 3.9 Explain in detail some common techniques to control the hardware directly.

Chapter 4

A DOS Device Driver Template

The intent of this chapter is to provide you with the tools you need to develop DOS device drivers quickly, accurately, and efficiently. A simple approach to accomplishing this goal is to develop a template for device drivers, then use and modify the template.

The template-based DOS device driver approach in this chapter was designed to be easily modified. In fact, the design goal of this DOS device driver was to isolate all invariant features of the DOS device driver from the features that you will want to modify. We use a multi-file approach to accomplish this goal.

To create a template-based DOS device driver we address the following topics:

- DOS makefile

- Segment headers

- Definitions

- Global data

- C environment

- Commands

- Ending marker.

As we discuss each topic in detail, we will present the code that goes with each topic. Once you understand the parts of a template-based DOS device driver, you will be able to use this method for developing your own DOS device drivers.

4.1 DOS Makefile

dos is the *makefile* file for the template-based DOS device driver. The `make`
utility uses a makefile.   And the makefile contains a list of commands and
dependencies — what needs to be done and in what order — to build an
executable program. We named our makefile `dos`.

We create a separate directory for each device driver we work on. We copy
the template files and the makefile into the directory. We make the necessary
modification on the files and then issue

```
make -fdos
```

to initiate the device driver build process. `make` is available with your TURBO
C package.

Here is our makefile.

```
#
#    Makefile For DOS Device Driver Template Written In C
#


#
#    Assembler Definitions
#

ASM     = \turbo\asm\tasm
AFLAGS  =


#
#    TURBO C Compiler Definitions
#
#    -c      Do Not Perform Link Step
#    -M      Produce Link/Load Map
#    -mt     Produce TINY Model Output
#    -S      Produce Assembler Module
#    -y      Produce Line Number Information
#    -Idir   Place To Search For Include Files

TURBO   = \turbo\c\tcc
TFLAGS  = -c -M -mt -S -y -I\turbo\c\include


#
#    Linker Definitions
#
```

```
LINK    = \turbo\c\tlink
LFLAGS  =

#
#   List Of Required Libraries
#

LIBS    = \turbo\c\lib\cs.lib

#
#   List Of Required Include Files
#
#   DOS_DD.H    DOS Device Driver Command Include File

INCS    = dos_dd.h

#
#   List Of Required Object Files
#
#   M1.OBJ      TURBO C Version Assembler Header For TINY Model
#   M2.OBJ      Modified C Assembler For DOS_DATA.C
#   M3.OBJ      Modified C Assembler For DOS_ENV.C
#   M4.OBJ      Modified C Assembler For DOS_DRVR.C
#   M5.OBJ      Modified C Assembler For DOS_END.C

OBJS    = m1.obj  m2.obj  m3.obj  m4.obj  m5.obj

#
#   Perform DOS Device Driver Linkage
#

dos.sys:    $(OBJS) $(INCS)
            $(LINK) $(LFLAGS) m1+m2+m3+m4+m5,dos.exe,,$(LIBS);
            erase  m3.*
            exe2bin  dos.exe  dos.sys

#
#   Perform DOS_HDR Assembly
#

m1.obj:     dos_hdr.asm
```

```
                copy  dos_hdr.asm  m1.asm
                $(ASM) $(AFLAGS)  m1.asm;


#
#    Perform DOS_DATA Compilation
#

m2.obj:         $(INCS)  dos_data.c
                $(TURBO) $(TFLAGS)  dos_data.c
                arrange  dos.arr  dos_data.asm  m2.asm
                erase  dos_data.asm
                $(ASM) $(AFLAGS)  m2.asm;


#
#    Perform DOS_ENV Compilation
#

m3.obj:         $(INCS)  dos_env.c
                $(TURBO) $(TFLAGS)  dos_env.c
                arrange  dos.arr  dos_env.asm  m3.asm
                erase  dos_env.asm
                $(ASM) $(AFLAGS)  m3.asm;


#
#    Perform DOS_DRVR Compilation
#

m4.obj:         $(INCS)  dos_drvr.c
                $(TURBO) $(TFLAGS)  dos_drvr.c
                arrange  dos.arr  dos_drvr.asm  m4.asm
                erase  dos_drvr.asm
                $(ASM) $(AFLAGS)  m4.asm;


#
#    Perform DOS_END Compilation
#

m5.obj:         $(INCS)  dos_end.c
                $(TURBO) $(TFLAGS) dos_end.c
                arrange  dos.arr  dos_end.asm  m5.asm
                erase  dos_end.asm
                $(ASM) $(AFLAGS)  m5.asm;
```

It is beyond the scope of this book to fully describe the operational characteristics of the **make** program. A number of good references are available for this utility, including a section in the TURBO C manual. Therefore, we will discuss only a small portion of the makefile in detail.

In the **dos** makefile you will find the following list of statements.

```
#
#   Perform DOS Device Driver Linkage
#

dos.sys:      $(OBJS) $(INCS)
              $(LINK) $(LFLAGS) m1+m2+m3+m4+m5,dos.exe,,$(LIBS);
              erase  m3.*
              exe2bin dos.exe  dos.sys
```

This set of statements informs the make program that **dos.sys** depends on the object files listed in the **OBJS=** statement as well as those listed in the **INCS=** statement. Once the **make** program has processed all the prerequisite statements to bring the object files and include files up to date, the linkage of the device driver begins.

The DOS linker is instructed to begin the linkage process on object files **m1** through **m5** with the linker flags specified in the **LFLAGS=** statement. The linker also uses the libraries listed in **LIBS=**. The resultant executable code is stored in the file **dos.exe**.

The location of your TURBO C compiler and libraries is up to you. However, you must modify **LIBS=** in the makefile for the make program to operate correctly.

4.2 Segment Headers

DOS device drivers require that the data segment be at location zero in the file. Because the data segment is not at location zero we need to move it around. As you recall, we discussed the **arrange** utility in Chapter 2. Our utility rearranges the order of segments in a .asm file. See Appendix C for more information.

For completeness we include a header file, **dos_hdr.asm**. The file rearranges the segments in the link file. You will notice this file contains assembler language pseudo-operations and no assembler language instructions. In other words, **dos_hdr.asm** is a passive element in the template-based DOS device driver.

Here is **dos_hdr.asm**.

```
        name          DOS_hdr
_DATA   segment word public 'DATA'
_d@ label             byte
_DATA   ends
_BSS    segment word public 'BSS'
_b@ label             byte
_BSS    ends
_TEXT   segment byte public 'CODE'
DGROUP  group         _DATA,_BSS,_TEXT
        assume        cs:DGROUP,ds:DGROUP,ss:DGROUP
_TEXT   ends
        end
```

4.3 Definitions

The file dos_dd.h contains the C structures and definitions that describe the entire DOS device driver environment. We include this file in the C files we use to create the template-based DOS device driver.

In previous sections you have encountered pieces of this file. For example, we have shown the C structure that describes the DOS device driver header. At that time, in Chapter 3, we called it struct DDH_struct. The real structure is struct DEVICE_HEADER_struct and it appears in dos_dd.h (Appendix F).

```
struct DEVICE_HEADER_struct
{
    struct DEVICE_HEADER_struct far *next_hdr;
    unsigned int  attribute;       /* Device Driver Attributes */
    unsigned int  dev_strat;       /* Pointer To Strategy Code */
    unsigned int  dev_int;         /* Pointer To Interrupt Code*/
    unsigned char name_unit [8];   /* Name/Unit Field          */
};
```

You will find this file contains all the C structures you will need to implement a DOS device driver. You will also see that REQ_struct describes DOS requests, commands, and packets. With those structures, developing visual was easy (see Appendix E).

The following C structure, REQ_struct, represents the DOS device driver command interface to pass commands around in a device driver. Each command has a unique structure in the variable portion of the DOS request structure.

```
struct REQ_struct
{
    unsigned char length;           /* Length In Bytes Of Req     */
    unsigned char unit;             /* Minor Device Unit Number */
    unsigned char command;          /* Device Command Code        */
    unsigned int  status;           /* Device Status Word         */
    unsigned char reserved [8];     /* Reserved For DOS           */
    union
    {
        struct    INIT_struct               init_req;
        struct    MEDIA_CHECK_struct        media_check_req;
        struct    BUILD_BPB_struct          build_bpb_req;
        struct    I_O_struct                i_o_req;
        struct    INPUT_NO_WAIT_struct      input_no_wait_req;
        struct    IOCTL_struct              ioctl_req;
        struct    L_D_MAP_struct            l_d_map_req;
    } req_type;
};
```

See Appendix F for a complete listing of dos_dd.h.

4.4 Global Data

One of the most important aspects of a DOS device driver is the DOS device driver header. This header must be at location zero in the .sys file, and it must be initialized for the device driver to operate correctly. The file dos_data.c allocates and initializes the device driver header. Note that the template-based DOS device driver is initialized as a block device driver. No particular significance is associated with this other than when the bit is not set it indicates a block rather than a character device driver (see Table 3.1 on page 37).

You will find that dos_data.c will have to be changed when you develop your own character device driver. However, if you skim forward to the chapter on character device drivers (Chapter 6) you will find the changes to this file are minimal.

dos_data.c serves another purpose. This file contains all the globally allocated data. It is important that you begin developing device drivers in a systematic way. The approach we take here has proven successful for both the programmer developing a DOS device driver and the programmer maintaining one. By conforming to the simple code and data separation technique we use, you will find your device drivers are reliable and easy to maintain.

Here is dos_data.c.

```
/* - - - - - - - - - - - - - - - - - - - - - - - - - - - - - - - -*/
/*                                                                 */
/*  PROGRAM :      D O S   D e v i c e   D r i v e r               */
/*                                                                 */
/*  REMARKS :      This file contains the set of command           */
/*          routines specified by the DOS Technical Reference      */
/*          Manual.                                                */
/*                                                                 */
/*             The following include file is required to           */
/*          compile this file :                                    */
/*          DOS_DD.H                                               */
/*                                                                 */
/* - - - - - - - - - - - - - - - - - - - - - - - - - - - - - - - -*/

#include    "dos_dd.h"                /* DOS  Command Structures  */

extern     void    far Strategy ();    /* Strategy Routine        */
extern     void    far Interrupt ();   /* Interrupt Routine       */

/* - - - - - - - - - - - - - - - - - - - - - - - - - - - - - - - -*/
/*                                                                 */
/*      Allocate And Initialize DOS Device Header                  */
/*                                                                 */
/* - - - - - - - - - - - - - - - - - - - - - - - - - - - - - - - -*/

/* DOS  Device  Header                                            */
struct  DEVICE_HEADER_struct  dos_header =
{
    (struct DEVICE_HEADER_struct far *) 0xFFFFFFFFL,
    0x2000,                           /* Non-IBM Format           */
    (unsigned int) Strategy,          /* Strategy Function        */
    (unsigned int) Interrupt,         /* Interrupt Function       */
    {                                 /* Unit/Name Field          */
        0x01,                         /* Initial Number Of Units  */
        0x00,                         /* Zero Remaining Entries   */
        0x00,                         /* Zero Remaining Entries   */
        0x00,                         /* Zero Remaining Entries   */
        0x00,                         /* Zero Remaining Entries   */
        0x00,                         /* Zero Remaining Entries   */
        0x00,                         /* Zero Remaining Entries   */
        0x00                          /* Zero Remaining Entries   */
    }
```

```
};

/* - - - - - - - - - - - - - - - - - - - - - - - - - - - - - - -*/
/*                                                               */
/*       DOS   Device Driver Global Data Region                 */
/*                                                               */
/* - - - - - - - - - - - - - - - - - - - - - - - - - - - - - - -*/

struct  BPB_struct  bpb =
{
    512,                        /* Bytes Per Sector            */
    1,                          /* Sectors Per Allocation Unit */
    1,                          /* Reserved Sectors            */
    2,                          /* Number Of FATS              */
    64,                         /* Number Of Root Dir Entries  */
    360,                        /* Number Of Sectors           */
    0xF0,                       /* Media Descriptor            */
    2,                          /* Number Of Sectors Per FAT   */
    1,                          /* Number Of Sectors Per Track */
    1,                          /* Number Of Heads             */
    1L,                         /* Number Of Hidden Sectors    */
    0L                          /* 32-Bit Number of Sectors    */
};

struct  BPB_struct  *bpb_ary [DEVICES] = { 0 };

unsigned int        rc;         /* Function Return Code        */
unsigned int        driver;     /* Global Driver Variable      */
unsigned int        SS_reg;     /* SS Register Variable        */
unsigned int        SP_reg;     /* SP Register Variable        */
unsigned int        ES_reg;     /* ES Register Variable        */
unsigned int        AX_reg;     /* AX Register Variable        */
unsigned int        BX_reg;     /* BX Register Variable        */
unsigned int        CX_reg;     /* CX Register Variable        */
unsigned int        DX_reg;     /* DX Register Variable        */
unsigned int        DS_reg;     /* DS Register Variable        */
unsigned int        SI_reg;     /* SI Register Variable        */

/* Local Device Driver Stack                                   */
unsigned int        local_stk [STK_SIZE];

struct REQ_struct  far *r_ptr;  /* DOS Request Packet Pointer  */
```

dos_data.c also contains variables that refer to machine registers and a structure bpb of type struct BPB_struct. We describe struct BPB_struct in Chapter 7.

4.5   C Environment

Without a doubt, the most critical portion of code in the entire template-based DOS device driver is contained in the dos_env.c file (Appendix F). This file contains the routines that are called directly by DOS whenever a DOS request must be processed by the device driver.

The code in the dos_env.c file is critical because it receives the DOS requests and transforms the current DOS environment, typically assembler language, into a usable C environment. DOS_Setup accomplishes this task.

The Strategy and Interrupt functions call DOS_Setup as soon as they receive a DOS request. DOS_Setup then saves the current operating environment and creates a new C environment, complete with its own local stack.

Here is DOS_Setup.

```
/* - - - - - - - - - - - - - - - - - - - - - - - - - - - - - - -*/
/*                                                               */
/*  FUNCTION:    D O S _ S e t u p                               */
/*                                                               */
/*  REMARKS :    DOS_Setup establishes a C environment prior to  */
/*          allowing the actual device driver routines to        */
/*          execute.                                             */
/*                                                               */
/*  INPUTS  :                                                    */
/*          which   0 : Strategy Entry; 1 : Interrupt Entry      */
/*          ES_tmp  Pointer To Request Packet                    */
/*          DS_tmp  Original DS Register Value                   */
/*          AX_tmp  Original AX Register Value                   */
/*                                                               */
/*  OUTPUTS :    Status  Must Be Set In The Request Packet       */
/*                                                               */
/*  NOTES   :    Register manipulations require this routine to  */
/*       be compiled with the TURBO C Compiler.                  */
/*                                                               */
/* - - - - - - - - - - - - - - - - - - - - - - - - - - - - - - -*/


void DOS_Setup (unsigned int which,
                unsigned int ES_tmp,
                unsigned int DS_tmp,
```

```c
                unsigned int AX_tmp)
{
    _AX = _CS;                  /* Obtain Code Segment      */
    _DS = _AX;                  /* Setup Data Segment       */

    BX_reg = _BX;               /* Save BX Register         */
    CX_reg = _CX;               /* Save CX Register         */
    DX_reg = _DX;               /* Save DX Register         */

    AX_reg = AX_tmp;            /* Save AX Register         */
    ES_reg = ES_tmp;            /* Save Request Pointer     */

    driver = which;             /* Move Value From Stack    */

    SS_reg = _SS;               /* Save Stack Segment       */
    SP_reg = _SP;               /* Save Stack Pointer       */

    disable ();                 /* Disable Interrupts       */
    _AX = _DS;                  /* Obtain Data Segment      */
    _SS = _AX;                  /* Setup New Stack          */
                                /* Set Stack Ptr Value      */
    _SP = (unsigned int) &local_stk [STK_SIZE];
    enable ();                  /* Enable Interrupts        */

    if (driver)
    {                           /* Interrupt Entry Point    */
        rc = 0x0000;            /* Clear Return Code        */
                                /* DOS Request Packet Ptr   */
        r_ptr = MK_FP (ES_reg, BX_reg);
        if (r_ptr->command >= DOS_CMDS)
        {
            rc = ERROR_BIT | UNKNOWN_CMD;
        }
        else
        {
            rc |= (*dos_cmd [r_ptr->command]) (r_ptr);
        }
                                /* Set Driver Complete Bit  */
        r_ptr->status = rc | DONE_BIT;
    }
    else
    {                           /* Strategy Entry Point     */
```

```
            /* Don't Save ES:BX Because It's Passed To Interrupt!!  */
    }

    disable ();                /* Disable Interrupts           */
    _SS = SS_reg;              /* Restore Entry Stack          */
    _SP = SP_reg;              /* Restore Entry Stack Ptr      */
    enable ();                 /* Enable Interrupts            */

    _DX = DX_reg;              /* Restore DX Register          */
    _CX = CX_reg;              /* Restore CX Register          */
    _BX = BX_reg;              /* Restore BX Register          */
    _AX = AX_reg;              /* Restore AX Register          */

    _ES = ES_tmp;              /* Restore ES Register          */
    _DS = DS_tmp;              /* Restore DS Register          */
}
```

You can see that DOS_Setup performs a number of critical operations in a small number of lines of code. You should be aware that this function is one of the reasons for using the *tiny model* in TURBO C. DOS_Setup will not work properly if you use another compiler model.

You can also see that DOS_Setup calls another function whose address is in the dos_cmd array. With the code written in this fashion, it is easy to isolate the DOS device driver command functions. All these functions are in the dos_drvr.c file (Appendix F).

A final note is in order here. Of all of the source files you will use, dos_env.c is the most difficult one to modify. You should not need to change such functions as DOS_Setup, Strategy, or Interrupt. If you change any of these functions, you will have changed the entire design of the template-based DOS device driver and you may find it difficult to debug.

4.6 Commands

The dos_drvr.c file contains all the functions for the DOS device driver commands (Appendix F). There is one C function for each command.

All functions have the same input parameter: a far pointer to the DOS request structure. Each function in this file performs the specified operation, then sets the appropriate return code in the status word of the DOS request structure.

You will find that the template-based DOS device driver includes a function stub, but no code, for each of the DOS device driver commands. Therefore, when you begin implementing your own DOS device drivers you simply copy the template-based DOS device driver files to another directory and add the code necessary to the stubs found in `dos_drvr.c`.

The `Init_cmd` function responds to the DOS INIT request command. The function is part of `dos_drvr.c`. All DOS device drivers must respond to the DOS INIT command to be functional. Therefore, this function is somewhat more than a stub. Nevertheless, the `Init_cmd` function conforms to the same interface as the rest of the functions in this file and can be viewed as representative of them.

```
/* - - - - - - - - - - - - - - - - - - - - - - - - - - - - - - -*/
/*                                                               */
/*  FUNCTION:   I n i t _ c m d                                  */
/*                                                               */
/*  REMARKS :                                                    */
/*                                                               */
/*  INPUTS  :   r_ptr    Pointer To Request Packet               */
/*                                                               */
/*  OUTPUTS :   Status  Returned In Function Return Value        */
/*                                                               */
/* - - - - - - - - - - - - - - - - - - - - - - - - - - - - - - -*/

unsigned int Init_cmd (struct REQ_struct far *r_ptr)
{
    r_ptr->req_type.init_req.num_of_units = 1;

    bpb_ary [0] = (unsigned int) &bpb;
    r_ptr->req_type.init_req.BPB_ptr =
                        MK_FP (_DS, (unsigned int) bpb_ary);

    r_ptr->req_type.init_req.end_ptr =
                        MK_FP (_DS, (unsigned int) End_code);

    return OP_COMPLETE;
}
```

4.7   Ending Marker

When DOS issues the INIT request the device driver must respond with its ending address. The code segment follows the data segment because we rearranged them with the **arrange** utility. Therefore, the ending address of the device driver is located somewhere within the code segment.

`dos_end.c` contains a C function named **End_code**. This file is linked last and truly becomes the end of the code segment. It is nothing more than a place holder that `Init_cmd` uses to determine the end of the template-based DOS device driver. Here is the function.

```
/* - - - - - - - - - - - - - - - - - - - - - - - - - - - - - - - -*/
/*                                                                 */
/*  FUNCTION:    E n d _ c o d e                                   */
/*                                                                 */
/*  REMARKS :    End_code is a place holder for the last routine   */
/*           and the last variable in the driver.                  */
/*                                                                 */
/*  INPUTS  :    None                                              */
/*                                                                 */
/*  OUTPUTS :    None                                              */
/*                                                                 */
/*  NOTES   :    End_code must be linked last!                     */
/*                                                                 */
/* - - - - - - - - - - - - - - - - - - - - - - - - - - - - - - - -*/

unsigned char end_data;

void    End_code (void)
{
}
```

4.8   Template Overview

When you use the template to build one of the device drivers we discuss in this book, you will create a `.sys` file with the arrangement we show in Table 4.1.

`dos_data.c` contains the device driver header: the address of the next header, the attribute byte for this device driver, the offsets for the `Strategy` and `Interrupt` functions, the device name (character device) or number of units (block device), and the remaining data.

`dos_env.c` contains data (an array of pointers to functions, `dos_cmd []`, that support DOS requests), the `DOS_Setup` function, and the `Strategy` and `Interrupt` functions (Appendix F).

`dos_drvr.c` contains the functions to support DOS requests in the device driver (Appendix F).

`dos_end.c` marks the end of the code in the device driver.

File	Description
dos_data.c	next_hdr attribute dev_strat (Strategy function offset) dev_int (Interrupt function offset) name_unit remaining dos_data.c data
dos_env.c	dos_env.c data DOS_Setup function Strategy function Interrupt function
dos_drvr.c	functions to support DOS requests
dos_end.c	function to mark end of device driver code

Table 4.1: Device Driver Format

4.9   Using the Template

To develop your own DOS device driver using the template you should create a separate directory where you will do the work. You can accomplish this with:

```
mkdir \my_dev
```

You should then copy the template-based DOS device driver source files into `my_dev` directory. If the template-based DOS device driver is in a directory `template`, you can copy the files from `template` to `my_dev` with the `copy` command.

```
copy \template \my_dev
```

Then you should make `my_dev` the current directory.

```
cd \my_dev
```

Next, you should modify the contents of the `dos_drvr.c` to perform the appropriate operations when DOS requests them. Then you should invoke **make** to create your new DOS device driver.

```
make -fdos
```

You may need to modify the DOS device driver header contained in `dos_data.c`. If your device driver requires modifications in any other file, the modifications should be easy.

4.10   Summary

DOS Makefile

A **make** utility is available with your TURBO C compiler. It uses a file that contains a list of commands and dependencies — what needs to be done and in what order — to build an executable program. The file that contains commands and dependencies is commonly referred to as the *makefile*. The makefile for our template-based device driver is **dos**. Check your compiler documentation for details on **make**, and see our makefile in Section 4.1.

Segment Headers

Device drivers require the data segment at location zero. We use our **arrange** utility to reorder the segments. In Section 4.2 we present a `.asm` file that shows the segments after they have been rearranged. That file is `dos_hdr.asm`.

Definitions

The C structures and definitions you need to implement a DOS device driver are in the dos_dd.h file.

Global Data

See dos_data.c in Section 4.4 for a listing of global data that a device driver requires.

C Environment

DOS sends a request to a device driver. We have to convert the request from assembler environment to C environment before the device driver services it. We use the DOS_Setup function (see Section 4.5) to convert requests.

Commands

In dos_drvr.c we implemented a function stub for each DOS command. Use this file to add the code for each command you need to implement in your device driver.

Ending Marker

The Init_cmd function needs to know where the code for the device driver ends. We use an empty function, End_code, to mark the spot and provide the address.

Using the Template

Now you have access to a template that facilitates the creation of DOS device drivers. This is the list of files that comprise the template:

- dos makefile (Section 4.1)

- Definitions file dos_dd.h (Section 4.3 and Appendix F)

- Global data file dos_data.c (Section 4.4 and Appendix F)

- C environment file dos_env.c (Section 4.5 and Appendix F)

- DOS commands file dos_drvr.c (Section 4.6 and Appendix F)

- Ending marker file dos_end.c (Section 4.7)

4.11   Exercises

Exercise 4.1 What is a *makefile*? Why use one?

Exercise 4.2 Why should you rearrange the order of segments in a device driver? How can you accomplish that?

Exercise 4.3 Why use the `dos_dd.h` file?

Exercise 4.4 List the main structures, and their contents, that are globally available in a device driver.

Exercise 4.5 Explain how `DOS_Setup` converts a request from assembler to C environment.

Exercise 4.6 What is the purpose of `dos_drvr.c`?

Exercise 4.7 What is the purpose of the `End_code` function?

Exercise 4.8 Show in a diagram the general flow/interaction between DOS and a device driver.

Chapter 5

What If It Doesn't Work?

We presented a template-based DOS device driver in the previous chapter. We discussed the steps necessary develop and modify that DOS device driver. However, we did not explain how to install the template-based DOS device driver in your system. Furthermore, the question of what to do if the device driver does not work was left unanswered. We address these topics in this chapter.

The template-based DOS device driver is like any other DOS device driver. To install a device driver you must have an entry defined in the `config.sys` file in your system.

`config.sys` is the system configuration file for DOS. You can use various commands in this file. The *DOS Reference Manual* discusses these commands. The command that we are most interested in is the `DEVICE=` command. This command informs DOS at initialization time that we would like to have an installable device driver loaded and initialized. To load and initialize the template-based DOS device driver in your system, you need the following entry in `config.sys`

        DEVICE=DOS.SYS

The relationship between DOS and the `config.sys` goes something like this. After the bootstrap process has loaded DOS into the system, DOS attempts to open the `config.sys` file. If the `config.sys` file is not present, then DOS completes its initialization process and displays the DOS prompt. If, however, `config.sys` is present, then DOS processes each command line in the file.

Whenever DOS encounters a `DEVICE=` command in `config.sys`, DOS attempts to load the specified DOS device driver into memory. Once the device driver is loaded, DOS issues the INIT request to the device driver. This request allows the DOS device driver to perform its initialization activities before DOS loads the next device driver.

This is an important concept, especially when part of the DOS device driver initialization process includes the allocation of physical memory. If another DOS device driver were loaded prior to the INIT request being sent, then the initializing DOS device driver would allocate the memory that is used by the next DOS device driver. Clearly, this would have a harmful effect on the operation of the system.

5.1   Installing your Device Driver

Whenever a new DOS device driver is installed in the system, the simplest problems to resolve are those that affect the `config.sys` file.

An example of this type of problem in `config.sys` is the absence of the `DEVICE=` statement for your DOS device driver. Every user-installable DOS device driver must have a `DEVICE=` statement in `config.sys`. If the `config.sys` file is not present in your system, then you must create one with your favorite editor or with the DOS `copy` command.

```
copy con: \config.sys
DEVICE=\DOS.SYS
ctrl-z
```

Press the ENTER key after each line you type in the example above. `ctrl-z` indicates the end of input for the `copy` command. This sequence creates a `config.sys` file with the `DEVICE=` statement for the template-based DOS device driver.

The next common problem concerning the `config.sys` file is that the location of the user-installable DOS device driver is not fully specified. In other words, in the previous example the template-based DOS device driver is named `DOS.SYS`, and it should be present in the root directory. However, if you have forgotten to copy the `DOS.SYS` file from your template development directory, then DOS will be unable to locate this device driver.

The following has proven to be a good method for maintaining a number of user-installable DOS device drivers. First, you should create a directory at the root-level which will contain all the drivers. Second, you should edit the makefiles for any of your own drivers to include a statement that will copy the driver into this directory. And third, you should edit your `config.sys` file to reflect the changes you have made.

For example, let's assume that we have created the `\DRIVERS` directory and have copied all the user-installable DOS device drivers into this directory. Then

```
DEVICE=\DRIVERS\DOS.SYS
```

in `config.sys` installs the template-based DOS device driver.

Another problem area in `config.sys` is the DOS device driver parameters. At system initialization time, each DOS device driver receives a pointer to the information following `DEVICE=` in `config.sys`. If you have installed a DOS device driver without providing a required option or parameter, then the DOS device driver may not install or function correctly.

To avoid this problem, be aware of the operational characteristics of the DOS device drivers you install in your system. Furthermore, make sure you understand each of the options you specify when installing DOS device drivers in your system.

5.2 Debugging your Device Driver

You can see that a number of points in the DOS device driver debugging process could cause a problem. Therefore, we will discuss each of the following items separately.

- Avoiding problems at initialization

- Using `visual` to find bugs

- Using imbedded debug statements.

5.2.1 Avoiding Problems at Initialization

You are most helpless as a DOS device driver implementer when the DOS device driver is being initialized. You are helpless because DOS has not completed its initialization process, so you cannot load or execute any debugging programs that might help if your DOS device driver does not initialize correctly.

This is the most difficult debugging process in the development of a DOS device driver. You are unable to employ the debug programs that you would typically use to detect and resolve a problem. You are also unable to request any DOS services because DOS has not completed its own initialization process. In short, this is a very difficult problem to solve. However, there are a number of steps you can take to reduce the complexity of this problem.

These are the steps.

1. Use the template's `Init_cmd` function.

2. Use `show_DDH` to find your driver.

3. Set breakpoints with a specialized device driver debugger or hardware in-circuit emulator.

4. Analyze driver and make changes.

5. Repeat steps 1 through 4.

Step 1 – You can begin the device driver initialization by using the initialization function of the template-based DOS device driver. This function will allow you to install your own DOS device driver. Once your DOS device driver is installed, you can proceed with Step 2.

Step 2 – Once your DOS device driver has been installed and DOS has completed its initialization you can execute the show_DDH program. This program will display the location of the Strategy and Interrupt functions of your DOS device driver. Write these addresses down. By the way, you will only see the offsets of these functions. Therefore, you must use the segment value of the DOS device driver header to obtain the complete address of these functions. The segment value of the DOS device driver header for your device driver is at the top of the screen when you run show_DDH.

Step 3 – Now you can execute your favorite DOS debug program. This will allow you to set breakpoints at the addresses you got from show_DDH. In other words, set the breakpoints at the location of your Strategy and Interrupt functions. After you have set the breakpoints, issue the debug command to continue. This allows you to begin exercising your DOS device driver.

Step 4 – Issue DOS-level commands that will cause your DOS device driver to execute. For example, the template-based DOS device driver is a block device. Therefore, DOS assigns a drive letter to your device driver after installing it. To execute the device driver, you have to copy some file to the assigned drive letter. This action will cause the previously set breakpoint to be executed and you will return to the debugger's environment. At this point you can trace through the operations of your DOS device driver.

Step 5 – Repeat steps 1–4 until your DOS device driver has been fully tested.

5.2.2   Using visual to Find Bugs

After the device driver initialization you can execute the visual utility, either with or without your debug program.

As you recall from Chapter 4, visual allows you to see the exact DOS requests issued to your DOS device driver. Often you can understand and isolate a bug simply by viewing these DOS requests and your DOS device driver's response to those requests.

You may find that a DOS request you did not implement in your device driver is being issued to your device driver. The oversight of not implementing all the possible requests a device driver may receive accounts for many of the operational errors in DOS device drivers.

Another problem area in DOS device drivers that can be seen using the `visual` utility is the lack of response to a specified request. In other words, you may find that you forgot to set the appropriate status bit in the DOS request status word. This oversight often causes DOS to retry the operation and finally issue an error concerning the problem.

At this stage in the development of a DOS device driver, you should read the description of the DOS device driver commands in great detail (see Appendix A and consult your *DOS Technical Reference Manual*). DOS is not a very forgiving program. You must conform to the specification defined within the DOS device driver commands for your DOS device driver to function correctly.

5.2.3 Using Imbedded Debug Statements

The previous sections describe the use of debug programs to analyze the operation of your DOS device driver. Although this is the preferred method of debugging a DOS device driver it is not the only method. Your DOS device driver can be implemented with imbedded debug statements. These statements are usually some type of output statement, such as `printf` in C. However, you must take certain precautions to imbed these statements into your DOS device driver.

In the introductory chapters we discussed some DOS features. In particular, we mentioned that DOS is not reentrant. Once DOS begins processing a command, it cannot call itself to perform another DOS function. This is an extremely important concept. We bring this point up again because most I/O statements in C, including `printf`, request DOS services. Well, you can see the problem. DOS is already processing one request and has invoked your device driver. We are not able to request DOS to process a second function until DOS has completed the first one. Therefore, when using C, you cannot imbed I/O statements in your DOS device driver.

The best way to provide imbedded debug statements is to avoid all C library routines and create your own library. The routines you create should not rely on DOS services. They should use only the BIOS interface level or the hardware interface level. The following C functions in `video.c` appear in the CONSOLE device driver and access only the BIOS interface level. You may find these functions useful in the development of your own DOS device drivers. The key is to remember that only the BIOS level interface or the hardware level interface can be used for imbedded debug statements in your DOS device drivers (See Section 8.4).

```
/* - - - - - - - - - - - - - - - - - - - - - - - - - - - - - -*/
/*                                                             */
/*  FUNCTION:   V i d e o . c                                  */
/*                                                             */
/*  REMARKS :   Video.c contains a number of TURBO C functions */
/*              that access the video BIOS.                    */
/*                                                             */
/* - - - - - - - - - - - - - - - - - - - - - - - - - - - - - -*/

#include    <dos.h>

/* - - - - - - - - - - - - - - - - - - - - - - - - - - - - - -*/
/*                                                             */
/*  FUNCTION:   A c t i v e _ p a g e                          */
/*                                                             */
/*  REMARKS :   Active_page returns the currently active page  */
/*              being used by the video adapter.               */
/*                                                             */
/* - - - - - - - - - - - - - - - - - - - - - - - - - - - - - -*/

int Active_page (void)
{
    unsigned char page;

    _AH = 0x0F;
    geninterrupt (0x10);     /* Invoke Video BIOS             */
    page = _BH;
    return page;             /* Return Currently Active Page  */
}
```

```
/* - - - - - - - - - - - - - - - - - - - - - - - - - - - - - - - -*/
/*                                                                  */
/*  FUNCTION:   G o t o _ X Y                                       */
/*                                                                  */
/*  REMARKS :   Goto_XY sets the cursor position to col, row.       */
/*          The position is set in the current display page.        */
/*                                                                  */
/* - - - - - - - - - - - - - - - - - - - - - - - - - - - - - - - -*/

void Goto_XY (int    col,
              int    row)
{
    _BH = Active_page ();    /* Set Video Display Page               */
    _DH = --row;             /* Set Video Display Row Position       */
    _DL = --col;             /* Set Video Column Position            */
    _AH = 0x02;
    geninterrupt (0x10);     /* Invoke Video BIOS                    */
}



/* - - - - - - - - - - - - - - - - - - - - - - - - - - - - - - - -*/
/*                                                                  */
/*  FUNCTION:   G e t _ c h a r                                     */
/*                                                                  */
/*  REMARKS :   Get_char reads the current character at the         */
/*          cursor and returns that character.                      */
/*                                                                  */
/* - - - - - - - - - - - - - - - - - - - - - - - - - - - - - - - -*/

char Get_char (void)
{
    unsigned char chr;

    _BH = Active_page ();    /* Set Video Display Page               */
    _AH = 0x08;              /* INT 10 Function                      */
    geninterrupt (0x10);     /* Invoke Video BIOS                    */
    chr = _AL;               /* Current Character                    */
    return chr;              /* Return The Current Character         */
}
```

```
/* - - - - - - - - - - - - - - - - - - - - - - - - - - - - - - - -*/
/*                                                                 */
/*  FUNCTION:   G e t _ k e y                                      */
/*                                                                 */
/*  REMARKS :   Get_key returns the next keystroke from the        */
/*          keyboard.                                              */
/*                                                                 */
/* - - - - - - - - - - - - - - - - - - - - - - - - - - - - - - - -*/

unsigned int Get_key (unsigned char mode)
{
    unsigned int key;

    _AH = mode;             /* INT 16 Function          */
    geninterrupt (0x16);    /* Invoke Video BIOS        */
    key = _AX;              /* Keystroke From Keyboard  */
    return key;             /* Return Key To Caller     */
}




/* - - - - - - - - - - - - - - - - - - - - - - - - - - - - - - - -*/
/*                                                                 */
/*  FUNCTION:   G e t _ a t t r                                    */
/*                                                                 */
/*  REMARKS :   Get_attr reads the current attribute from the      */
/*          active page and returns the attribute.                */
/*                                                                 */
/* - - - - - - - - - - - - - - - - - - - - - - - - - - - - - - - -*/

char Get_attr (void)
{
    unsigned char attr;

    _BH = Active_page ();   /* Set Video Display Page       */
    _AH = 0x08;             /* INT 10 Function              */
    geninterrupt (0x10);    /* Invoke Video BIOS            */
    attr = _AH;             /* Current Attribute            */
    return attr;            /* Return The Current Attribute */
}
```

```
/* - - - - - - - - - - - - - - - - - - - - - - - - - - - - - - -*/
/*                                                               */
/*  FUNCTION:    G e t _ X                                       */
/*                                                               */
/*  REMARKS :   Get_X returns the X position (column) of the     */
/*            cursor in the current display page.                */
/*                                                               */
/* - - - - - - - - - - - - - - - - - - - - - - - - - - - - - - -*/

int Get_X (void)
{
    unsigned char col;

    _BH = Active_page ();    /* Set Video Display Page         */
    _AH = 0x03;              /* INT 10 Function                */
    geninterrupt (0x10);     /* Invoke Video BIOS              */
    col = _DL;
    return ++col;            /* Return Column Position Of Cursor */
}
```

```
/* - - - - - - - - - - - - - - - - - - - - - - - - - - - - - - -*/
/*                                                                */
/*  FUNCTION:    G e t _ Y                                        */
/*                                                                */
/*  REMARKS :    Get_Y returns the Y position (row) of the        */
/*            cursor in the current display page.                 */
/*                                                                */
/* - - - - - - - - - - - - - - - - - - - - - - - - - - - - - - -*/

int Get_Y (void)
{
    unsigned char row;

    _BH = Active_page ();    /* Set Video Display Page          */
    _AH = 0x03;              /* INT 10 Function                 */
    geninterrupt (0x10);     /* Invoke Video BIOS               */
    row = _DH;
    return ++row;            /* Return Row Position Of Cursor   */
}




/* - - - - - - - - - - - - - - - - - - - - - - - - - - - - - - -*/
/*                                                                */
/*  FUNCTION:    G e t _ m o d e                                  */
/*                                                                */
/*  REMARKS :    Get_mode gets the current video mode of the      */
/*            adapter.                                            */
/*                                                                */
/* - - - - - - - - - - - - - - - - - - - - - - - - - - - - - - -*/

unsigned char Get_mode (void)
{
    unsigned char mode;

    _AH = 0x0F;              /* INT 10 Function                 */
    geninterrupt (0x10);     /* Invoke Video BIOS               */
    mode = _AL;              /* Current Video State (Mode)      */
    return mode;             /* Return The Current Mode         */
}
```

```c
/* - - - - - - - - - - - - - - - - - - - - - - - - - - - - - - - -*/
/*                                                                 */
/*  FUNCTION:   S e t _ m o d e                                    */
/*                                                                 */
/*  REMARKS :   Set_mode sets the current video mode of the        */
/*          adapter.                                               */
/*                                                                 */
/* - - - - - - - - - - - - - - - - - - - - - - - - - - - - - - - -*/

void Set_mode (unsigned char mode)
{
    _AL = mode;
    _AH = 0x00;
    geninterrupt (0x10);    /* Invoke Video BIOS                   */
}




/* - - - - - - - - - - - - - - - - - - - - - - - - - - - - - - - -*/
/*                                                                 */
/*  FUNCTION:   C l e a r _ s c r e e n                            */
/*                                                                 */
/*  REMARKS :   Clear_screen clears the active display             */
/*          page (screen) in the video adapter.                    */
/*                                                                 */
/* - - - - - - - - - - - - - - - - - - - - - - - - - - - - - - - -*/

void Clear_screen (void)
{
    unsigned char   mode;    /* Video Mode Of Adapter              */

    mode = Get_mode ();      /* Obtain Current Video State         */
    _BH = 0x00;              /* Set Attribute To Black             */
    _CX = 0x0000;
    _DX = 0x184F;            /* Rows = 24, Columns = 79            */
    _AX = 0x0600;            /* Clear All 25 Rows                  */
    geninterrupt (0x10);     /* Invoke Video BIOS                  */
    Set_mode (mode);         /* Restore Video Mode If Disturbed    */
    Goto_XY (1, 1);          /* Set Cursor In Upper Left Corner    */
}
```

```
/* - - - - - - - - - - - - - - - - - - - - - - - - - - - - - - - - -*/
/*                                                                    */
/*  FUNCTION:    W r i t e _ c h r                                    */
/*                                                                    */
/*  REMARKS :    Write_chr writes the character argument at the       */
/*               current cursor position.                             */
/*                                                                    */
/* - - - - - - - - - - - - - - - - - - - - - - - - - - - - - - - - -*/

void Write_chr (unsigned char chr)
{
    unsigned char attr;

    attr = Get_attr ();
    _BL  = attr;              /* Establish Character Color       */
    _AL  = chr;              /* Move Character To AL Register    */
    _AH  = 0x0E;             /* Write Character To Active Page   */
    geninterrupt (0x10);     /* Invoke Video BIOS               */
}
```

```
/* - - - - - - - - - - - - - - - - - - - - - - - - - - - - - - - -*/
/*                                                                 */
/*  FUNCTION:    W r i t e _ t t y                                 */
/*                                                                 */
/*  REMARKS :    Write_tty writes the string argument at the       */
/*               cursor position.                                  */
/*                                                                 */
/* - - - - - - - - - - - - - - - - - - - - - - - - - - - - - - - -*/

static  unsigned int    es_static;
static  unsigned int    bp_static;

void Write_tty (unsigned char *str)
{
    unsigned char   x;
    unsigned char   y;
    unsigned int    len;
    unsigned char   page;
    unsigned char   attr;

    x = Get_X ();
    y = Get_Y ();
    len = strlen (str);
    page = Active_page ();
    attr = Get_attr ();

    es_static = _ES;        /* Save ES Register (Globally)      */
    bp_static = _BP;        /* Save BP Register (Globally)      */

    _CX = len;              /* Establish Length Of String       */
    _DH = --y;              /* Establish Cursor Row Positon      */
    _DL = --x;              /* Establish Cursor Column Position  */
    _BH = page;             /* Establish Active Video Page      */
    _BL = attr;             /* Establish Character Color        */
    _ES = _DS;              /* Set ES Register To DS Register   */
    _BP = str;              /* Establish String Offset          */
    _AX = 0x1301;           /* Write Character String           */
    geninterrupt (0x10);    /* Invoke Video BIOS                */
    _BP = bp_static;        /* Restore BP Register              */
    _ES = es_static;        /* Restore ES Register              */
}
```

5.3   DOS Device Driver Debug Programs

We have discussed a number of techniques that can be applied to debug DOS device drivers. However, none of them included an adequate form of debugging the DOS device driver during its initialization phase. For this type of debugging, you have to use specialized device driver debug programs or hardware in-circuit emulators.

For the remainder of this section we will address software debug programs that can be used to debug DOS device drivers during their initialization phase. A number of issues arise when discussing this topic. We will attempt to elaborate on the critical ones.

The most important issue is how the debug program gains control of the system before the DOS device driver is loaded and initialized. Two basic methods can accomplish this. First, the debug program can relocate itself into high physical memory, then set the maximum amount of memory in the system below itself. In this way, the debug program is protected when it requests the system to reboot itself.

Second, the debug program becomes a DOS-compatible device driver and is loaded into the system before the DOS device driver under test. This is a simple task: all that is required is to insert a `DEVICE=` statement for the debug program into the `config.sys` before the DOS device driver's `DEVICE=` statement.

A number of other alternative approaches also produce the same response from the system, but they are variations of the above methods. No matter which method you use to debug the device driver, you must not request the service of DOS. Remember, DOS cannot service the second request until the first one has been processed!

Presenting a specialized debug program of the type we have described is, regrettably, beyond the scope of this text. Therefore, we suggest you use the methods we discussed earlier to debug your DOS device drivers. If those methods are insufficient then you should investigate debug programs that meet the criteria set forth in this section.

5.4   Summary

config.sys

You need a `config.sys` with a `DEVICE=` line to inform DOS of your device driver. Our device driver is `dos.sys`. Consequently we have the line:

        DEVICE=DOS.SYS

in `config.sys`; otherwise, DOS will not find our device driver.

Debugging

Use the `Init_cmd` function to initialize your device driver. Then use `show_DDH` to find your device driver in the system. Once you find your device driver and the addresses for the `Interrupt` and the `Strategy` functions, you can use your favorite debugger to trace your device driver.

Use the `visual` utility to see the exact DOS requests issued to your device driver.

Avoid imbedded debug statements that invoke DOS services. Avoid C library routines in general. Create your own library routines that use the BIOS interface level. See `video.c` in Section 5.2.3 and the CONSOLE device driver.

5.5 Exercises

Exercise 5.1 Explain the purpose of `config.sys` on your DOS system.

Exercise 5.2 Explain what happens during the initialization of a device driver.

Exercise 5.3 How can you find the addresses of `Strategy` and `Interrupt` functions once your device driver has been initialized?

Exercise 5.4 What are imbedded debug statements? What kinds of statements should you avoid in a device driver?

Exercise 5.5 We use the BIOS interface for the functions in `video.c`. Take a look at those functions and add other functions you might need.

Chapter 6

DOS Character Device Drivers

In this chapter we will use the template-based DOS device driver to implement a completely functional DOS character device driver.

If you want to build the character device driver as we discuss it, you may want to create a `console` directory. We will perform our development work in this directory. To start, we copy the template-based device driver files into `console`.

This is the list of the source files that we need to create the CONSOLE character device driver:

- `console`

- `dos_hdr.asm`

- `dos_dd.h`

- `console.h`

- `dos_data.c`

- `dos_env.c`

- `dos_drvr.c`

- `dos_end.c`

We will examine the differences between the template-based DOS device driver and the CONSOLE character device driver. From this examination, you will see the benefits of using the template and the fundamental differences between a DOS block device driver and a DOS character device driver. First, let's review the DOS device driver headers.

6.1   Character Device Driver Headers

It is important that we understand the differences between a DOS block device driver and a DOS character device driver. The program show_DDH displays the following information for a block device driver :

```
Device Driver Entry (0070:01B6)


Next Device Driver   : 0070:01CA
Device Attributes    : 0840
Device Strategy Offset   : 05DC
Device Interrupt Offset : 0634
Device Driver Name   :
```

This is the device driver header for the drive letters A:, B:, C:, and D: in the system that we use.

For a character device driver, show_DDH displays the following information:

```
Device Driver Entry (0070:016E)


Next Device Driver   : 0070:0180
Device Attributes    : 8013
Device Strategy Offset   : 05DC
Device Interrupt Offset : 05E7
Device Driver Name   : CON
```

Note the differences between the two DOS device driver headers. The second header has the name field filled in. This is the header for the console device and has the name CON. Also note that the device attributes of the two DOS device driver headers are radically different.

The DOS block device driver header attributes indicate that this device driver can handle removable media and that the Get and Set logical device map requests are enabled. What this means is that this device driver can handle floppy diskette drives as well as hard disk drives.

The DOS character device driver header attributes, on the other hand, indicate that this device driver is the device driver responsible for both the standard input and standard output functions of the system. In other words, this device driver controls the display and the keyboard.

It is this type of DOS character device driver that we implement in this section. And our device driver will take the place of the existing CONSOLE device driver in the system.

6.2 Character Device Driver Commands

The template-based DOS device driver implemented a function for all possible DOS requests. DOS will issue a subset of those requests to the driver when the driver is a block device driver; DOS will issue another subset of those requests when the driver is a character device driver. Here is the list of requests (with command codes) that DOS may issue to the CONSOLE character device driver:

- (00) Initialize

- (03) IOCTL Input

- (04) Input From Device

- (05) Input Without Waiting

- (06) Obtain Input Status

- (07) Flush Input Buffer

- (08) Output To Device

- (09) Output And Verify Data

- (10) Obtain Output Status

- (11) Flush Output Buffer

- (12) IOCTL Output

- (13) Open Device

- (14) Close Device

- (19) IOCTL To Device

Of these requests that DOS can issue to a character device driver, some are not applicable to the CONSOLE device driver. For example, we do not have to Open Device or Close Device. Consequently, the CONSOLE character device driver implements the following:

- (00) Initialize

- (04) Input From Device

- (05) Input Without Waiting

- (07) Flush Input Buffer

- (08) Output To Device

- (09) Output And Verify Data

The remaining DOS requests for the CONSOLE character device drivers are implemented to return an *unknown command* status.

Now we know the scope of our task. Let's begin the implementation of the new CONSOLE device driver for DOS.

6.3   CONSOLE Character Device Driver

The new CONSOLE character device driver will perform the same basic tasks as the existing CONSOLE character device driver. It will receive input from the keyboard and display it on the monitor. Whenever a program writes to the monitor, the new driver will accept the output characters and display them on the monitor.

The major difference between the two CONSOLE character device drivers is that the new one will display the key in the upper right hand corner of the monitor as well as at the current cursor location. The reason for this difference is we want to demonstrate the implementation of a fully functional DOS character device driver, but with some functional characteristics not found in the existing one. This is not to imply that this is some spectacular work of art, but rather that it is a functional and complete device driver you can implement yourself.

We have to make several modifications to the template-based DOS device driver to turn it into the new CONSOLE device driver. Some of the files do not change. Here is the list of all the files with information about their status.

- `console` – This is the makefile. It has a new include file, `console.h`. We also changed the name of the device driver from `dos.sys` to `console.sys` (Appendix G).

- `console.h` – This is an include file. It contains constants we need for this device driver. We created a new file instead of changing `dos_dd.h` (Appendix G).

- `dos_dd.h` – No change.

- `dos_hdr.asm` – No change.

- `dos_end.c` – No change.

- `dos_data.c` – This file contains three minor modifications. First, we changed the device driver header to indicate a character device that is both the standard input and the standard output device. Second, we

changed the name/unit field of the device driver header to contain the
name of the character device, CON. Third, we eliminated the BPB-related
information in this file because it does not pertain to character device
drivers (Appendix G).

- **dos_env.c** – We changed this file to indicate that it is not necessary to
  have all the DOS request functions of the template present in each DOS
  device driver. Therefore, only the required DOS request functions are
  referenced in this file. Note that this file could have been left unchanged
  (Appendix G).

- **dos_drvr.c** – We changed this file extensively. The rest of this section
  discusses the modifications (Appendix G).

The initialization of a DOS character device driver is different from that of
a DOS block device driver. Therefore, we changed the initialization function.
Here is the new function.

```
unsigned int Init_cmd (struct REQ_struct far *r_ptr)
{
    unsigned int    save_x;
    unsigned int    save_y;

    save_x = Get_X ();
    save_y = Get_Y ();

    Clear_screen ();
    Goto_XY (5, 5);
    Write_tty ("New Console Device Driver (CON:) Installed ...");
    Goto_XY (save_x, save_y);

    r_ptr->req_type.init_req.end_ptr =
                    MK_FP (_DS, (unsigned int) End_code);

    return OP_COMPLETE;
}
```

We use in **Init_cmd** the video routines we discussed earlier. The only
significant activity this function performs is to set the ending address of the
CONSOLE device driver.

The input function also changed. **Input_cmd** now tests for keystrokes in
the keyboard buffer. If **Input_cmd** finds a keystroke it reads it, places it in
the request buffer, increments the transfer count, and displays the character at
location (78,1) on the monitor. Here is the modified function:

```
unsigned int Input_cmd (struct REQ_struct far *r_ptr)
{
    unsigned int    i;
    unsigned int    key;
    unsigned char   chr;
    unsigned int    save_x;
    unsigned int    save_y;

    for (i = 0; i < r_ptr->req_type.i_o_req.count; i++)
    {
        key = Get_key (0);   /* Obtain Next Key Stroke            */

        if (key & 0xFF)      /* Normal Mode Key Strokes           */
        {
            chr = key & 0xFF;
        }
        else                 /* Extended Function Key Strokes     */
        {
            chr = key >> 8;
        }
        *r_ptr->req_type.i_o_req.buffer_ptr++ = chr;
        save_x = Get_X ();
        save_y = Get_Y ();
        Goto_XY (78, 1);
        Write_chr (chr);
        Goto_XY (save_x, save_y);
    }

    return OP_COMPLETE;
}
```

The `Input_no_wait_cmd` function is similar to `Input_cmd`, but with one significant difference. If the keyboard buffer is empty, then the return status must include the BUSY bit set to indicate this situation to DOS. Here is the function:

```
unsigned int Input_no_wait_cmd (struct REQ_struct far *r_ptr)
{
    unsigned int    rc;
    unsigned int    key;
    unsigned char   chr;
    unsigned int    far *head_ptr;
    unsigned int    far *tail_ptr;

    head_ptr = MK_FP (BIOS_DATA, KBD_HEAD);
    tail_ptr = MK_FP (BIOS_DATA, KBD_TAIL);

    if (*head_ptr == *tail_ptr)
    {                           /* Keyboard Buffer Empty         */
        rc = BUSY_BIT;          /* Indicate Buffer Empty         */
    }
    else
    {                           /* Characters In KBD Buffer      */
        rc = OP_COMPLETE;       /* Indicate Characters In Buffer */
        key = Get_key (1);      /* Obtain Next Key Stroke        */

        if (key & 0xFF)         /* Normal Mode Key Strokes       */
        {
            chr = key & 0xFF;
        }
        else                    /* Extended Function Key Strokes */
        {
            chr = key >> 8;
        }

        r_ptr->req_type.input_no_wait_req.byte_read = chr;
    }

    return rc;
}
```

The `Input_flush_cmd` function simply flushes the keyboard buffer. The function accomplishes this task by altering the low-level BIOS data region pointers. This is not a recommended approach, but we included it to demonstrate various ways of using BIOS interface and hardware interface. The preferred method would have been to invoke the BIOS keyboard function (INT 16) requesting the next character in the buffer until the buffer is empty.

```
unsigned int Input_flush_cmd (struct REQ_struct far *r_ptr)
{
    unsigned int    far *head_ptr;
    unsigned int    far *tail_ptr;

    head_ptr = MK_FP (BIOS_DATA, KBD_HEAD);
    tail_ptr = MK_FP (BIOS_DATA, KBD_TAIL);

    *tail_ptr = *head_ptr;

    return OP_COMPLETE;
}
```

Finally, `Output_cmd` supports the requests Output To Device and Output And Verify Data. The function accesses the data buffer and writes the character argument to the current cursor position.

```
unsigned int Output_cmd (struct REQ_struct far *r_ptr)
{
    unsigned int    i;
    unsigned char   chr;

    for (i = 0; i < r_ptr->req_type.i_o_req.count; i++)
    {
        chr = *r_ptr->req_type.i_o_req.buffer_ptr++;

        Write_chr (chr);
    }

    return OP_COMPLETE;
}
```

Developing the new DOS CONSOLE character device driver required about one hour of work. Most of the work involved selecting the functions to delete within the template and modifying the remaining ones.

6.4   Summary

Character Device Driver Headers

Use the `show_DDH` to find the device driver headers in your system. The character device drivers have device driver names; block device drivers use the name field to indicate the number of units they support.

Character Device Driver Commands

See the *DOS Technical Reference Manual* to find the commands DOS may issue to a character device driver.

CONSOLE Character Device Driver

Files in the CONSOLE character device driver:

- `console` – It is the makefile (Appendix G).

- `console.h` – Contains constants and definitions for the CONSOLE driver (Appendix G).

- `dos_dd.h` – No change

- `dos_hdr.asm` – No change

- `dos_end.c` – No change

- `dos_data.c` – Because this is a character device driver it has a name field; the BPB-related information was eliminated (Appendix G).

- `dos_env.c` – Although we removed the unnecessary DOS request functions, this file could be left unchanged (Appendix G).

- `dos_drvr.c` – Changed extensively (Appendix G).

6.5 Exercises

Exercise 6.1 Run `show_DDH` on your system. Find the character device drivers installed. Explain the attributes of each device.

Exercise 6.2 List the commands DOS may issue to a character device driver.

Exercise 6.3 List the commands DOS may issue to the CONSOLE device driver.

Exercise 6.4 What files do you need to implement the CONSOLE device driver? Which template files do you have to change?

Exercise 6.5 Explain the changes in `dos_drvr.c` for the CONSOLE device driver.

Exercise 6.6 Use the `make` utility to build the CONSOLE device driver on your system.

Exercise 6.7 Explain the fundamental differences between character and block device drivers. List the DOS requests that apply only to character device drivers. List the DOS requests that apply only to block device drivers. List the DOS requests that apply to either device driver.

Chapter 7

Disk/Diskette Fundamentals

This chapter introduces the concepts and terminology related to secondary storage devices. The primary storage device is the disk drive or direct access storage device (DASD).

There are a many types of secondary storage devices. However, most of these devices have a great deal in common. This chapter focuses on the most common aspects of these devices and describes how DOS manages storage devices.

We begin with the vocabulary used to describe secondary storage devices. This vocabulary is complicated by the terms DOS uses to describe various aspects of these devices. Once we have presented the technical jargon, the rest of the chapter will follow a "hands-on" approach to understanding the characteristics of disks and their relationship to DOS.

7.1 The Jargon

Today's DOS-based personal computers use a number of different secondary storage devices. Each of these secondary storage devices has its own physical characteristics. This section presents the terminology used to describe these features.

7.1.1 DASD Types

The different types of secondary storage devices can best be described by the following DASD type matrix.

	Magnetic Media	*Optical Media*
Flexible Media	Floppy Diskette	Digital Paper
Rigid Media	Hard Disk	CD-ROM, WORM
Removable Media	Hard Disk	CD-ROM, WORM
Non-Removable Media	Hard Disk	
Write-Only Media		WORM
Read-Write Media	Diskette, Hard Disk	Magneto-Optic

You can see from this matrix that there are a number of different types of DASDs. The two major recording technologies listed in the matrix are magnetic and optical. A number of other types of recording technologies, such as semiconductor, are not listed in the matrix. These technologies will emerge as costs decrease.

7.1.2 DASD Form Factors

The number of different shapes and sizes of DASDs far outnumbers the types of DASD devices. However, the personal computer industry has been instrumental in presenting a set of de facto standards for DASDs.

The following table presents the most popular DASD form factors adopted by the personal computer industry.

	Full Height	*Half Height*	*Third Height*
8.00" DASD	Diskette		
	Hard Disk		
5.25" DASD	Diskette	Diskette	
	Hard Disk	Hard Disk	
	CD-ROM	CD-ROM	
3.50" DASD		Diskette	Diskette
		Hard Disk	

The form factor is driven primarily by how DASD is used. Reduced size provides a number of benefits, such as reduced material costs, reduced power consumption, and a host of others.

7.1.3 DASD Physical Layout

It is important to understand the internal characteristics of a DASD. Each of the DASDs we have discussed has two major components. The first is the drive and the second is the media that the drive reads and/or writes.

The drive must write the data or read the data in a specified format. The rest of the discussion will focus on the physical data format on the media.

The media consists of one or more circular surfaces. Each surface is similar to a standard phonograph record. The surfaces have a number of concentric recording tracks; the read and/or read/write head of the drive must be positioned to one of these tracks before an operation can be performed.

Each track on a surface is formatted into a number of sectors. These sectors can vary in size from 128 bytes to 4,096 bytes. DOS is capable of handling sector sizes of 128, 256, 512, and 1,024 bytes. The typical sector size for DOS DASDs is 512 bytes.

A DASD must have a read and/or a read/write head associated with each surface in the drive — unless one wishes to turn the media over on a single-headed drive. This is where we get the terms single-sided and double-sided. If the DASD (usually a floppy diskette drive) had only one head, it was termed a single-sided diskette drive. If two heads were present, then the DASD was termed double-sided because both sides of the media could be accessed.

In larger devices, such as hard disks, it is very common to have multiple surfaces. This is accomplished by having multiple pieces of circular media, referred to as platters, contained in the same drive. Each of these platters has two sides, or surfaces, and requires that a head be associated with each.

7.1.4 DASD Storage Capacity

The final physical characteristic of a DASD is its actual capacity. Calculating the capacity of a DASD requires an understanding of the terms presented in the preceding section. The following equation represents the storage capacity for a given DASD.

$$Storage = \frac{Sectors}{Track} \times \frac{Tracks}{Surface} \times Surfaces$$

The storage capacity calculation above is in terms of sectors. If you want the results in bytes, then multiply this value by the number of bytes per sector (sector size).

7.2 DOS View Of DASDs

The information we have presented so far has focused on the physical characteristics of DASDs. This section begins to address the logical aspects of a DASD.

The term logical means that an operating system does not attempt to support all DASDs as separate and unique devices. Operating systems, including DOS, attempt to support a general class of devices. DOS supports both character and block device types, with DASDs classified as block devices.

DOS can support a myriad of DASDs by architecting an operating system structure that accounts for the differences between the various block devices. This structure is referred to as the BIOS Parameter Block (BPB) because it is used by the BIOS service routines as well as DOS. The following C structure describes the contents of a BPB.

```
struct  BPB_struct
{
        unsigned int  bps;                /* Bytes Per Sector       */
        unsigned char spau;               /* Sectors Per Alloc. Unit */
        unsigned int  rs;                 /* Reserved Sectors        */
        unsigned char num_FATs;           /* Number Of FATS          */
        unsigned int  root_entries;       /* # Of Root Dir Entries   */
        unsigned int  num_sectors;        /* Number Of Sectors       */
        unsigned char media_descriptor;/* Media Descriptor         */
        unsigned int  spfat;              /* # Of Sectors Per FAT    */
        unsigned int  spt;                /* # Of Sectors Per Track  */
        unsigned int  heads;              /* Number Of Heads         */
        unsigned long hidden;             /* Number Of Hidden Sectors */
        unsigned long num_sectors_32;     /* 32-Bit Number of Sectors */
};
```

The following is a list of the fields in the BPB that are related to the physical characteristics of the DASD.

- Number of bytes per sector (bps)

- Number of sectors per track (spt)

- Number of heads (heads)

- Number of sectors (num_sectors)

- Number of sectors (num_sectors_32)

- Type of media (media_descriptor)

All of these items are critical values that ensure the correct operation of DOS on various DASDs. The remainder of the entries in the BPB define a logical partitioning or format of data on the DASD that is relevant only in a DOS environment. The remaining entries in the BPB are discussed in the following sections.

7.3 DOS Disk Organization

A DASD operating in a DOS environment has the following major logical sections.

- Partition table

- DOS boot record

- DOS file allocation table (FAT)

- DOS root directory

- DOS file system data

Each logical section of a DOS DASD is defined from fields in the BPB. For example, the hidden field of the BPB specifies the number of sectors from the beginning of the device that are not a part of the logical DOS block device. The spfat field of the BPB specifies the size of the DOS File Allocation Table (FAT) with the num_FATs indicating the number of FATs on the device.

In general, a logical DOS block device can be represented by the following diagram.

DASD partition table
. . .
DOS boot record
DOS file allocation table (FAT)
Possibly second DOS FAT
DOS root directory
DOS file system data

7.3.1 DASD Partition Table

The partition table is not specific to the DOS environment. The partition table is an architected approach that allows the main storage device to be partitioned into multiple operating environments. In other words, the partition table makes it possible to divide your hard disk into a DOS environment as well as a UNIX environment. You can then activate either environment. This capability provides you with two environments (only one is active at a time) without requiring two separate machines.

The partition table is nothing more than a structure located on the first sector of the DASD that provides the following information.

- The number of partitions

- The type of partitions

- The active partition

- The location of the partition

- The size of the partition

The following C structure represents the format and contents of a partition table entry.

```
struct   p_entry
{
    unsigned char  boot_ID;        /* Boot Indicator          */
    unsigned char  boot_HSC [3];   /* Head, Sec, Cyl Of Boot Rec */
    unsigned char  system_ID;      /* Owning System ID        */
    unsigned char  end_HSC [3];    /* Head, Sec, Cyl Of Last Sec */
    unsigned long  sector_offset;  /* Sector Offset From Phys 0 */
    unsigned long  sector_length;  /* Sector Length Of Partition */
};
```

The boot_HSC field of the partition table indicates the head, sector, and cylinder of the boot record for that specific partition; the end_HSC field indicates the head, sector, and cylinder of the end of the partition. The boot_ID field indicates whether the partition is the active or bootable partition.

A specific DASD device can have up to four partitions. The location of the partition table entries is specified in the following structure.

```
struct   partition
{
    unsigned char  code [446];     /* Boot Code For Device (Disk) */
    struct p_entry p_tbl [MAXPART]; /* Partition Table Entries  */
    unsigned int   signature;      /* Valid Partition Signature  */
};
```

7.3.2 DOS Boot Record

A DOS boot record is a complete BPB that has been prepended with a jump instruction around the BPB and an Original Equipment Manufacturer (OEM) identifier. OEM simply identifies the company or supplier of the DOS operating system.

The following C structure describes the content and format of the DOS boot record.

```
struct  BOOT_struct
{
    unsigned char  entry_point [3];  /* Jump To Begin. Boot Code */
    unsigned char  oem [8];          /* OEM Name And Version     */
    unsigned int   bps;              /* Unsigned Chars Per Sector*/
    unsigned char  spau;             /* Sectors Per Alloc. Unit  */
    unsigned int   res_sectors;      /* Number Of Reserved Sector*/
    unsigned char  num_FATs;         /* Number Of FATs           */
    unsigned int   root_files;       /* Number Of Files Root Dir.*/
    unsigned int   volume_size;      /* Number Of Sectors On Vol.*/
    unsigned char  media_byte;       /* Media Descriptor Byte    */
    unsigned int   spf;              /* Number Of Sectors Per FAT*/
    unsigned int   spt;              /* Number Of Secs. Per Track*/
    unsigned int   hpc;              /* Number Of Heads Per Cyl. */
    unsigned long  hidden;           /* Number Of Hidden Sectors */
    unsigned long  volume_size_32;   /* 32-Bit Volume Size       */
};
```

The BPB portion of the DOS boot record begins with the third field. It was discussed in Section 7.2.

7.3.3 DOS File Allocation Table

The DOS File Allocation Table (FAT) is the mechanism DOS uses to manage DASD space. The basic concept of the FAT is that the directory entry points to the first DOS File Allocation Unit of the file.

A DOS File Allocation Unit is typically referred to as an Allocation Unit (AU) or, simply, a cluster. The AU represents the allocation of a specific number of sectors to the specified file. The exact number of sectors each AU represents is given in the **spau** field of the BPB. Therefore, if a file contains one byte of data and the **spau** field in the BPB is eight, then the file has actually allocated eight sectors or 4,096 bytes, assuming the sector size is 512 bytes.

In short, DOS manages disk space in terms of allocation units, or clusters, rather than in terms of actual sectors. We can determine the actual sectors allocated using the following equation.

$$sector = (AU \times spau) + first\_data\_sector$$

Remember that the file system data DOS manages is not located at the beginning of the disk. The file system data follows the boot record, the FAT(s), and the root directory.

If a file requires more than one AU, then the location in the FAT (which is pointed to by the file's directory entry) will contain the number or index of the next AU. The last AU contains 0xFFF when DOS uses 12-bit cluster numbers and contains 0xFFFF when DOS uses 16-bit cluster numbers. This scheme allows a file to physically allocate its actual size through an AU chaining process.

It should be noted that this sequential chaining of AUs has caused a great deal of controversy, especially in DOS environments with very large DASDs. The controversy arises because the AU chain for a specified file must be traversed in order for any given datum in the file to be extracted. This is a very time-consuming operation!

7.3.4 DOS Root Directory

As we mentioned in the previous section, the file directory entry points to the beginning of the file allocation chain. Each file must have a DOS directory entry. Because DOS is a hierarchical file system, it is possible to locate any file by beginning the search at the root directory.

The following C structure indicates the format and content of a DOS directory entry.

```
struct   d_entry
{
    unsigned char   f_name [8];     /* File's Name            */
    unsigned char   f_ext [3];      /* File's Extension       */
    unsigned char   f_attribute;    /* File's Attribute       */
    unsigned char   f_res [10];     /* DOS Reserved Region    */
    unsigned int    f_time;         /* Time Last Changed      */
    unsigned int    f_date;         /* Date Last Changed      */
    unsigned int    f_FAT;          /* Starting FAT Entry     */
    unsigned long   f_size;         /* File's Size (bytes)    */
};
```

The `dos_fat` program presented in Appendix I uses these structures to implement a DOS FAT traversal. The program allows you to enter the name of a file, then watch as the program repeatedly chains through the FAT searching for the specified file.

7.3.5 DOS File System Data

The DOS file system consists of data that has been organized by the application programs as a stream of bytes. DOS allocates space for the specified file in terms of clusters or allocation units (AUs). And like UNIX, DOS does not impose any predefined file format on the files.

Predefined file format (required by some operating systems) means that you must define the structure of your data. In other words, you might have to specify that the data in your file has fixed length records. Therefore, you must specify the size of the maximum fixed-length record. From this, the operating system deduces that each record requires this same amount of data.

You can see the potential for large amounts of wasted DASD space with this type of predefined file format. DOS, on the other hand, allows the application to determine the format of the file data.

7.4 Summary

DOS View of DASDs

DOS supports character and block devices. DASDs are block devices, and DOS and BIOS use BPB to pass information about a device.

DOS Disk Organization

- Partition table

- DOS boot record

- DOS file allocation table(s) (FAT)

- DOS root directory

- DOS file system data

DASD Partition Table

The partition table is a structure located on the first sector of the DASD. It contains

```
struct   partition
{
    unsigned char   code [446];  /* Boot Code For Device (Disk)  */
    struct p_entry  p_tbl [MAXPART]; /* Partition Table Entries  */
    unsigned int    signature;   /* Valid Partition Signature    */
};
```

The structure p_entry is presented on page 102.

DOS File Allocation Table

The File Allocation Table (FAT) is the mechanism DOS uses to manage DASD space. DOS allocates non-contiguous space for a file in a sequence of clusters, or allocation units (AU). Each AU in the FAT has the index of the next AU for the file. The last AU contains 0xFFF when DOS uses 12-bit cluster numbers and contains 0xFFFF when DOS uses 16-bit cluster numbers.

DOS Root Directory

Each file has a DOS directory entry. Each directory entry points to the beginning of the file allocation chain (f_FAT in d_entry, page 104). Appendix I contains the source code for the dos_fat program. The program uses d_entry and the FAT to locate a file.

7.5   Exercises

Exercise 7.1 Find the number of sectors, tracks, and surfaces for your DASDs, then use the storage formula we presented in Section 7.1.4 to calculate their capacities.

Exercise 7.2 Use a diagram to show the relation between a directory entry and FAT for a file that has three non-contiguous AUs.

Exercise 7.3 Explain the use of BPB_struct in block devices.

Exercise 7.4 Compile the dos_fat program. Use the program to locate a file you know exists in your system.

Chapter 8

DOS Block Device Drivers

In this chapter we introduce the concepts of DOS block device drivers. We will use the template-based DOS device driver to implement a completely functional DOS block device driver.

If you want to build the block device driver as we discuss it, you may want to create a `ram_disk` directory. We will perform our development work in this directory. To start, we copy the template-based device driver files into `ram_disk`.

This is the list of the source files that we need to create the RAM_DISK block device driver:

- `ram_disk`

- `dos_hdr.asm`

- `dos_dd.h`

- `dos_data.c`

- `dos_env.c`

- `dos_drvr.c`

- `dos_end.c`

We will examine the differences between the template-based DOS device driver and the RAM_DISK DOS block device driver. First, we will review DOS device driver headers.

107

8.1   Block Device Driver Headers

It is important that we understand the differences between a DOS block device driver and a DOS character device driver. The program `show_DDH` displays the following information for a block device driver :

```
Device Driver Entry (0070:01B6)

Next Device Driver   : 0070:01CA
Device Attributes    : 0840
Device Strategy Offset  : 05DC
Device Interrupt Offset : 0634
Device Driver Name   :
```

This DOS device driver header is the same one that we used to illustrate the differences between character device driver headers and block device driver headers in Chapter 6. The important point to remember is that the block device driver headers place the number of units they support, rather than the name of the device, in the name/unit field of the header as in the following DOS character device driver header.

For a character device driver, `show_DDH` displays the following information:

```
Device Driver Entry (0070:016E)

Next Device Driver   : 0070:0180
Device Attributes    : 8013
Device Strategy Offset  : 05DC
Device Interrupt Offset : 05E7
Device Driver Name   : CON
```

The RAM_DISK, or virtual disk, device driver we implement in this chapter creates a simple block device driver header that allows it to support only one unit.

8.2   How DOS Finds A Block Device

The approach DOS uses to locate a specific DOS block device or drive letter is quite different than that of the DOS character device search strategy.

DOS maintains an internal data structure referred to as the Device Parameter Block (DPB) array. This array has an element for each DOS drive letter or DOS block device. DOS initially creates two entries in this array, which account for drives A: and B:. If the system supports a hard disk, then DOS creates a third element for drive C:.

Each element of the DPB array contains vital information concerning that specific drive. In other words, you would find the following type of information in an element of the DPB array.

- Logical number (A: = 0, ..., Z: = 25)

- Device driver unit

- Sectors per allocation unit

- Sector size

- Type of media

- Number of FATs

- Sector number of FAT

- Sector number of data

- Sector number of root directory

- Number of sectors per FAT

- Number of allocation units

- Number of root directory entries

- Address of the device driver header

When DOS begins to install the device drivers listed in the `config.sys` file, it determines whether the device driver is a block device. If the device driver is for a block device, then DOS creates a DPB for each unit the block device driver supports. Each of these DPBs is initialized with the above information, including the address of the newly installed block device driver header.

Whenever DOS receives a request to access a specific DOS drive, DOS can service that request without searching through the complete DOS device driver header list. DOS simply indexes into the DPB array and locates the appropriate DOS device driver header address. Using this address, DOS constructs either the `Strategy` function or the `Interrupt` function address by accessing the DOS device driver header's `Strategy` or `Interrupt` function offsets. Once DOS has created the `Strategy` or `Interrupt` function address, then it performs a far call to this address.

The approach DOS employs to find DOS block devices is an efficient and effective one. It reduces the need to continually read and re-read vital information from the media and reduces the initial search time required to locate the specified device driver routines.

8.3   Block Device Driver Commands

The template-based DOS device driver implemented a function for all possible
DOS requests. DOS will issue a subset of those requests to the driver when the
driver is a block device driver; DOS will issue another subset of those requests
when the driver is a character device driver. Here is the list of request (with
command codes) that DOS may issue to the RAM_DISK block device driver:

- (00) Initialize

- (01) Check Media

- (02) Build BPB

- (03) IOCTL Input

- (04) Input From Device

- (08) Output To Device

- (09) Output And Verify Data

- (12) IOCTL Output

- (13) Open Device

- (14) Close Device

- (15) Check if Media is Removable

- (19) IOCTL To Device

- (23) Get Logical Device Map

- (24) Set Logical Device Map

Of these requests that DOS can issue to a block device driver, most are not
applicable to the RAM_DISK device driver. For example, we do not have to
Check Media, Open Device, or Close Device. In fact, the RAM_DISK block
device driver has to implement only one:

- (00) Initialize

The remaining DOS requests for the RAM_DISK block device driver are
implemented to pass the requests to the installed VDISK device driver.

8.4 RAM_DISK Block Device Driver

The RAM_DISK device driver is different from other device drivers that we have presented. The uniqueness of the RAM_DISK device driver is neither because it is a DOS block device driver nor because it simulates a physical disk drive by allocating a large RAM buffer. RAM_DISK is unique because it demonstrates the ability of DOS device drivers to build upon the functionality of other installed DOS device drivers!

The RAM_DISK device driver is a block device driver that performs the following functions.

- Installs if `vdisk.sys` is installed

- Deinstalls if `vdisk.sys` is not installed

- Builds DOS requests for `vdisk.sys`

- Issues DOS requests to `vdisk.sys`

The RAM_DISK device driver detects whether the IBM `vdisk.sys` (virtual disk device driver) is installed in the system. If it is, then the RAM_DISK device driver creates a DOS device driver request (command) to obtain the size and functional characteristics of the installed virtual disk. This is accomplished by issuing a Build BPB command to the `vdisk.sys` device driver.

The results of the Build BPB command are then copied into the RAM disk's internal BPB structure at initialization (INIT) time. The local BPB information is then returned to DOS indicating that DOS now has the virtual disk installed (`vdisk.sys`) as well as a disk that looks exactly like the virtual disk (`ram_disk.sys`). The major difference between the two installed block devices is that only one of the block device drivers will be doing all of the work! And that is `vdisk.sys`.

Although this might sound like a shell game, it does have a significant number of uses. For example, it is possible to create a DOS block device driver using the same concepts that will pass the device driver requests to two or more installed device drivers. In essence, this will allow you to automatically back up one device to any number of DOS devices (shadow write) without complex hardware or software.

The details of the RAM_DISK device driver appear in Appendix J.

We need to make one comment about the use of a DOS service call (INT 21) from within the RAM_DISK device driver. You may recall that we cautioned against employing any of these services. It happens that a few of these DOS services can be safely invoked from within a DOS device driver at INIT time.

The following is a list of the DOS services that can be employed from within a DOS device driver without damaging the operational integrity of the operating system.

- (0x01) Keyboard Input

- (0x02) Display Output

- (0x03) Auxiliary Input

- (0x04) Auxiliary Output

- (0x05) Printer Output

- (0x06) Direct Console I/O

- (0x07) Direct Console Input

- (0x08) Console Input

- (0x09) Print String

- (0x0a) Buffered Keyboard Input

- (0x0b) Check Standard Input Status

- (0x0c) Clear Keyboard Buffer

- (0x30) Get DOS Version Number

The above DOS services should be used only during the initialization of the DOS device driver.

We have to make a number of modifications to the template-based DOS device driver to turn it into the new RAM_DISK device driver. Some of the files do not change. Here is the list of all the files with information about their status.

- `ram_disk` – This is the makefile. We changed the name of the device driver from `dos.sys` to `ram_disk.sys` (Appendix J).

- `dos_dd.h` – No change.

- `dos_hdr.asm` – No change.

- `dos_end.c` – No change.

- `dos_data.c` – We added a few global variables that this driver needs (Appendix J).

- `dos_env.c` – We changed this file to indicate that it is not necessary to have all the DOS request functions of the template present in each DOS device driver. Therefore, only the required DOS request function is referenced in this file. Note that this file could have been left unchanged (Appendix J).

- `dos_drvr.c` – We changed this file to include only `Unknown_cmd` and `Init_cmd` functions (Appendix J).

After we initialize the device driver, we forward any request that comes in to `vdisk.sys`:

```
unsigned int Unknown_cmd (struct REQ_struct far *r_ptr)
{
    v_call = MK_FP (FP_SEG (vdisk), vdisk->dev_strat);
    _ES = FP_SEG (r_ptr);
    _BX = FP_OFF (r_ptr);
    v_call ();

    v_call = MK_FP (FP_SEG (vdisk), vdisk->dev_int);
    _ES = FP_SEG (r_ptr);
    _BX = FP_OFF (r_ptr);
    v_call ();
}
```

Here are the new variables for `dos_data.c`:

```
void                             (far *v_call) (void);
struct REQ_struct                tmp_req = { 0 };
struct DEVICE_HEADER_struct far *vdisk = { 0 };

unsigned char   vdisk_str [ ] = "VDISK";
unsigned char   found_msg [ ] = "\r\nVDISK Found\r\n"
                                "Driver Installed\r\n\r\n$";
unsigned char   error_msg [ ] = "\r\nVDISK Not Found\r\n"
                                "Driver Not Installed\r\n\r\n$";
```

8.5 SHADOW Block Device Driver

If you want to build the block device driver as we discuss it, you may want to create a **shadow** directory. We will perform our development work in this directory. To start, we copy the template-based device driver files into **shadow**.

This is the list of the source files that we need to create the SHADOW block device driver.

- shadow

- dos_hdr.asm

- dos_dd.h

- dos_data.c

- dos_env.c

- dos_drvr.c

- dos_end.c

The SHADOW device driver implements *shadow* writing; that is, it writes to two devices at the same time (this is the *n*-plexing concept we discuss in Chapter 10 — in this case *n* is 2).

The SHADOW device driver is a block device driver that allows you to write something on drive A:, then writes a back up copy of the information on drive B:. The only requirement is that drive A: and drive B: are identical drives. We have this requirement because we execute the DOS command issued to drive A:, then we change the unit number and issue the command again to drive B:.

We have to make a number of modifications to the template-based DOS device driver to turn it into the new SHADOW device driver. Some of the files do not change. Here is the list of all the files with information about their status.

- **shadow** – This is the makefile. We changed the name of the device driver from **dos.sys** to **shadow.sys** (Appendix K).

- **dos_dd.h** – No change.

- **dos_hdr.asm** – No change.

- **dos_end.c** – No change.

- **dos_data.c** – We added a few global variables this driver needs (Appendix K).

- **dos_env.c** – We changed this file to indicate that it is not necessary to have all the DOS request functions of the template present in each DOS device driver. Therefore, only functions **Init_cmd**, **Unknown_cmd**, and **Output_cmd** are referenced in this file (Appendix K).

- **dos_drvr.c** – This file changed like **dos_drvr.c** in RAM_DISK. It contains three functions: **Unknown_cmd**, **Output_cmd**, and **Init_cmd**. (Appendix K).

We modified three functions in `dos_drvr.c`: Init_cmd, Unknown_cmd, and Output_cmd.

Init_cmd appears in Appendix K. The Unknown_cmd function forwards commands to the device driver handling drive A:. Unknown_cmd is similar to the Unknown_cmd function in RAM_DISK:

```
unsigned int Unknown_cmd (struct REQ_struct far *r_ptr)
{
    v_call = MK_FP (FP_SEG (ddh_ptr), ddh_ptr->dev_strat);
    _ES = FP_SEG (r_ptr);
    _BX = FP_OFF (r_ptr);
    v_call ();

    v_call = MK_FP (FP_SEG (ddh_ptr), ddh_ptr->dev_int);
    _ES = FP_SEG (r_ptr);
    _BX = FP_OFF (r_ptr);
    v_call ();
}
```

Shadow write requires that we implement two output commands: the Output Command and the Output Verify Command. Output_cmd routes the output request to Unknown_cmd — it writes to drive A:. If the output request succeeds, Output_cmd changes the unit to drive B: and routes the output request again to Unknown_cmd. Here is Output_cmd.

```
unsigned int Output_cmd (struct REQ_struct far *r_ptr)
{
    unsigned char    unit;

    unit = r_ptr->unit;
    r_ptr->unit = DRIVE_A;
    r_ptr->status = OP_COMPLETE;

    Unknown_cmd (r_ptr);            /* Initial Write To A Drive*/

    if (!(r_ptr->status & ERROR_BIT))
    {
        r_ptr->unit = DRIVE_B;
        r_ptr->status = OP_COMPLETE;

        Unknown_cmd (r_ptr);        /* Shadow Write To B Drive */
    }
```

```
    r_ptr->unit = unit;
}
```

8.6   Summary

How DOS Finds a Block Device

DOS uses an internal Device Parameter Block (DPB) array with information
about block devices. The array contains one element for each DOS drive letter.
Each entry in the DPB array points to the appropriate device driver header.
To access the DPB array, DOS uses the logical number for a block device and
follows the pointer to the device driver header.

RAM_DISK Block Device Driver

Files in the RAM_DISK block device driver:

- `ram_disk` – It is the makefile (Appendix J).

- `dos_dd.h` – No change

- `dos_hdr.asm` – No change

- `dos_end.c` – No change

- `dos_data.c` – The template file already indicates it is a block device driver.
  We added some global variables RAM_DISK uses (Appendix J).

- `dos_env.c` – We modified the array of pointers to functions (`dos_cmd []`)
  because RAM_DISK uses only two functions: `Init_cmd` and `Unknown_cmd`
  (Appendix J).

- `dos_drvr.c` – We use only two functions: `Init_cmd` and `Unknown_cmd`
  (Appendix J).

SHADOW Block Device Driver

Files in the SHADOW block device driver:

- `shadow` – It is the makefile (Appendix K).

- `dos_dd.h` – No change

- `dos_hdr.asm` – No change

- `dos_end.c` – No change

- `dos_data.c` – We added a few global variables this driver needs (Appendix K).

- `dos_env.c` – We modified the array of pointers to functions (`dos_cmd []`) because SHADOW uses only three functions: `Init_cmd`, `Unknown_cmd`, and `Output_cmd` (Appendix K).

- `dos_drvr.c` – We use only three functions: `Init_cmd`, `Unknown_cmd`, and `Output_cmd` (Appendix K).

8.7 Exercises

Exercise 8.1 Run `show_DDH` on your system. Find the block device drivers installed. Explain the attributes of each driver.

Exercise 8.2 List the commands DOS may issue to a block device driver.

Exercise 8.3 Explain DPB. When does DOS create it? How does DOS use it?

Exercise 8.4 What files do you need to implement the RAM_DISK device driver? Which template files do you have to change?

Exercise 8.5 We could have left `dos_data.c` unchanged in the RAM_DISK device driver. How would you handle the extra global variables the driver needs?

Exercise 8.6 Explain the changes in `dos_drvr.c` for the RAM_DISK device driver.

Exercise 8.7 Use the `make` utility to build the RAM_DISK device driver on your system.

Chapter 9

DOS Device Driver Test Methodology

We have developed a couple of device drivers in this text so far. However, we have not yet proposed a formalized device driver test methodology. So, we propose such a methodology now, and we attempt to demonstrate its use and potential benefits.

Our device driver test methodology is based on a bottom-up approach that consists of the following three phases.

1. Device driver debug process

2. Device driver command exercise

3. Device driver exercise.

The device driver debug process normally starts with ad hoc testing. Ad hoc testing is a type of testing where the programmer checks random parts of the code without following every possible path available in the program. Ad hoc testing ensures that your driver is functionally stable through frequently executed program paths.

The next step exercises the driver with specific DOS requests. This is the second-level testing.

The third-level testing uses DOS API service requests in an exhaustive manner and in a combinatorial sequence.

The three phase test methodology reduces the number of errors in the DOS device drivers you implement and improves their level of functional conformance.

119

9.1   Device Driver Debug Process

The most important step in this device driver test methodology is to ensure the device driver can be correctly installed in a DOS environment. If the device driver can be correctly installed it is because it conforms to the structural characteristics of DOS device drivers and that it can process the DOS initialization request. If we derive the driver from the template-based device driver we presented earlier, then we meet both requirements.

The more we test a device driver, the better are the chances we will find fewer errors. However, the ad hoc device driver testing that is typically performed on DOS device drivers is only the first step in the test methodology proposed here. Ad hoc testing is not a substitute for a formalized, repeatable test scenario.

The ad hoc testing process can incorporate many of the techniques described in Chapter 5. Those techniques allow you to develop a DOS device driver and monitor all aspects of the DOS device driver request/response dialog.

Once you complete the ad hoc device driver testing, you are ready to begin the more sophisticated device driver command interface testing. We describe this type of testing next.

9.2   Device Driver Command Exercise

It is difficult to force DOS to issue a specific device driver request to a device driver. Typically, the ad hoc testing attempts to force DOS to issue such requests to the device driver under test. This is attempted by invoking DOS commands, such as `copy`, `chkdsk`, and the like.

Invoking DOS commands to test a driver places the actual device driver requests in a secondary role. The primary role in this type of testing is the execution of DOS applications that use the device driver under test, and not the requests the device driver is processing.

A production device driver must be exercised in conformance with the DOS device driver command interface definition. Therefore, this test methodology requires that the test application be able to create a specific DOS request and issue it directly to the DOS device driver under test. Furthermore, the test application must verify that the DOS device driver responds correctly to the DOS request.

It is easy to develop such a test application. For example, on several occasions we have used the `show_DDH` program to gather information about device drivers loaded in the system. If we run `show_DDH`, we can obtain the addresses of the `Strategy` and `Interrupt` functions of the device driver under test. Then we can create a DOS request structure, initialize it to the desired DOS device driver command, set the `ES` and `BX` registers to the address of the DOS request structure.

Finally we can perform a far call to the **Strategy** function, then perform a far call to the **Interrupt** function.

The above technique allows the test application to simulate the DOS service manager without involving DOS directly. With this approach we can issue every defined DOS request to the device driver under test and review the response to that request. We can then analyze the device driver's response to determine if it conforms to the DOS device driver specifications.

If the device driver conforms with the DOS device driver specifications, then this phase of the test methodology is complete. However, if the DOS device driver does not conform, then you have isolated the input to the driver and the response from the driver that is in error. With this information, you can change the DOS device driver and begin the test procedure again.

9.3 Device Driver Exercise

The device driver testing we just discussed cannot account for error conditions caused by the order of the requests and application interfacing conflicts. Therefore, the final phase of testing in the device driver test methodology involves DOS API-initiated device operations.

DOS API-initiated device operations is a set of DOS device driver requests that are issued as a result of DOS API service requests. The approach is to create a test application that requests all DOS API services that can cause DOS to issue a device driver request. This test application then executes these DOS API services in an exhaustive manner as well as in a combinatorial sequence.

The incorporation of this form of DOS device driver testing ensures that your DOS device driver is functionally stable (ad hoc testing), conforms with the DOS device driver specification (second-level testing), and is not sensitive to ordering or context (third-level testing).

If you submit your DOS device driver to the level of testing we described in this chapter, you will produce a DOS device driver that is better tested than most device drivers available today.

9.4 Summary

Device Driver Testing

1. Install the device driver.

2. Perform ad hoc testing to verify the driver is functionally stable.

3. Perform second-level testing. Issue DOS request directly to the device driver under test.

4. Perform third-level testing. Use DOS API service requests to issue device driver requests in an exhaustive manner as well as in a combinatorial sequence.

9.5   Exercises

Exercise 9.1 Install the CONSOLE device driver. Perform ad hoc and command exercise testing. Then use DOS API-initiated device operations to test the device driver.

Chapter 10

DOS Device Driver Projects

In this chapter we present suggestions for DOS device driver projects. The projects follow the same implementation techniques we used to develop the template-based device driver.

Many projects are possible. Here is a representative set of DOS device drivers.

- *n*-plexing devices

- Logical device concatenation

- Device espionage

- CD-ROM support

- New technology support.

Each of the proposed projects has a practical as well as a theoretical basis. A device driver that can solve the age-old problem of providing a single logical device view of multiple physical devices would certainly be useful as well as having its theoretical merits.

The concept of DOS device driver leveraging is also exploited in two of the proposed projects. Device driver leveraging means the DOS device driver does not implement functions that already exist in other DOS device drivers. The device driver simply constructs a DOS request and simulates the function DOS performs when issuing the DOS request to the other DOS device driver.

With these projects we intend to present some general design and implementation guidelines you might find useful when you develop your own device drivers.

10.1   *n*-plexing DOS Devices

The concept of *n*-plexing physical devices is not a new one. Most implementations of the *n*-plexing concept are restricted to the case where *n* is 2. In other words, duplex operations.

Many applications of *n*-plexing capability can be found, especially at the DOS device driver level rather than at the application level. For example, in systems that require some level of redundancy it is important to have the shadow write capability that is implied in duplex operations to a device.

Another useful application of this capability is related to the duplication industry. It would be nice to have a standard application write to one specific device and have *n* exact copies made at the same time. Without such a device driver, the application has the responsibility of issuing writes to *n* devices.

In more advanced use of an *n*-plexing the DOS device driver would write to both a local disk and a remote disk at the same time. In other words, it is possible for the *n*-plexing DOS device driver to write to its local disk drive while at the same time propagating a copy of the same data to a remote disk via a local area network or a mainframe host connection. This sort of capability allows automatic backups.

The issues that surround this type of implementation are not overwhelming. For example, the *n*-plexing device driver must be able to find the DOS device driver headers of other DOS device drivers in the system. This is not difficult — remember the `show_DDH` example. We can use the same concept during the initialization phase of a DOS device driver.

Once we locate the device driver headers for the target device drivers then it is easy to route the DOS requests to the *n* target DOS device drivers. You will find this approach provides a great deal of flexibility, yet it is simple to implement.

10.2   Logical Device Concatenation

Have you ever had a device that is large enough? This device driver project will not solve the problem of capacity completely, but will ease it. The general idea is that *n* physical devices are logically concatenated through a single DOS device driver.

There must be a number of applications for this type of DOS device driver. We made this statement because companies have gone to great lengths to provide a DOS command that provides similar function. Namely, the DOS command `join`. This command allows a physical device to be joined to the logical file structure of another device, resulting in a common file system view of the physical devices.

A logical device concatenation driver provides a single DOS drive letter that represents the entire set of physical devices, or any subset desired. This allows you to forget about separate drive letters forever. In fact, it is possible to create the DOS device driver that allows the format process to occur on the collection of physical devices.

The technical issues related to this DOS device driver are similar in nature to the issues for n-plexing devices. One of the issues omitted in that section concerns the elimination of DOS drive letters for the specific physical devices. In other words, once the controlling DOS device driver is installed you would not like any DOS requests to go directly to the physical devices without coming through this DOS device driver. Therefore, it is necessary to eliminate the original DOS drive letters and maintain only the one representing the collection of physical devices.

We can use a number of techniques to achieve the above effect in the system. However, most of them require some features that are specific to a DOS version. Consequently, we will not attempt to present their details.

10.3 DOS Device Espionage

Considerable discussion has centered around "viruses" and various damaging programs. It is possible to combat a significant amount of potentially damaging influence by developing and installing a device driver that performs a special type of espionage.

It is possible to write a device driver to monitor the operations of all the DOS device drivers in the system. Because these device drivers are the software portal to the outside, it is reasonable to assume that if the proper monitoring techniques are applied, then the system achieves a greater level of security.

These are the types of operations that such a device driver monitor could do.

- Elimination of TSR disk writes

- Data integrity (read after write)

- Elimination of device driver hooking.

Each of these items can be implemented by a DOS device driver. This is not to imply that by implementing these three items your system immediately becomes secure. The intention is to provide you with a small list of representative operations that can be added to, and will collectively improve, the security of your system.

10.4   CD-ROM Support For DOS Devices

CD-ROMs provide a very inexpensive form of long-term mass storage. However, a number of very difficult problems are associated with the use of CD-ROMs in DOS-based systems.

The first technical issue CD-ROMs present is how to access the data on the CD-ROM. The CD-ROM has roughly 600 megabytes of data organized in a CD-ROM standard format. This format is alien to the DOS file format. Therefore, there is difficulty in treating the CD-ROM simply as a write-protected disk drive.

The next technical issue relates to the physical format of the data contained on the CD-ROM. The typical CD-ROM has data written in 2048-byte sectors. Therefore, under a DOS FAT system it is possible to access only 128 megabytes of the CD-ROM, even if the logical format of the data on the CD-ROM permitted access. The 128 megabytes is computed by multiplying the maximum number of allocation units in DOS (64K) by the size of the allocation unit (2K).

Although DOS allows the allocation unit to be larger than 2048 bytes, it is difficult to increase this value for a CD-ROM. The problem that occurs is this: if the allocation unit is increased beyond the 2K value, then an allocation unit could contain both the end of a file as well as the start of another file. As the allocation unit approaches a larger value, it is theoretically possible for complete files to be contained within one allocation unit as well as the start and end of other files. Clearly, DOS is not capable of addressing the complex allocation unit decoding required to resolve this issue without the support of an intelligent device driver.

10.5   Supporting New Technology

The last area of DOS device driver projects is the leading edge. This area includes the development of DOS device drivers that support new technology. For example, the small computer system interface (SCSI) adapters are continually in need of a DOS device driver to control them.

Another new technology that has not received a reasonable amount of DOS device driver support is the write-once-read-many (WORM) optical disks. These devices provide large quantities of mass storage, but can only be written once. Therefore, the current directory update operations of DOS must be buffered or physically chained to different sectors on the WORM.

In each of these cases it is important to remember that the DOS device driver is responsible for compensating for the idiosyncrasies of the attached device or adapter. Therefore, as new technology emerges there will always be a need for the development of DOS device drivers to support that technology. Furthermore, the more effectively the DOS device driver addresses the new technology, the more successful the technology will become.

10.6 Summary

DOS Device Driver Projects

- n-plexing DOS devices – write to one device and have the same information copied to n devices

- Logical device concatenation – logically concatenate a number of physical devices with a device driver allowing access to the devices using one name

- DOS device espionage – a device driver that monitors the operations of all the DOS device drivers in the system

- CD-ROM support for DOS devices – inexpensive form of long-term mass storage

- Supporting new technology – SCSI, WORM, etc.

10.7 Exercises

Exercise 10.1 Select one of the device driver projects we have suggested and implement it.

Part III

DOS WORM Device Driver

Chapter 11

WORM Fundamentals

We have discussed several DOS device drivers in Part II. Now we present
the concepts, design, and implementation of a full-function Write-Once-Read-
Many (WORM) DOS device driver for the IBM 3363 WORM and its associated
adapter.

WORM devices have a number of interesting characteristics that have forced
operating systems, in particular device drivers, to take a new look at classical
device models. It is for this reason that we include a WORM device driver in
this text. The ability to develop a full-function WORM device driver utilizing
the methodology we presented in previous chapters demonstrates the robustness
of the method. Furthermore, the flexibility inherent in the method allows new
technology to be addressed in new ways.

The fundamental concept of WORM technology is that any given sector on
the media may be written only once. Typically, the process of writing data to
a sector of a WORM device is accomplished by a process termed *obliteration*.
In other words, a laser in the WORM device actually obliterates or damages
portions of the surface of the media. The results of this process are permanent,
and any attempt to write over the data will result in the destruction of both the
original data and the new data.

Although the operating principles of a WORM device are easy to understand
it is difficult to grasp the overall impact of WORM devices on the system's
software without a detailed analysis.

11.1 DOS File System Services - A Closer Look

The incorporation of any secondary storage device or new mass-storage technology into an operating environment is dictated largely by the file system services

131

and architecture. The DOS environment is no exception. Therefore, before we
attempt to develop a DOS device driver for the IBM 3363 WORM we must
understand the relationship between the DOS file system services and the DOS
device driver commands.

In the previous chapters we focused on the DOS device driver command
interface. The intent was to present the information about DOS device drivers
in a self-contained and manageable way. However, new technology, such as
WORM, often affects the entire operating environment. The potential of such
affects forces us to review the technology with respect to every abstract interface
in the operating environment.

It is important to analyze all file-related DOS services prior to embarking on
the development of a DOS device driver for a new device. And it is relatively
simple to develop a complete set of programs, such as the one that follows, that
invoke a specific DOS service.

You recall that an application program requests DOS services via the
interrupt 0x21 interface. The DOS services we are interested in are the ones
that will ultimately invoke a DOS device driver to gain access to a specific
device. As an example, the following program (**dos_del**) uses DOS services to
delete the file **foo.txt**.

```
#include     <stdio.h>
#include     <dos.h>

#define      DELETE_FILE 0x41

void main ()
{
    int              ret;
    union REGS       regs;
    struct SREGS     sregs;
    char             *filename = "foo.txt";

    regs.h.ah = DELETE_FILE;
    regs.x.dx = (unsigned int) filename;
    sregs.ds = _DS;
    ret = intdosx (&regs, &regs, &sregs);
```

```
    if (regs.x.cflag)
    {
        printf ("Operation Failed - Status : %04X\n", ret);
    }
    else
    {
        printf ("Operation Succeeded\n");
    }
}
```

We will use `dos_del` to determine the relationship between the DOS services interface and the DOS device driver command interface when we try to delete a file. Here is the order of events:

- Create `foo.txt`

- Execute the `visual` utility

- Execute `dos_del` to delete `foo.txt`

- Reboot the system to remove the `visual` utility

11.2   DOS FAT File System

If you executed `dos_del` (presented in the previous section), you noticed output commands being issued to the device driver. The purpose of these write operations is the topic of this section.

During the execution of `dos_del` you noticed commands used to determine the existence and location of the file `foo.txt`. After locating the file, DOS performs the following operations (not necessarily in this order).

- Erase file (update DOS directory)

- Free space (update FAT number 1)

- Free space (update FAT number 2)

If you execute `visual` and begin to perform file operations, such as copy and erase, you will notice a number of device driver output commands to low-numbered sectors. These output operations are related primarily to the DOS directory updates as well as the File Allocation Table (FAT) management.

It should be obvious that if a WORM device is treated the same as a magnetic device in the DOS operating environment, then the entire DOS directory and FAT will become corrupted due to sector rewrites! Therefore, a DOS device driver that supports a WORM device must resolve this problem. We address this problem in the next chapter.

11.3   Summary

- Interrupt 0x21 provides DOS file services

- DOS file system services may issue many device driver commands

- `visual` verifies the DOS device driver commands that are executed for a single DOS file service

11.4   Exercises

Exercise 11.1 List the file service commands available in DOS.

Exercise 11.2 Run `visual`. Then run `dos_del` and identify the commands executed.

Exercise 11.3 Choose a storage device you are familiar with and find out which DOS file services you can invoke for that device.

Exercise 11.4 Before reading the next chapter, consider how you would solve the rewrite problem in a WORM file allocation table.

Chapter 12

WORM Device Driver Architecture

The previous chapter described the problem that WORM device drivers must overcome when dealing with classical file system directories. The tendency has been to develop very complex file systems to accommodate WORM devices. The major problem with developing yet another file system is that the new file system is alien to most operating systems. This situation typically prohibits the user from using standard commands while accessing the WORM device.

Either the device driver must compensate for the WORM device's peculiarities and conform to the operating environment's perception of the Direct Access Storage Device (DASD), or a completely new file system environment must be developed, including the commands to manage that environment. The architectural approach we present in this chapter achieves operating system conformance at the device driver level. This approach allows all DOS commands to function properly without exceptions.

12.1   The DOS BPB In Review

The most important question a developer faces during the design of a DOS device driver for a new device is "How should the device appear to DOS?" In other words: "How does DOS perceive the device when viewing it through the new device driver?" DOS develops its perception of the device from the information provided in the DOS BIOS Parameter Block (BPB) in the DOS device driver.

In the case of the IBM 3363 WORM, the information required to construct the DOS BPB comes from the specification of the device itself — the *IBM 3363 Optical Disk Drive* hardware technical reference manual. Here is a summary of

135

this type of information.

Capacity	200,000,000	bytes
Track Size	11,776	bytes
Sector Size	512	bytes
Number of Heads	1	
Number of Tracks	17,100	
Sectors/Track	23	

Although it would be nice to define a DOS BPB that fully describes the capacity of the IBM 3363 WORM, the BPB would not allow for any type of free sector management. Because DOS will continue to write and rewrite the same sector multiple times, the device driver must implement some type of sector reallocation algorithm — and that requires media space. Therefore, the DOS BPB must not define the actual capacity of the IBM 3363 WORM.

The WORM device driver attempts to give DOS the perception of a 32-megabyte magnetic storage device. The rest of the sectors on the IBM 3363 WORM constitute the free sector pool that is used for reallocation of previously written sectors. In other words, the DOS BPB defined in the device driver accounts for only the first 32 megabytes of storage space on the IBM 3363 WORM with the remainder being managed by the device driver on an as-needed basis. Table 12.1 illustrates this architecture.

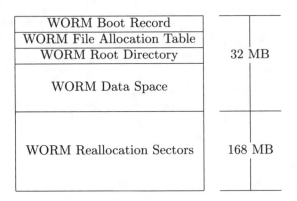

Table 12.1: WORM information

12.2   IBM 3363 Device Driver Architecture

We started to address the design of the device driver for the IBM 3363 WORM in the previous section. However, we did not discuss the free space management algorithms. These algorithms are the heart of the device driver. Another way to look at it is to view DOS as managing the first 32 megabytes of the WORM, and the free space management algorithms embedded in the device driver as managing the remaining 168 megabytes of space.

Numerous methods can be applied to the space management of write-once media. Each of these methods provides its own set of advantages and disadvantages. If we were developing this device driver for production use, we would typically conform to a development process that is similar to the following one.

- Perform market research

- Develop marketing requirements

- Develop initial design points

- Perform marketing/development review

- Develop defined product

Although each step is crucial to the success of a product, we take the liberty to simply state our assumptions, then develop the product without a great deal of fuss. The following list represents the major assumptions and/or design points this WORM device driver attempts to address.

- Demonstrate device driver design flexibility

- Functionally emulate a read/write disk drive

- Minimize device driver implementation effort

- Minimize optical media usage

The optical media free space (sector) management algorithms realize, in part, the above design goals while maintaining simplicity in the design and implementation of the device driver. To accomplish this, we modified the read and write operations of the device driver to include a level of processing indirection. This level of processing indirection allows reads and writes of physical sector locations to be transformed into reads and writes of sectors other than the ones specified.

The concept of inserting a level of processing indirection is not new. This concept is used in all memory mapping hardware to transform logical addresses into physical addresses. And that is the approach we take in this device driver. The application, or DOS itself, specifies a particular physical sector to read or write. To the device driver this is not a physical sector, but a logical one.

Therefore, the driver performs a table look-up to determine which physical sector it should read or write.

But, where is the look-up table stored? The device driver augments the optical media characteristics of the WORM with the magnetic media characteristics of floppy diskettes. This unique combination of mass-storage media characteristics allows the device driver to save the table on magnetic media while fully using the optical media for data storage.

Although it is simple to develop a WORM device driver, we have tried to demonstrate a more powerful concept: a device driver can create an abstract device from the devices present in the system.

12.3   Typical Problems with WORM Devices

You have become aware of a number of problems that WORM devices pose. However, some problems are more subtle than others. For example, a file that is created in the root directory will alter the FATs as well as the root directory. Both the FATs and the root directory are located at the beginning of the DOS disk. Therefore, it is easy to track the additions and deletions made to root-level items by watching the contents of the first few sectors of the media.

What happens when subdirectories are allowed in the file system? Subdirectories are nothing more than files that have been allocated from the data portion of the disk and contain directory entries. An entry can again be a directory. This means that subdirectories can appear anywhere on the media. Therefore, it is impossible to tell from the sector location whether you are accessing a file or a directory.

For this reason many WORM device drivers and file managers provide only a flat file system. A flat file system has only one level. In other words, if you specify that subdirectories are not allowed and that all operations must occur in the root directory, then you have created a flat file system.

Our device driver fully supports all aspects of the DOS file system. It allows the full use of subdirectories, as well as the root directory, without limitations.

12.4   Summary

We covered the specifications for the IBM 3363 WORM and the design of the WORM device driver. We follow the template we described in Chapter 4. Our device driver solution stores the look-up table on floppy diskettes to avoid FAT updates on the WORM device.

12.5 Exercises

Exercise 12.1 List the device specifications for the IBM 3363 WORM.

Exercise 12.2 Explain how you will use the BPB with a WORM device.

Exercise 12.3 Explain how we propose to solve the write-once problem when supporting FATs. Develop other possible solutions.

Chapter 13

DOS WORM Device Driver

The previous chapters have provided information about the operating environment as well as the operating characteristics of WORM devices. The operating system's perception of the WORM device is defined by the WORM device driver.

We can apply numerous design and implementation strategies to WORM devices. We offer one approach that demonstrates the robustness of the DOS device driver implementation philosophy presented in this book, rather than the full exploitation of WORM device technology.

Our design approach has a number of interesting characteristics that may be found in the device drivers we outlined earlier. This chapter collects a number of useful concepts and demonstrates how they might be combined into a device driver that addresses new technological problems.

13.1 DOS WORM Device Driver Concept

The basic concept of the WORM device driver is to present the WORM device to the operating system as a 32-megabyte magnetic device. This is accomplished by creating on the diskette drive a read-write file that represents the current state of the optical media. In other words, whenever the driver rewrites the optical surface, it updates the diskette file to indicate the actual optical sector in use.

We use the following algorithm to read from the WORM device.

```
Break operation into single sectors
For each sector do
    Read the magnetic file indexed by sector number
    Obtain actual sector number from magnetic file
Read actual sector from optical media
```

We use the following algorithm to write to the WORM device.

```
Break operation into single sectors
For each sector do
    Read the magnetic file indexed by sector number
    Obtain actual sector number from magnetic file
    If sector is not written then
        Write the currently addressed optical sector
    If sector is written then
        Find a free (blank) optical sector
        Update the magnetic file to indicate the change
    Write the data in the selected free optical sector
```

This algorithm gives us full use of the optical surface while the device appears to be a standard read/write media. The algorithm is analogous to the algorithms used in defective sector reallocation.

Note that the low-level access to the floppy diskette drive and the IBM 3363 WORM drive is through the BIOS interface. Appendix H describes the BIOS interface for the floppy disk drive while Appendix L describes the BIOS interface for the IBM 3363 WORM drive.

13.2   DOS WORM Device Driver Header

The device driver header we use for the WORM device driver is the same one we provided in the template (Chapter 4). Remember, the template includes a device driver header that specifies a block device in the attribute word of the header. The WORM device driver is attempting to present itself to DOS as a magnetic block device which allows us to use the template header.

The file dos_data.c indicates what the DOS device driver header looks like. Here is the dos_header structure.

```
struct  DEVICE_HEADER_struct  dos_header =
{
    (struct DEVICE_HEADER_struct far *) 0xFFFFFFFFL,
    0x2000,                         /* Non-IBM Format           */
    (unsigned int) Strategy,        /* Strategy Function        */
    (unsigned int) Interrupt,       /* Interrupt Function       */
    {                               /* Unit/Name Field          */
        0x01,                       /* Initial Number Of Units  */
        0x00,                       /* Zero Remaining Entries   */
        0x00,                       /* Zero Remaining Entries   */
        0x00,                       /* Zero Remaining Entries   */
        0x00,                       /* Zero Remaining Entries   */
        0x00,                       /* Zero Remaining Entries   */
        0x00,                       /* Zero Remaining Entries   */
        0x00                        /* Zero Remaining Entries   */
    }
};
```

Once again we capitalize on the benefits of the template-based approach to writing DOS device drivers.

13.3 DOS WORM Device Driver Commands

The DOS WORM device driver is a block device driver. Consequently, it does not require any of the character device driver commands. Furthermore, a number of the standard DOS device driver commands are not necessary in this implementation. Therefore, the DOS device driver command processing functions in `dos_drvr.c` have been reduced to the following list.

- (00) Initialize

- (01) Check Media

- (02) Build BPB

- (04) Input From Device

- (08) Output To Device

This list of commands must be augmented with the following functions.

- `Unknown_cmd`

- `Which_sector`

- Check_sector

- Send_command

The `Unknown_cmd` function processes DOS device driver commands that are not implemented by the device driver. `Which_sector` reads the diskette and determines the actual optical sector to be used in the operation. `Check_sector` checks an optical sector. If the optical sector has been written, the function `Check_sector` attempts to reallocate that sector prior to execution of the actual write operation. Finally, `Send_command` sends the constructed command block to the IBM 3363 WORM device through the BIOS interface.

The use of these additional functions is best illustrated by analyzing the `Input_cmd` and `Output_cmd` functions. Here is the `Input_cmd` function.

```
/* - - - - - - - - - - - - - - - - - - - - - - - - - - - - - - -*/
/*                                                               */
/*  FUNCTION:    I n p u t _ c m d                               */
/*                                                               */
/*  REMARKS :                                                    */
/*                                                               */
/*  INPUTS  :    r_ptr    Pointer To Request Packet              */
/*                                                               */
/*  OUTPUTS :    Status  Returned In Function Return Value       */
/*                                                               */
/* - - - - - - - - - - - - - - - - - - - - - - - - - - - - - - -*/

unsigned int Input_cmd (struct REQ_struct far *r_ptr)
{
    unsigned int    i;
    unsigned int    rc;
    unsigned int    cnt;
    unsigned long   sec;

    cnt = r_ptr->req_type.i_o_req.count;
    if (cnt > 127)                          /* > 64 Kbytes          */
    {
        r_ptr->req_type.i_o_req.count = 127;
        cnt = 127;
    }

    sec = r_ptr->req_type.i_o_req.start_sector + bpb.hidden;

    if ((sec > bpb.num_sectors) ||
```

```
            ((sec + cnt) > bpb.num_sectors))
    {
        r_ptr->req_type.i_o_req.count = 0x0000;
        return (STATUS_SNF);
    }

    for (i = 0, rc = 0; i < cnt; i++, sec++)
    {
        rc |= Send_command (r_ptr->req_type.i_o_req.buffer_ptr,
                Which_sector (sec), 1, READ_3363);
    }

    if (rc != STATUS_NO_ERROR)
    {
        rc = Xlate_error (rc);
        r_ptr->req_type.i_o_req.count = 0x0000;
    }

    return rc;
}
```

In `Output_cmd` we use the function `Check_sector` to allow the reallocation of the optical sector, if necessary, prior to the actual sector write operation. Here is the `Output_cmd` function.

```
/* - - - - - - - - - - - - - - - - - - - - - - - - - - - - - - -*/
/*                                                               */
/*  FUNCTION:   O u t p u t _ c m d                              */
/*                                                               */
/*  REMARKS :                                                    */
/*                                                               */
/*  INPUTS  :   r_ptr   Pointer To Request Packet                */
/*                                                               */
/*  OUTPUTS :   Status  Returned In Function Return Value        */
/*                                                               */
/* - - - - - - - - - - - - - - - - - - - - - - - - - - - - - - -*/

unsigned int Output_cmd (struct REQ_struct far *r_ptr)
{
    unsigned int    i;
    unsigned int    rc;
    unsigned int    cnt;
```

```
    unsigned long    sec;

    cnt = r_ptr->req_type.i_o_req.count;
    if (cnt > 127)                         /* > 64 Kbytes         */
    {
        r_ptr->req_type.i_o_req.count = 127;
        cnt = 127;
    }


    sec = r_ptr->req_type.i_o_req.start_sector + bpb.hidden;

    if ((sec > bpb.num_sectors) ||
        ((sec + cnt) > bpb.num_sectors))
    {
        r_ptr->req_type.i_o_req.count = 0x0000;
        return (STATUS_SNF);
    }

    for (i = 0, rc = 0; i < cnt; i++, sec++)
    {
        rc |= Send_command (r_ptr->req_type.i_o_req.buffer_ptr,
                Check_sector (sec), 1, WRITE_3363);
    }

    if (rc != STATUS_NO_ERROR)
    {
        rc = Xlate_error (rc);
        r_ptr->req_type.i_o_req.count = 0x0000;
    }

    return rc;
}
```

13.4   DOS WORM Device Driver Control Flow

The control flow and general operation of the DOS WORM device driver are
identical to that of the template-based device driver. The only twist added
to the device driver is that DOS is tricked into thinking that the device it is
addressing is something other than what it is.

You will find that the technique of representing device characteristics
differently than the actual characteristics of the device is very useful. In fact,

for most new technologies that are unknown to existing operating systems this technique is the only way to integrate these technologies into the operating environment.

The other technique we use in this device driver is the combination of two or more physical device characteristics to achieve the desired results. In short, it was necessary to have a read/write media that could store the logical-to-actual sector transformation table. We accomplished that by using the diskette drive. Clearly, any read/write media, including RAM, would have achieved the same results.

The important point to remember is that you are the one that creates the implementation of the abstract device being accessed. Only your imagination limits how that can be accomplished.

13.5 DOS WORM Device Driver Files

We must make a number of modifications to the template-based DOS device driver to turn it into the new WORM device driver. Some of the files do not change. Here is the list of all the files, with information about their status.

- worm – This is the makefile. We changed the name of the device driver from dos.sys to worm.sys (Appendix M).

- dos_dd.h – No change.

- dos_hdr.asm – No change.

- dos_end.c – No change.

- dos_data.c – We added a few global variables this driver needs (Appendix M).

- dos_env.c – We changed this file to indicate that it is not necessary to have all the DOS request functions of the template present in each DOS device driver. Therefore, only functions Init_cmd, Media_check_cmd, Build_bpb_cmd, Input_cmd, Output_cmd, and Unknown_cmd are referenced in this file (Appendix M).

- We created a new file, worm.h, which contains definitions for the WORM device driver (Appendix M).

- dos_drvr.c – This file contains six functions that implement commands: Init_cmd, Media_check_cmd, Build_bpb_cmd, Input_cmd, Output_cmd, and Unknown_cmd.

  The file dos_drvr.c also contains the ancillary functions Which_sector, Check_sector, and Send_command. (Appendix M).

13.6   What If It Doesn't Work?

The most difficult challenge you will face if the DOS WORM device driver does
not work is to isolate the device that is responsible for the error condition. In
general, accesses to the magnetic disk through the BIOS interrupt 0x13 are quite
reliable. It is usually the new device or the combination of device operations that
cause the problem.

It is important to follow the problem determination process presented in
Chapter 5. You remember that you must analyze each component in the system
separately and convince yourself that they work properly before attempting to
analyze the entire device driver.

For this particular device driver both the diskette drive and the IBM 3363
WORM must be exercised separately. It is easy to exercise the diskette drive.
You can employ any of the following techniques.

- Perform DOS operations to the A: drive

- Use the disk BIOS function stand-alone

- Use disk utilities you may have available

- Write your own test programs

It is far more difficult to test the IBM 3363 WORM device. The first step is
to run the IBM-supplied diagnostics. However, running the diagnostics will not
allow you to sequence through the IBM 3363 commands that the DOS WORM
device driver is sending to the IBM 3363. Some type of stand-alone test program
is required to perform this type of test. The following example is a rudimentary
form of such a program.

```
/* - - - - - - - - - - - - - - - - - - - - - - - - - / - - - - - - -*/
/*                                                                    */
/*   PROGRAM :        T s t _ 3 3 6 3                                 */
/*                                                                    */
/*   REMARKS :        This program exercises the IBM 3363 Optical     */
/*            Disk BIOS.                                              */
/*                                                                    */
/* - - - - - - - - - - - - - - - - - - - - - - - - - - - - - - - -*/

#include         <dos.h>
#include         <stdio.h>
#include         <string.h>

#define BUF_SIZE      512

unsigned char    filename [64];
unsigned char    rw_buf [BUF_SIZE];
void             (far *bios_ptr) (void);

Set_Buffer ()
{
    unsigned int     i;

    for (i = 0; i < BUF_SIZE; i++)
    {
        rw_buf [i] = 0x3535;
    }
}

main ()
{
    unsigned int     seg;
    unsigned int     ofs;
    unsigned int     far *i_ptr;

    unsigned char    ah_reg;
    unsigned char    al_reg;
    unsigned char    dh_reg;
    unsigned char    dl_reg;
    unsigned int     cx_reg;
    unsigned int     es_reg;
    unsigned int     bx_reg;
```

```
unsigned char    ah_ret;
unsigned char    al_ret;
unsigned char    bh_ret;
unsigned char    bl_ret;
unsigned char    ch_ret;
unsigned char    cl_ret;
unsigned char    dh_ret;
unsigned char    dl_ret;

i_ptr = MK_FP (0x0040, 0x00B0);
ofs = *i_ptr++;
seg = *i_ptr;

bios_ptr = MK_FP (seg, ofs);

for ( ; ; )
{
    printf ("\nDo You Wish To Quit (y/n)? ");
    scanf (" %c", filename);
    printf ("\n");
    if ((*filename == 'y')  ||
        (*filename == 'Y'))
    {
        break;
    }
    else
    {
        Set_Buffer ();
        printf ("\nEnter Command Code (Hex) : ");
        scanf (" %x", &ah_reg);

        printf ("\nEnter Block Count (Hex) : ");
        scanf (" %x", &al_reg);

        printf ("\nEnter Track Address (Hex) : ");
        scanf (" %x", &cx_reg);

        printf ("\nEnter Sector Address (Hex) : ");
        scanf (" %x", &dh_reg);

        printf ("\nEnter Drive Address (Hex) : ");
```

```
            scanf (" %x", &dl_reg);

            es_reg = _DS;
            bx_reg = (unsigned int) rw_buf;

            _ES = es_reg;
            _BX = bx_reg;
            _CX = cx_reg;
            _DH = dh_reg;
            _DL = dl_reg;
            _AH = ah_reg;
            _AL = al_reg;

            bios_ptr ();

            ah_ret = _AH;
            al_ret = _AL;
            bh_ret = _BH;
            bl_ret = _BL;
            ch_ret = _CH;
            cl_ret = _CL;
            dh_ret = _DH;
            dl_ret = _DL;

            printf ("\n\t\tBIOS Return Values\n\n");
            printf ("\tAH : %02x\tAL : %02x\n", ah_ret, al_ret);
            printf ("\tBH : %02x\tBL : %02x\n", bh_ret, bl_ret);
            printf ("\tCH : %02x\tCL : %02x\n", ch_ret, cl_ret);
            printf ("\tDH : %02x\tDL : %02x\n", dh_ret, dl_ret);
        }
    }
    printf ("Program Complete\n");
}
```

This program has proven invaluable during the development of the DOS WORM device driver for the IBM 3363. Although it is not very elegant, it is flexible enough to allow the user of an IBM 3363 WORM to fully exercise its command list.

If all else fails you will find that you must resort to a software debugger or hardware debugger to uncover your more subtle nemesis.

13.7   Summary

DOS WORM Device Driver Commands

We use five commands to implement the WORM device driver.

- (00) Initialize

- (01) Check Media

- (02) Build BPB

- (04) Input From Device

- (08) Output To Device

We also included the function `Unknown_cmd` in `dos_drvr.c` and three ancillary routines: `Which_sector`, `Check_sector`, and `Send_command`. See Appendix M.

DOS WORM Device Driver Files

Files in the WORM block device driver:

- `worm` – This is the makefile (Appendix M).

- `dos_dd.h` – No change.

- `dos_hdr.asm` – No change.

- `dos_end.c` – No change.

- `dos_data.c` – We added a few global variables this driver needs (Appendix M).

- `dos_env.c` – We modified the array of pointers to functions (`dos_cmd[]`). WORM uses six functions: `Init_cmd`, `Media_check_cmd`, `Build_bpb_cmd`, `Input_cmd`, `Output_cmd`, and `Unknown_cmd` (Appendix M).

- `worm.h` – This file contains definitions for the WORM device driver (Appendix M).

- `dos_drvr.c` – We use six functions and three auxiliary routines. The functions are `Init_cmd`, `Media_check_cmd`, `Build_bpb_cmd`, `Input_cmd`, `Output_cmd`, and `Unknown_cmd` (Appendix M).

13.8   Exercises

Exercise 13.1 List the commands the WORM device driver supports.

Exercise 13.2 Run `tst_3363` to exercise each individual command in the WORM device driver.

Exercise 13.3 Explain the major changes we made in the template device driver files to create the WORM device driver.

Appendix A

Device Driver Commands

This is a summary of DOS device driver commands. The command field appears in the request header. We discussed the structure `REQ_struct` on page 45. One of the members of that structure is `command` and the command is a small number that tells DOS the type of service requested. In Table A.1 cd identifies character device commands and bd, block device commands; other commands apply to either type of driver.

Consult your *DOS Technical Reference Manual* for details.

Value	Description
00	Initialize
bd 01	Check Media
bd 02	Build BPB
03	IOCTL Input
04	Input From Device
cd 05	Input Without Waiting
cd 06	Obtain Input Status
cd 07	Flush Input Buffer
08	Output To Device
09	Output And Verify Data
cd 10	Obtain Output Status
cd 11	Flush Output Buffer
12	IOCTL Output
13	Open Device
14	Close Device
bd 15	Check If Media Is Removable
19	IOCTL To Device
23	Get Logical Device Map
24	Set Logical Device Map

Table A.1: DOS Device Driver Commands

Appendix B

Device Driver Interface

DOS uses a request header to pass information to a device driver. We use the structure `REQ_struct` to hold the information. The first five fields are fixed (we discussed them on page 45). The union `req_type` holds the variable part of the request. It is variable because different commands require different kinds of information. In the next few pages we will show you request headers for various commands — they represent a small set from Appendix A. First, here is the full structure for the request header.

```
struct REQ_struct
{
    unsigned char length;           /* Length In Bytes Of Req    */
    unsigned char unit;             /* Minor Device Unit Number  */
    unsigned char command;          /* Device Command Code       */
    unsigned int  status;           /* Device Status Word        */
    unsigned char reserved [8];     /* Reserved For DOS          */
    union
    {
        struct    INIT_struct            init_req;
        struct    MEDIA_CHECK_struct     media_check_req;
        struct    BUILD_BPB_struct       build_bpb_req;
        struct    I_O_struct             i_o_req;
        struct    INPUT_NO_WAIT_struct   input_no_wait_req;
        struct    IOCTL_struct           ioctl_req;
        struct    L_D_MAP_struct         l_d_map_req;
    } req_type;
};
```

INIT Command - input values

- INIT command uses the structure `INIT_struct` to hold the variable part of `REQ_struct`.

- See `INIT_struct` in `dos_dd.h` (Appendix F).

- The variable part of the structure `REQ_struct` follows the variable `reserved`.

- XX identifies input values you do not have to supply and output values DOS does not provide; the other input values you must supply.

`length`	1234	length in bytes of header plus variable data
`unit`	XX	minor device number (block devices only)
`command`	00	command code
`status`	XX	status after execution
`reserved`	XX	
`num_of_units`	01	number of units
`end_ptr`	1234:5678	ending address of the driver
`BPB_ptr`	1234:5678	pointer to arguments to initialize
`drive_num`	01	driver number
`config_err`	XX	config.sys error flag

INIT Command - output values

- INIT command uses the structure `INIT_struct` to hold the variable part of `REQ_struct`.

- See `INIT_struct` in `dos_dd.h` (Appendix F).

- The variable part of the structure `REQ_struct` follows the variable `reserved`.

- XX identifies input values you do not have to supply and output values DOS does not provide; the other input values you must supply.

length	1234	length in bytes of header plus variable data
unit	XX	minor device number (block devices only)
command	00	command code
status	00	status after execution
reserved	XX	
num_of_units	01	number of units
end_ptr	1234:5678	ending address of the driver
BPB_ptr	1234:5678	pointer to arguments
drive_num	01	driver number
config_err	00	config.sys error flag

CHECK MEDIA Command - input values

- CHECK MEDIA command uses the structure `MEDIA_CHECK_struct` to hold the variable part of `REQ_struct`.

- See `MEDIA_CHECK_struct` in `dos_dd.h` (Appendix F).

- The variable part of the structure `REQ_struct` follows the variable `reserved`.

- XX identifies input values you do not have to supply and output values DOS does not provide; the other input values you must supply.

`length`	1234	length in bytes of header plus variable data
`unit`	01	minor device number (block devices only)
`command`	01	command code
`status`	XX	status after execution
`reserved`	XX	
`media_byte`	01	media descriptor from DOS
`return_info`	XX	returns information about media
`return_ptr`	XXXX:XXXX	pointer to previous volume id

CHECK MEDIA Command - output values

- CHECK MEDIA command uses the structure `MEDIA_CHECK_struct` to hold the variable part of `REQ_struct`.

- See `MEDIA_CHECK_struct` in `dos_dd.h` (Appendix F).

- The variable part of the structure `REQ_struct` follows the variable `reserved`.

- XX identifies input values you do not have to supply and output values DOS does not provide; the other input values you must supply.

length	1234	length in bytes of header plus variable data
unit	01	minor device number (block devices only)
command	01	command code
status	00	status after execution
reserved	XX	
media_byte	01	media descriptor from DOS
return_info	55	returns information about media
return_ptr	1234:5678	pointer to previous volume id

Build BPB Command - input values

- Build BPB command uses the structure `BUILD_BPB_struct` to hold the variable part of `REQ_struct`.

- See `BUILD_BPB_struct` in `dos_dd.h` (Appendix F).

- The variable part of the structure `REQ_struct` follows the variable `reserved`.

- XX identifies input values you do not have to supply and output values DOS does not provide; the other input values you must supply.

length	1234	length in bytes of header plus variable data
unit	01	minor device number (block devices only)
command	02	command code
status	XX	status after execution
reserved	XX	
media_byte	01	media descriptor from DOS
buffer_ptr	1234:5678	buffer address (transfer address)
BPB_table	XXXX:XXXX	pointer to BPB table

Build BPB Command - output values

- Build BPB command uses the structure `BUILD_BPB_struct` to hold the variable part of `REQ_struct`.

- See `BUILD_BPB_struct` in `dos_dd.h` (Appendix F).

- The variable part of the structure `REQ_struct` follows the variable `reserved`.

- XX identifies input values you do not have to supply and output values DOS does not provide; the other input values you must supply.

`length`	1234	length in bytes of header plus variable data
`unit`	01	minor device number (block devices only)
`command`	02	command code
`status`	00	status after execution
`reserved`	XX	
`media_byte`	01	media descriptor from DOS
`buffer_ptr`	1234:5678	buffer address (transfer address)
`BPB_table`	1234:5678	pointer to BPB table

INPUT Command - input values

- INPUT command uses the structure `I_O_struct` to hold the variable part of `REQ_struct`.

- See `I_O_struct` in `dos_dd.h` (Appendix F).

- The variable part of the structure `REQ_struct` follows the variable `reserved`.

- XX identifies input values you do not have to supply and output values DOS does not provide; the other input values you must supply.

length	1234	length in bytes of header plus variable data
unit	00	minor device number (block devices only)
command	04	command code
status	XX	status after execution
reserved	XX	
media_byte	01	media descriptor from DOS
buffer_ptr	1234:5678	pointer to buffer
count	XXXX	byte/sector count
start_sector	1234	starting sector number
vol_id_ptr	1234:5678	pointer to volume id
start_sector_32	12345678	32-bit starting sector

INPUT Command - output values

- INPUT command uses the structure `I_O_struct` to hold the variable part of `REQ_struct`.

- See `I_O_struct` in `dos_dd.h` (Appendix F).

- The variable part of the structure `REQ_struct` follows the variable `reserved`.

- XX identifies input values you do not have to supply and output values DOS does not provide; the other input values you must supply.

length	1234	length in bytes of header plus variable data
unit	00	minor device number (block devices only)
command	04	command code
status	00	status after execution
reserved	XX	
media_byte	01	media descriptor from DOS
buffer_ptr	1234:5678	pointer to buffer
count	1234	byte/sector count
start_sector	1234	starting sector number
vol_id_ptr	1234:5678	pointer to volume id
start_sector_32	12345678	32-bit starting sector

INPUT NO WAIT Command - input values

- INPUT NO WAIT command uses the structure `INPUT_NO_WAIT_struct` to hold the variable part of `REQ_struct`.

- See `INPUT_NO_WAIT_struct` in `dos_dd.h` (Appendix F).

- The variable part of the structure `REQ_struct` follows the variable `reserved`.

- XX identifies input values you do not have to supply and output values DOS does not provide; the other input values you must supply.

length	1234	length in bytes of header plus variable data
unit	XX	minor device number (block devices only)
command	05	command code
status	00	status after execution
reserved	XX	
media_byte	XX	byte read from device

INPUT NO WAIT Command - output values

- INPUT NO WAIT command uses the structure `INPUT_NO_WAIT_struct` to hold the variable part of `REQ_struct`.

- See `INPUT_NO_WAIT_struct` in `dos_dd.h` (Appendix F).

- The variable part of the structure `REQ_struct` follows the variable `reserved`.

- XX identifies input values you do not have to supply and output values DOS does not provide; the other input values you must supply.

length	1234	length in bytes of header plus variable data
unit	XX	minor device number (block devices only)
command	05	command code
status	00	status after execution
reserved	XX	
media_byte	55	byte read from device

Appendix C

arrange Utility

Here is the source listing for the **arrange** utility.

```c
#include    <stdio.h>
#include    <string.h>
#include    <stdlib.h>

#include    "calls.h"           /* function call prototypes      */

#define     MAXCMDS     100 /* maximum number of cmds allowed    */
#define     MAXLINE     100 /* maximum number of char in a line */

char *progname;                 /* name of this program          */

/* arrange: utility to arrange segments in a .asm file           */
void main(int argc, char *argv[])
{
    char *cmds[MAXCMDS];
    FILE *fp_cmds, *fp_in, *fp_out;

    progname = argv[0];
    if (argc != 4)
        Error ("Usage:  %s cmds input output", progname);
    if ((fp_cmds = fopen(argv[1], "r")) == NULL)
        Error ("Cannot open command file %s", argv[1]);
    if ((fp_in = fopen(argv[2], "r")) == NULL)
        Error ("Cannot open input file %s", argv[2]);
    if ((fp_out = fopen(argv[3], "w")) == NULL)
```

```
        Error ("Cannot open output file %s", argv[3]);

    Read_Cmds (cmds, MAXCMDS, fp_cmds);
    Run_Cmds (cmds, fp_in, fp_out);
}




/* Read_Cmds: read command file into an array of pointers     */
void Read_Cmds(char *cmds[], int limit, FILE *fp_cmds)
{
    int  nl = 0;                        /* number of lines     */
    char line[MAXLINE];

    while (fgets (line, MAXLINE, fp_cmds))
    {
        cmds[nl] = strdup (line);   /* allocate space for line */
        if (!cmds[nl])
            Error ("strdup failed at line %s", line);
        if (++nl >= limit)
            Error ("Read_Cmds: too many commands", "");
    }
    cmds[nl] = NULL;
}




/* Run_Cmds: run the commands accumulated in the array cmds    */
void Run_Cmds(char *cmds[], FILE *fp_in, FILE *fp_out)
{
    char line[MAXLINE];

    while (fgets (line, MAXLINE, fp_in))
    {
        Apply_Cmds (cmds, line);
        fputs (line, fp_out);
    }
}
```

```
/* Apply_Cmds: apply commands in cmds[] to contents of line    */
void Apply_Cmds(char *cmds[], char *line)
{
    int i;
    char *p;

    for (i = 0; p = cmds[i]; i++)
    {
        switch(*p)
        {
            case 's':
                Substitute (++p, line);
                break;
            default:
                Error ("Unknown command %s", p);
                break;
        }
    }
}



/* Error: print error message and terminate the program        */
void Error(char *s1, char *s2)
{
    fprintf (stderr, "%s: ", progname);
    fprintf (stderr, s1, s2);
    exit (1);
}
```

```c
/* Substitute: substitute first string in line by the second    */
void Substitute(char *s, char *line)
{
    char *p;
    int  i, slen;
    char delimiter = *s;
    char source[MAXLINE], target[MAXLINE], tmpstr[MAXLINE];

    for (i = 0, s++; *s != '\n' && *s != delimiter; i++)
        source[i] = *s++;
    source[i] = '\0';
    if ((slen = strlen (source)) <= 0)
        Error ("Line %s, source cannot be empty", s);
    for (i = 0, s++; *s != '\n' && *s != delimiter; i++)
        target[i] = *s++;
    target[i] = '\0';
    for (p = strstr (line, source); p; p = strstr (p+1, source))
    {
        strcpy (tmpstr, p+slen);
        strcpy (p, target);
        strcat (p, tmpstr);
    }
}
```

The **arrange** utility expects three arguments:

- the file name that contains the substitute commands

- the input file

- the output file

For example, in the **dos** makefile for the template we use

```
arrange  dos.arr  dos_data.asm  m2.asm
```

to arrange the segments in **dos_data.asm**. The file **m2.asm** contains the modifications.

Here are the contents of **dos.arr** that we use.

```
s/DGROUP     group    _DATA,_BSS/DGROUP    group    _DATA,_BSS,_TEXT/
s/assume    cs:_TEXT/assume cs:DGROUP/
s/dw    @/dw     DGROUP:@/
s/dw    _Init_cmd/dw DGROUP:_Init_cmd/
s/dw    _Media_check_cmd/dw DGROUP:_Media_check_cmd/
s/dw    _Build_bpb_cmd/dw DGROUP:_Build_bpb_cmd/
s/dw    _Ioctl_input_cmd/dw DGROUP:_Ioctl_input_cmd/
s/dw    _Input_cmd/dw DGROUP:_Input_cmd/
s/dw    _Input_no_wait_cmd/dw DGROUP:_Input_no_wait_cmd/
s/dw    _Input_status_cmd/dw DGROUP:_Input_status_cmd/
s/dw    _Input_flush_cmd/dw DGROUP:_Input_flush_cmd/
s/dw    _Output_cmd/dw DGROUP:_Output_cmd/
s/dw    _Output_verify_cmd/dw DGROUP:_Output_verify_cmd/
s/dw    _Output_status_cmd/dw DGROUP:_Output_status_cmd/
s/dw    _Output_flush_cmd/dw DGROUP:_Output_flush_cmd/
s/dw    _Ioctl_output_cmd/dw DGROUP:_Ioctl_output_cmd/
s/dw    _Dev_open_cmd/dw DGROUP:_Dev_open_cmd/
s/dw    _Dev_close_cmd/dw DGROUP:_Dev_close_cmd/
s/dw    _Remove_media_cmd/dw DGROUP:_Remove_media_cmd/
s/dw    _Ioctl_cmd/dw DGROUP:_Ioctl_cmd/
s/dw    _Unknown_cmd/dw DGROUP:_Unknown_cmd/
s/dw    _Get_l_d_map_cmd/dw DGROUP:_Get_l_d_map_cmd/
s/dw    _Set_l_d_map_cmd/dw DGROUP:_Set_l_d_map_cmd/
s/offset _/offset DGROUP:_/
s/offset @/offset DGROUP:@/
```

Appendix D

DOS API

This is a summary of DOS API (Application Programming Interface). To use a DOS function, load the *Function* value in **AH** (unless otherwise noted), load other registers as indicated, and issue INT 21. The *Function* values are in hexadecimal. Please see your *DOS Technical Reference Manual* for details.

Function	*Input Registers*	*Output Registers*	*Description*
00	CS		program terminate points to PSP
01		AL	keyboard input character from standard input device
02	DL		display output character
03		AL	auxiliary input character from auxiliary device
04	DL		auxiliary output character
05	DL		printer output character

Function	Input Registers	Output Registers	Description
06			direct console I/O
	DL		0xFF for console input
	DL		0x00-0xFE for console output
		AL	depends on DL
07			direct console input without echo
		AL	character from standard input device
08			console input without echo
		AL	character from standard input device
09			print string
	DS		segment for character string
	DX		offset for character string
0A			buffered keyboard input
	DS		segment for input buffer
	DX		offset for input buffer
0B			check standard input status
		AL	0xFF if character is available
		AL	0x00 if character is not available
0C			clear kbd buffer and invoke kbd function
	AL		function number
0D			disk reset
0E			select disk
	DL		drive number
		AL	total number of drives
0F			open file
	DS		segment for unopened FCB
	DX		offset for unopened FCB
		AL	0x00 if file opened
		AL	0xFF if file not opened
10			close file
	DS		segment for opened FCB
	DX		offset for opened FCB
		AL	0x00 if file is found
		AL	0xFF if file not is found

Function	Input Registers	Output Registers	Description
11			search for first entry
	DS		segment for unopened FCB
	DX		offset for unopened FCB
		AL	0x00 if matching filename found
		AL	0xFF if matching filename not found
12			search for next entry
	DS		segment for unopened FCB
	DX		offset for unopened FCB
		AL	0x00 if matching filename found
		AL	0xFF if matching filename not found
13			delete file
	DS		segment for unopened FCB
	DX		offset for unopened FCB
		AL	0x00 if file deleted
		AL	0xFF if file not found
14			sequential read
	DS		segment for opened FCB
	DX		offset for opened FCB
		AL	0x00 if read successfully completed
		AL	0x01 if EOF (no data read)
		AL	0x02 if DTA too small (read canceled)
		AL	0x03 if EOF (partial record read)
15			sequential write
	DS		segment for opened FCB
	DX		offset for opened FCB
		AL	0x00 if write successfully completed
		AL	0x01 if diskette is full (write canceled)
		AL	0x02 if DTA too small (write canceled)
16			create file
	DS		segment for unopened FCB
	DX		offset for unopened FCB
		AL	0x00 if file created
		AL	0xFF if file not created

Function	Input Registers	Output Registers	Description
17			rename file
	DS		segment for a modified FCB
	DX		offset for a modified FCB
		AL	0x00 if file renamed
		AL	0xFF if file not renamed
19			current disk
		AL	current default drive
1A			set disk transfer address
	DS		segment for disk transfer address
	DX		offset for disk transfer address
1B			allocation table information
		DS	segment for media descriptor byte
		BX	offset for media descriptor byte
		DX	number of allocation units
		AL	number of sectors/allocation unit
		CX	size of physical sector
1C			allocation table info for a device
	DL		drive number
		DS	segment for media descriptor byte
		BX	offset for media descriptor byte
		DX	number of allocation units
		AL	number of sectors/allocation unit
		CX	size of physical sector
21			random read
	DS		segment for an opened FCB
	DX		offset for an opened FCB
		AL	0x00 if read successfully completed
		AL	0x01 if EOF (no data read)
		AL	0x02 if DTA too small (read canceled)
		AL	0x03 if EOF (partial record read)
22			random write
	DS		segment for opened FCB
	DX		offset for opened FCB
		AL	0x00 if write successfully completed
		AL	0x01 if diskette is full (write canceled)
		AL	0x02 if DTA too small (write canceled)

Function	Input Registers	Output Registers	Description
23			file size
	DS		segment for unopened FCB
	DX		offset for unopened FCB
		AL	0x00 if the directory entry found
		AL	0xFF if the directory entry not found
24			set relative record field
	DS		segment for opened FCB
	DX		offset for opened FCB
25			set interrupt vector
	DS		segment for interrupt handling routine
	DX		offset for interrupt handling routine
	AL		interrupt number
26			create new program segment
	DX		segment number for new segment
27			random block read
	DS		segment for opened FCB
	DX		offset for opened FCB
	CX		number of records to read
		AL	0x00 if read successfully completed
		AL	0x01 if EOF (no data read)
		AL	0x02 if DTA too small (read canceled)
		AL	0x03 if EOF (partial record read)
		CX	actual number of records read
28			random block write
	DS		segment for opened FCB
	DX		offset for opened FCB
	CX		number of records to write
		AL	0x00 if write successfully completed
		AL	0x01 if diskette is full
		AL	0x02 if DTA too small
		CX	actual number of records written

Function	Input Registers	Output Registers	Description
29			parse filename
	DS		segment for command line to parse
	SI		offset for command line to parse
	ES		segment for portion of memory (target)
	DI		offset for portion of memory (target)
	AL		bit value to control parsing
		AL	0x00 if no global filename characters
		AL	0x01 if global filename characters
		AL	0xFF if driver specified is invalid
		DS	segment first character after filename
		SI	offset first character after filename
		ES	segment first byte of formatted FCB
		DI	offset first byte of formatted FCB
2A			get date
		AL	day of the week
		CX	year
		DH	month
		DL	day
2B			set date
	CX		year
	DH		month
	DL		day
		AL	0x00 if date was valid
		AL	0xFF if date was not valid
2C			get time
		CH	hour
		CL	minutes
		DH	seconds
		DL	hundredths
2D			set time
	CH		hour
	CL		minutes
	DH		seconds
	DL		hundredths
		AL	0x00 if time was valid
		AL	0xFF if time was not valid

Function	Input Registers	Output Registers	Description
2E			set/reset verify switch
	AL		0x00 to set verify OFF
	AL		0x01 to set verify ON
2F			get disk transfer address (DTA)
		ES	segment for current DTA
		BX	offset for current DTA
30			get DOS version number
		BX	0x0000
		CX	0x0000
		AL	major version number
		AH	minor version number
31			terminate process and remain resident
	AL		return code
	DX		memory size in paragraphs
33			ctrl-break check
	AL		0x00 to request current state
	AL		0x01 to set the current state
	DL		0x00 to set the current state OFF
	DL		0x01 to set the current state ON
		DL	0x00 the current state is OFF
		DL	0x01 the current state is ON
35			get vector
	AL		interrupt number
		ES	segment for interrupt handling routine
		BX	offset for interrupt handling routine
36			get disk free space
	DL		drive number
		BX	available clusters
		DX	clusters/driver
		CX	bytes/sector
		AX	0xFFFF if drive number is invalid
		AX	number of sectors per cluster

Function	Input Registers	Output Registers	Description
38			return country-dependent information
	DS		segment for 32-byte memory area
	DX		offset for 32-byte memory area
	AL		function code
		AX	error code if carry flag is set
		DS	segment country data if flag not set
		DX	offset country data if flag not set
39			create subdirectory (mkdir)
	DS		segment for an ASCIIZ string
	DX		offset for an ASCIIZ string
		AX	error code if carry flag is set
3A			remove subdirectory (rmdir)
	DS		segment for an ASCIIZ string
	DX		offset for an ASCIIZ string
		AX	error code if carry flag is set
3B			change current directory (chdir)
	DS		segment for an ASCIIZ string
	DX		offset for an ASCIIZ string
		AX	error code if carry flag is set
3C			create a file (creat)
	DS		segment for an ASCIIZ string
	DX		offset for an ASCIIZ string
	CX		attribute of the file
		AX	error code if carry flag is set
		AX	16-bit handle if carry flag is not set
3D			open a file
	DS		segment for an ASCIIZ string
	DX		offset for an ASCIIZ string
	AL		access code
		AX	error code if carry flag is set
		AX	16-bit handle if carry flag is not set
3E			close a file handle
	BX		file handle returned by open or create
		AX	error code if carry flag is set

Function	Input Registers	Output Registers	Description
3F			read from a file or device
	BX		file handle
	DS		segment for buffer address
	DX		offset for buffer address
	CX		number of bytes to read
		AX	error code if carry flag is set
		AX	number of bytes read
40			write to a file or device
	BX		file handle
	DS		segment for data address
	DX		offset for data address
	CX		number of bytes to write
		AX	error code if carry flag is set
		AX	number of bytes written
41			delete a file from a directory
	DS		segment for an ASCIIZ string
	DX		offset for an ASCIIZ string
		AX	error code if carry flag is set
42			move file read write pointer
	CX		distance (offset) to move (high)
	DX		distance (offset) to move (low)
	AL		method of moving
	BX		file handle
		AX	error code if carry flag is set
		DX	new location if carry not set (high)
		AX	new location if carry not set (low)
43			change file mode
	DS		segment for an ASCIIZ string
	DX		offset for an ASCIIZ string
	CX		attribute
	AL		function code
		AX	error code if carry flag is set
		CX	current attribute of file

Function	Input Registers	Output Registers	Description
44			I/O control for devices (IOCTL)
	DS		data or segment for buffer
	DX		data or offset for buffer
	CX		number of bytes to read or write
	BX		file handle
	BL		drive number
	AL		function value
		AX	error code if carry flag is set
		AX	error code if 0xFF
		AX	number of bytes transferred
45			duplicate file handle
	BX		file handle
		AX	error code if carry flag is set
		AX	new file handle if carry flag not set
46			force a duplicate of a handle
	BX		existing file handle
	CX		second file handle
		AX	error code if carry flag is set
47			get current directory
	DS		segment for a 64-byte user memory area
	SI		offset for a 64-byte user memory area
	DL		drive number
		AX	error code if carry flag is set
		DS	segment for full path name
		SI	offset for full path name
48			allocate memory
	BX		number of paragraphs of memory request
		AX	error code if carry flag is set
		AX	AX:0 points to allocated memory block
		BX	size of largest block, if allocation fails
49			free allocated memory
	ES		segment for the block to be returned
		AX	error code if carry flag is set

Function	Input Registers	Output Registers	Description
4A			modify allocated memory blocks
	ES		segment for the block
	BX		new request block size in paragraphs
		AX	error code if carry flag is set
		BX	maximum pool size if call fails
4B			load or execute a program
	DS		segment for an ASCIIZ string
	DX		offset for an ASCIIZ string
	ES		segment for parameter block
	BX		offset for parameter block
	AL		function code
		AX	error code if carry flag is set
4C			terminate a process
	AL		return code
4D			get return code of a subprocess
		AX	return code
4E			find first matching file
	DS		segment for an ASCIIZ string
	DX		offset for an ASCIIZ string
	CX		attribute
		AX	error code if carry flag is set
4F			find next matching file
			(function uses DTA from previous call)
		AX	error code if carry flag is set
54			get verify setting
		AL	0x00 if verify is OFF
		AL	0x01 if verify is ON

Function	Input Registers	Output Registers	Description
56			rename a file
	DS		segment for an ASCIIZ old name
	DX		offset for an ASCIIZ old name
	ES		segment for an ASCIIZ new name
	DI		offset for an ASCIIZ new name
		AX	error code if carry flag is set
57			get/set a file's date and time
	AL		0x00 if get date and time
	AL		0x01 if set date and time
	BX		file handle
	CX		time to be set if AL=0x01
	DX		date to be set if AL=0x01
		AX	error code if carry flag is set
		CX	time received if AL=0x00
		DX	date received if AL=0x00
59			get extended error
	BX		0x0000 (version 3.00 and 3.10)
		AX	extended error code
		BH	error class
		BL	suggested action
		CH	locus
5A			create unique file
	DS		segment for an ASCIIZ path name
	DX		offset for an ASCIIZ path name
	CX		attribute
		AX	error code if carry flag is set
		DS	segment for string with filename
		DX	offset for string with filename
5B			create a new file
	DS		segment for an ASCIIZ path name
	DX		offset for an ASCIIZ path name
	CX		attribute
		AX	error code if carry flag is set

Function	Input Registers	Output Registers	Description
5C			lock/unlock file access
	AL		0x00 to lock
	AL		0x01 to unlock
	BX		file handle
	CX		offset high
	DX		offset low
	SI		length high
	DI		length low
		AX	error code if carry flag is set
62			get program segment prefix address
		BX	segment address of executing process

Function codes with four hexadecimal digits must be loaded in the **AX** register.

Function	Input Registers	Output Registers	Description
5E00			get machine name
	DS		segment for buffer for computer name
	DX		offset for buffer for computer name
		AX	error code if carry flag is set
		DS	segment for buffer with computer name
		DX	offset for buffer with computer name
		CH	0x00 if name not defined
		CH	not 0x00 if name/number defined
		CL	NETBIOS name number for the name
5E02			set printer
	BX		redirection list index
	CX		length of setup string
	DS		segment for printer setup buffer
	SI		offset for printer setup buffer
		AX	error code if carry flag is set

Function	Input Registers	Output Registers	Description
5E03			get printer
	BX		redirection list index
	ES		segment for printer setup buffer
	DI		offset for printer setup buffer
		AX	error code if carry flag is set
		CX	length of data returned
		ES	segment for buffer with setup string
		DI	offset for buffer with setup string
5F02			get redirection list entry
	BX		redirection index
	DS		segment for 128-byte local device name
	SI		offset for 128-byte local device name
	ES		segment for 128-byte network name
	DI		offset for 128-byte network name
		AX	error code if carry flag is set
		BH	bit 0 is 0 if device is valid
		BH	bit 0 is 1 if device is not valid
		BL	device type
		CX	stored parm value
		DS	segment for ASCIIZ local device name
		SI	offset for ASCIIZ local device name
		ES	segment for ASCIIZ network name
		DI	offset for ASCIIZ network name
5F03			redirect device
	BL		0x03 if printer device
	BL		0x04 if file device
	CX		value to save for caller
	DS		segment for ASCIIZ device name
	SI		offset for ASCIIZ device name
	ES		segment for destination network path
	DI		offset for destination network path
		AX	error code if carry flag is set
5F04			cancel redirection
	DS		segment for ASCIIZ device name or path
	SI		offset for ASCIIZ device name or path
		AX	error code if carry flag is set

Appendix E

visual Utility

Here is the source listing for the visual utility.

```
/* - - - - - - - - - - - - - - - - - - - - - - - - - - - - - - -*/
/*                                                               */
/*  PROGRAM :   V i s u a l                                      */
/*                                                               */
/*  REMARKS :   Visual is a program that interposes itself       */
/*        between DOS and the device drivers in the system.      */
/*        Once installed VISUAL displays the device driver       */
/*        requests and the results for that request.             */
/*                                                               */
/*  NOTES   :   tcc -mt -y -M  visual.c                          */
/*                                                               */
/* - - - - - - - - - - - - - - - - - - - - - - - - - - - - - - -*/

#include     <dos.h>
#include     <bios.h>
#include     <alloc.h>
#include     <stdio.h>
#include     <stdlib.h>
#include     <string.h>

#include     "dos_dd.h"

#define     TRUE      0x01
#define     FALSE     0x00
#define     MAX_NEW   0x05
```

```
#define     MAX_STK      0x100



/* - - - - - - - - - - - - - - - - - - - - - - - - - - - - - - -*/
/*                                                               */
/*      Program's "New" Device Headers (Replaces Old)            */
/*                                                               */
/* - - - - - - - - - - - - - - - - - - - - - - - - - - - - - - -*/

struct new_dh_struct
{
    struct DEVICE_HEADER_struct      dh;
    void                             (far * drv_ptr) ();
};


/* - - - - - - - - - - - - - - - - - - - - - - - - - - - - - - -*/
/*                                                               */
/*      DOS Internal Variables Block Structure                   */
/*                                                               */
/* - - - - - - - - - - - - - - - - - - - - - - - - - - - - - - -*/

struct DOS_struct
{
    unsigned char                    reserved [34];
    struct DEVICE_HEADER_struct far *ddh_ptr;
};
```

```
/* - - - - - - - - - - - - - - - - - - - - - - - - - - - - - - - -*/
/*                                                                  */
/*  Array Of "New" Device Headers                                   */
/*  To Replace Block Device Headers                                 */
/*                                                                  */
/* - - - - - - - - - - - - - - - - - - - - - - - - - - - - - - - -*/

void    far Driver_00 ();
void    far Driver_01 ();
void    far Driver_02 ();
void    far Driver_03 ();
void    far Driver_04 ();

struct new_dh_struct new_dh_ary [MAX_NEW] =
{
    {   /* 00 */
        {
            MK_FP (0, 0),               /* Next Device Header   */
            0x0000,                     /* Attribute            */
            FP_OFF (Driver_00),         /* Strategy Routine     */
            FP_OFF (Driver_00)          /* Interrupt Routine    */
        },
        Driver_00
    },
    {   /* 01 */
        {
            MK_FP (0, 0),               /* Next Device Header   */
            0x0000,                     /* Attribute            */
            FP_OFF (Driver_01),         /* Strategy Routine     */
            FP_OFF (Driver_01)          /* Interrupt Routine    */
        },
        Driver_01
    },
    {   /* 02 */
        {
            MK_FP (0, 0),               /* Next Device Header   */
            0x0000,                     /* Attribute            */
            FP_OFF (Driver_02),         /* Strategy Routine     */
            FP_OFF (Driver_02)          /* Interrupt Routine    */
        },
        Driver_02
    },
```

```
{   /* 03 */
    {
        MK_FP (0, 0),                  /* Next Device Header  */
        0x0000,                        /* Attribute           */
        FP_OFF (Driver_03),            /* Strategy Routine    */
        FP_OFF (Driver_03)             /* Interrupt Routine   */
    },
    Driver_03
},
{   /* 04 */
    {
        MK_FP (0, 0),                  /* Next Device Header  */
        0x0000,                        /* Attribute           */
        FP_OFF (Driver_04),            /* Strategy Routine    */
        FP_OFF (Driver_04)             /* Interrupt Routine   */
    },
    Driver_04
}
};
```

```
/* - - - - - - - - - - - - - - - - - - - - - - - - - - - - - -*/
/*                                                             */
/*  Miscellaneous Program Data Regions (Global Data In General) */
/*                                                             */
/* - - - - - - - - - - - - - - - - - - - - - - - - - - - - - -*/

char    *cmd_ary [] =
{
        "INIT     ",            /* Device Driver Command  0 */
        "MEDIA CHK",            /* Device Driver Command  1 */
        "BUILD BPB",            /* Device Driver Command  2 */
        "IOCTL INP",            /* Device Driver Command  3 */
        "INPUT    ",            /* Device Driver Command  4 */
        "IN NOWAIT",            /* Device Driver Command  5 */
        "INP STAT ",            /* Device Driver Command  6 */
        "INP FLUSH",            /* Device Driver Command  7 */
        "OUTPUT   ",            /* Device Driver Command  8 */
        "OUT VERFY",            /* Device Driver Command  9 */
        "OUT STAT ",            /* Device Driver Command 10 */
        "OUT FLUSH",            /* Device Driver Command 11 */
        "IOCTL OUT",            /* Device Driver Command 12 */
        "DEV OPEN ",            /* Device Driver Command 13 */
        "DEV CLOSE",            /* Device Driver Command 14 */
        "RM MEDIA ",            /* Device Driver Command 15 */
        " res  16 ",            /* Device Driver Command 16 */
        " res  17 ",            /* Device Driver Command 17 */
        " res  18 ",            /* Device Driver Command 18 */
        "IOCTL    ",            /* Device Driver Command 19 */
        " res  20 ",            /* Device Driver Command 20 */
        " res  21 ",            /* Device Driver Command 21 */
        " res  22 ",            /* Device Driver Command 22 */
        "GET LDMAP",            /* Device Driver Command 23 */
        "SET LDMAP",            /* Device Driver Command 24 */
        " res  25 ",            /* Device Driver Command 25 */
        " res  26 "             /* Device Driver Command 26 */
};
```

```
char    *req_display [] =
{
                "-------------------------------",
                "            : Input  : Output   ",
                "-------------------------------",
                " Length  :          :          ",
                "-------------------------------",
                " Unit    :          :          ",
                "-------------------------------",
                " Command :          :          ",
                "-------------------------------",
                " Status  :          :          ",
                "-------------------------------",
                " 1st Field:         :          ",
                "-------------------------------",
                " 2nd Field:         :          ",
                "-------------------------------",
                " 3rd Field:         :          ",
                "-------------------------------",
                " 4th Field:         :          ",
                "-------------------------------",
                " 5th Field:         :          ",
                "-------------------------------"

};
```

```
/* - - - - - - - - - - - - - - - - - - - - - - - - - - - - -*/
/*                                                           */
/*      Global Program Data Region (Continued)               */
/*                                                           */
/* - - - - - - - - - - - - - - - - - - - - - - - - - - - - -*/

unsigned int        stack [MAX_STK];    /* Driver Stack Area   */
unsigned int        flag [MAX_NEW];     /* Strategy/Intrpt Flag */
unsigned int        driver;             /* Global Driver Variable */

unsigned int        SS_reg;        /* SS Register Variable   */
unsigned int        SP_reg;        /* SP Register Variable   */
unsigned int        ES_reg;        /* ES Register Variable   */
unsigned int        AX_reg;        /* AX Register Variable   */
unsigned int        BX_reg;        /* BX Register Variable   */
unsigned int        CX_reg;        /* CX Register Variable   */
unsigned int        DX_reg;        /* DX Register Variable   */
unsigned int        DS_reg;        /* DS Register Variable   */

/* Array Of DOS Requests                                     */
struct  REQ_struct  far *req_ary [MAX_NEW];
```

```
/* - - - - - - - - - - - - - - - - - - - - - - - - - - - - - - - -*/
/*                                                                */
/*  FUNCTION:    D i s p l a y _ r e q u e s t                    */
/*                                                                */
/*  REMARKS :   Display_request displays the DOS request header   */
/*        and associated data on the screen for each DOS call     */
/*        to the RCD device driver.                               */
/*                                                                */
/* - - - - - - - - - - - - - - - - - - - - - - - - - - - - - - -*/

void     Display_request (struct REQ_struct   far *req_ptr,
                          unsigned int         io_flag)
{
    unsigned int    i;
    unsigned int    x;
    unsigned int    y;

    if (io_flag)
    {
        for (i = 1; i < 22; i++)
        {
            gotoxy (49, i);
            cputs (req_display [(i - 1)]);
        }
        x = 60;
    }
    else
    {
        x = 70;
    }

    gotoxy (x, 4);
    cprintf ("%02X", req_ptr->length);

    gotoxy (x, 6);
    cprintf ("%c", ('A' + req_ptr->unit));

    gotoxy (x, 8);
    cprintf ("%s", cmd_ary [req_ptr->command]);

    gotoxy (x, 10);
    cprintf ("%02X", req_ptr->status);
```

```
switch (req_ptr->command)
{
    case    INIT :                   /* Device Driver INIT       */
        gotoxy (50, 12);
        cprintf (" Units  ");
        gotoxy (x, 12);
        cprintf ("%02X",
                 req_ptr->req_type.init_req.num_of_units);

        gotoxy (50, 14);
        cprintf ("End  Addr");
        gotoxy (x, 14);
        cprintf ("%Fp", req_ptr->req_type.init_req.end_ptr);

        gotoxy (50, 16);
        cprintf ("BPB   Ptr");
        gotoxy (x, 16);
        cprintf ("%Fp", req_ptr->req_type.init_req.BPB_ptr);

        gotoxy (50, 18);
        cprintf ("Drive   #");
        gotoxy (x, 18);
        cprintf ("%02X",
                 req_ptr->req_type.init_req.drive_num);

        gotoxy (50, 20);
        cprintf ("ConfigErr");
        gotoxy (x, 20);
        cprintf ("%04X",
                 req_ptr->req_type.init_req.config_err);

        break;

    case    MEDIA_CHECK :            /* Device Driver MEDIA CHK */
        gotoxy (50, 12);
        cprintf ("MediaByte");
        gotoxy (x, 12);
        cprintf ("%02X",
             req_ptr->req_type.media_check_req.media_byte);

        gotoxy (50, 14);
```

```
            cprintf ("Media Chk");
            gotoxy (x, 14);
            cprintf ("%02X",
                req_ptr->req_type.media_check_req.return_info);

            gotoxy (50, 16);
            cprintf ("Vol IDPtr");
            gotoxy (x, 16);
            cprintf ("%Fp",
                req_ptr->req_type.media_check_req.return_ptr);

            break;

    case    BUILD_BPB :              /* Device Driver BUILD BPB  */
            gotoxy (50, 12);
            cprintf ("MediaByte");
            gotoxy (x, 12);
            cprintf ("%02X",
                req_ptr->req_type.build_bpb_req.media_byte);

            gotoxy (50, 14);
            cprintf ("BufferPtr");
            gotoxy (x, 14);
            cprintf ("%Fp",
                req_ptr->req_type.build_bpb_req.buffer_ptr);

            gotoxy (50, 16);
            cprintf ("BPBTblPtr");
            gotoxy (x, 16);
            cprintf ("%Fp",
                req_ptr->req_type.build_bpb_req.BPB_table);

            break;

    case    INPUT :                  /* Device Driver INPUT       */
    case    OUTPUT :                 /* Device Driver OUTPUT      */
    case    IOCTL_INPUT :            /* Device Driver IOCTL INP   */
    case    IOCTL_OUTPUT :           /* Device Driver IOCTL OUT   */
    case    OUTPUT_VERIFY :          /* Device Driver OUT VERIFY  */
            gotoxy (50, 12);
            cprintf ("MediaByte");
            gotoxy (x, 12);
```

```
        cprintf ("%02X",
                req_ptr->req_type.i_o_req.media_byte);

        gotoxy (50, 14);
        cprintf ("BufferPtr");
        gotoxy (x, 14);
        cprintf ("%Fp",
                req_ptr->req_type.i_o_req.buffer_ptr);

        gotoxy (50, 16);
        cprintf ("XferCount");
        gotoxy (x, 16);
        cprintf ("%04X", req_ptr->req_type.i_o_req.count);

        gotoxy (50, 18);
        cprintf ("StartSect");
        gotoxy (x, 18);
        if (req_ptr->req_type.i_o_req.start_sector == 0xFFFF)
        {
            cprintf ("%08lX",
              req_ptr->req_type.i_o_req.start_sector_32);
        }
        else
        {
            cprintf ("%04X",
              req_ptr->req_type.i_o_req.start_sector);
        }

        gotoxy (50, 20);
        cprintf ("Vol IDPtr");
        gotoxy (x, 20);
        cprintf ("%Fp", req_ptr->req_type.i_o_req.vol_id_ptr);

        break;

    case   IOCTL :                  /* Device Driver IOCTL      */
        gotoxy (50, 12);
        cprintf ("MajorFunc");
        gotoxy (x, 12);
        cprintf ("%02X",
            req_ptr->req_type.ioctl_req.major_func);
```

```
            gotoxy (50, 14);
            cprintf ("MinorFunc");
            gotoxy (x, 14);
            cprintf ("%02X",
                req_ptr->req_type.ioctl_req.minor_func);

            gotoxy (50, 16);
            cprintf ("SI RegVal");
            gotoxy (x, 16);
            cprintf ("%04X", req_ptr->req_type.ioctl_req.SI_reg);

            gotoxy (50, 18);
            cprintf ("DI RegVal");
            gotoxy (x, 18);
            cprintf ("%04X", req_ptr->req_type.ioctl_req.DI_reg);

            gotoxy (50, 20);
            cprintf ("RequstPtr");
            gotoxy (x, 20);
            cprintf ("%Fp",
                req_ptr->req_type.ioctl_req.ioctl_req_ptr);

            break;

    case    GET_L_D_MAP :           /* Device Driver GET LD Map */
    case    SET_L_D_MAP :           /* Device Driver SET LD Map */
            gotoxy (50, 12);
            cprintf ("Unit Code");
            gotoxy (x, 12);
            cprintf ("%02X",
                req_ptr->req_type.l_d_map_req.unit_code);

            gotoxy (50, 14);
            cprintf ("Cmnd Code");
            gotoxy (x, 14);
            cprintf ("%02X",
                req_ptr->req_type.l_d_map_req.cmd_code);

            gotoxy (50, 16);
            cprintf ("Status    ");
            gotoxy (x, 16);
            cprintf ("%04X",
```

```
                            req_ptr->req_type.l_d_map_req.status);

            break;

        case    DEV_OPEN :              /* Device Open Command       */
        case    DEV_CLOSE :             /* Device Close Command      */
        case    INPUT_FLUSH :           /* Character Devices Only    */
        case    INPUT_STATUS :          /* Character Devices Only    */
        case    OUTPUT_FLUSH :          /* Character Devices Only    */
        case    REMOVE_MEDIA :          /* Removable Media           */
        case    OUTPUT_STATUS :         /* Character Devices Only    */
        case    INPUT_NO_WAIT :         /* No Wait Input--Char Only */
            break;

        default :
            break;
    }
    getch ();
}
```

```
/* - - - - - - - - - - - - - - - - - - - - - - - - - - - - - - - - -*/
/*                                                                    */
/*  FUNCTION:    C o m m o n _ d r i v e r                            */
/*                                                                    */
/*  REMARKS :    Common_driver processes all DOS requests from        */
/*        each of the respective drivers (00 - 04).                   */
/*        Each driver calls Common_driver with its driver            */
/*        number.  This is used as the index into the common         */
/*        driver tables.                                             */
/*                                                                    */
/* - - - - - - - - - - - - - - - - - - - - - - - - - - - - - - - - -*/

void    Common_driver (unsigned int driver,
                       unsigned int ES_reg,
                       unsigned int BX_reg)
{
    int                 x;
    int                 y;
    void                (far * Strategy_rtn) ();
    void                (far * Interrupt_rtn) ();
    struct REQ_struct   far *req_ptr;

    x = wherex ();
    y = wherey ();

    if (flag [driver] == 0)
    {
        flag [driver]++;
        req_ary [driver] = MK_FP (ES_reg, BX_reg);

        Strategy_rtn = MK_FP (FP_SEG (
                        new_dh_ary [driver].dh.next_hdr),
                        new_dh_ary [driver].dh.dev_strat);
        _ES = ES_reg;
        _BX = BX_reg;
        Strategy_rtn ();
    }
    else
    {
        flag [driver] = 0;
        req_ptr = req_ary [driver];
```

```
            ES_reg = FP_SEG (req_ptr);
            BX_reg = FP_OFF (req_ptr);
            Display_request (req_ptr, TRUE);
            Interrupt_rtn = MK_FP (FP_SEG (
                            new_dh_ary [driver].dh.next_hdr),
                            new_dh_ary [driver].dh.dev_int);
            _ES = ES_reg;
            _BX = BX_reg;
            Interrupt_rtn ();
            Display_request (req_ptr, FALSE);
        }
    gotoxy (x, y);
}
```

```
/* - - - - - - - - - - - - - - - - - - - - - - - - - - - - - - - -*/
/*                                                                 */
/* FUNCTION:   D O S _ S e t u p                                   */
/*                                                                 */
/* REMARKS :   DOS_Setup transforms O/S dependent requests to      */
/*        character and block devices.                             */
/*                                                                 */
/* INPUTS  :   CX  Contains Type (<0x80 Is Character)              */
/*             ES:BX   Is Pointer To Request Packet                */
/*                                                                 */
/* OUTPUTS :   Status  Must Be Set In The Request Packet           */
/*             RETF    Must Be Used To Return From Strategy         */
/*                                                                 */
/* - - - - - - - - - - - - - - - - - - - - - - - - - - - - - - - -*/

void    DOS_Setup (unsigned int which,
                   unsigned int ES_tmp,
                   unsigned int DS_tmp,
                   unsigned int AX_tmp)
{
    _AX = _CS;                          /* Obtain Code Segment     */
    _DS = _AX;                          /* Setup Data Segment      */

    BX_reg = _BX;                       /* Save BX Register        */
    CX_reg = _CX;                       /* Save CX Register        */
    DX_reg = _DX;                       /* Save DX Register        */

    AX_reg = AX_tmp;                    /* Save AX Register        */
    ES_reg = ES_tmp;                    /* Save Request Pointer    */

    driver = which;                     /* Move Value From Stack    */

    SS_reg = _SS;                       /* Save Stack Segment      */
    SP_reg = _SP;                       /* Save Stack Pointer      */

    disable ();                         /* Disable Interrupts      */
    _AX = _DS;                          /* Obtain Data Segment     */
    _SS = _AX;                          /* Setup New Stack         */
                                        /* Set Stack Pointer Value */
    _SP = (unsigned int) &stack [MAX_STK];
    enable ();                          /* Enable Interrupts       */
```

```
    Common_driver (driver, ES_reg, BX_reg);

    disable ();                     /* Disable Interrupts     */
    _SS = SS_reg;                   /* Restore Entry Stack    */
    _SP = SP_reg;                   /* Restore Entry Stack Ptr */
    enable ();                      /* Enable Interrupts      */

    _DX = DX_reg;                   /* Restore DX Register    */
    _CX = CX_reg;                   /* Restore CX Register    */
    _BX = BX_reg;                   /* Restore BX Register    */
    _AX = AX_reg;                   /* Restore AX Register    */

    _ES = ES_tmp;                   /* Restore ES Register    */
    _DS = DS_tmp;                   /* Restore DS Register    */
}
```

```
/* - - - - - - - - - - - - - - - - - - - - - - - - - - - - - - -*/
/*                                                              */
/*  FUNCTION:   D r i v e r _ 0 X                               */
/*                                                              */
/*  REMARKS :   Driver_0X accepts all DOS requests for the      */
/*              first block device driver in the device header  */
/*              chain (X is in the range 0-4).                  */
/*                                                              */
/* - - - - - - - - - - - - - - - - - - - - - - - - - - - - - - -*/

void far    Driver_00 (void)
{
    DOS_Setup (0x00, _ES, _DS, _AX);
}

void far    Driver_01 (void)
{
    DOS_Setup (0x01, _ES, _DS, _AX);
}

void far    Driver_02 (void)
{
    DOS_Setup (0x02, _ES, _DS, _AX);
}

void far    Driver_03 (void)
{
    DOS_Setup (0x03, _ES, _DS, _AX);
}

void far    Driver_04 (void)
{
    DOS_Setup (0x04, _ES, _DS, _AX);
}
```

```
/* - - - - - - - - - - - - - - - - - - - - - - - - - - - - - - - -*/
/*                                                                 */
/*  FUNCTION:     P r i n t _ H D R                                */
/*                                                                 */
/*  REMARKS :   Print_HDR displays (prints) the contents of the */
/*          currently addressed device header.                     */
/*                                                                 */
/* - - - - - - - - - - - - - - - - - - - - - - - - - - - - - - - -*/

void     Print_HDR (struct DEVICE_HEADER_struct  far *hdr_ptr)
{
    char          tmp_str [32];
    unsigned int    i;

    printf ("\n\t\t* * * D e v i c e    H e a d e r * * *");
    printf ("\n\t\t   ( A d d r e s s  : %Fp )\n\n", hdr_ptr);
    printf ("Next Header\t: %Fp\n", hdr_ptr->next_hdr);
    printf ("Attribute\t: %04X\n", hdr_ptr->attribute);
    printf ("Strategy Addr\t: %Np\n", hdr_ptr->dev_strat);
    printf ("Interrupt Addr\t: %Np\n", hdr_ptr->dev_int);
    printf ("Name/Unit Bytes\t: ");
    for (i = 0; i < 8; i++)
    {
        tmp_str [i] = hdr_ptr->name_unit.char_ary [i];
        printf ("%02X ", hdr_ptr->name_unit.char_ary [i]);
    }
    printf ("\t");
    tmp_str [8] = '\0';
    printf ("%s\n", tmp_str);
}
```

```
/* - - - - - - - - - - - - - - - - - - - - - - - - - - - - - - - - -*/
/*                                                                   */
/*  FUNCTION:    C h e c k _ H D R                                   */
/*                                                                   */
/*  REMARKS :    Check_HDR checks the current device header to       */
/*          see if it is a block device driver.                      */
/*          If so, it unlinks it from the device header chain and    */
/*          links in one of the new device headers that allow this   */
/*          program to process the requests prior to passing them    */
/*          on to the original device driver.                        */
/*                                                                   */
/* - - - - - - - - - - - - - - - - - - - - - - - - - - - - - - - - -*/

void    Check_HDR (struct DEVICE_HEADER_struct  far *hdr_ptr)
{
                                      /* Device Header Pointers   */
    struct DEVICE_HEADER_struct  far *tmp_ptr;
    struct DEVICE_HEADER_struct  far *LPT3_ptr;

    printf ("\n\n\t\t\tC h e c k _ H D R\n");

    tmp_ptr = hdr_ptr;
    while (FP_OFF (hdr_ptr) != 0xFFFF)
    {
        if ((hdr_ptr->name_unit.int_ary [0] == 0x504C)  &&
            (hdr_ptr->name_unit.int_ary [1] == 0x3354)  &&
            (hdr_ptr->name_unit.int_ary [2] == 0x2020)  &&
            (hdr_ptr->name_unit.int_ary [3] == 0x2020))
        {
            LPT3_ptr = hdr_ptr;
        }
#ifdef  DEBUG
        Print_HDR (hdr_ptr);
#endif
        hdr_ptr = hdr_ptr->next_hdr;
    }

    hdr_ptr = tmp_ptr;
    while (FP_OFF (hdr_ptr) != 0xFFFF)
    {
        if ((hdr_ptr->attribute & 0x0800)  &&
            (driver < MAX_NEW))
```

```
     {
         tmp_ptr = &new_dh_ary [driver].dh;

         tmp_ptr->next_hdr  = hdr_ptr;
         tmp_ptr->attribute = hdr_ptr->attribute;
         tmp_ptr->dev_strat = hdr_ptr->dev_strat;
         tmp_ptr->dev_int   = hdr_ptr->dev_int;
         tmp_ptr->name_unit.int_ary [0] =
                     hdr_ptr->name_unit.int_ary [0];
         tmp_ptr->name_unit.int_ary [1] =
                     hdr_ptr->name_unit.int_ary [1];
         tmp_ptr->name_unit.int_ary [2] =
                     hdr_ptr->name_unit.int_ary [2];
         tmp_ptr->name_unit.int_ary [3] =
                     hdr_ptr->name_unit.int_ary [3];

         if (FP_SEG (hdr_ptr) == FP_SEG (LPT3_ptr))
         {
             hdr_ptr->dev_strat = (FP_OFF (LPT3_ptr) + 0x0B);
             hdr_ptr->dev_int = hdr_ptr->dev_strat;
             LPT3_ptr->name_unit.char_ary [1] = 0xEA;
             LPT3_ptr->name_unit.int_ary [1] =
                 FP_OFF (new_dh_ary [driver].drv_ptr);
             LPT3_ptr->name_unit.int_ary [2] =
                 FP_SEG (new_dh_ary [driver].drv_ptr);
         }
         else
         {
             hdr_ptr->dev_strat = (FP_OFF (hdr_ptr) + 0x0B);
             hdr_ptr->dev_int = hdr_ptr->dev_strat;
             hdr_ptr->name_unit.char_ary [1] = 0xEA;
             hdr_ptr->name_unit.int_ary [1] =
                 FP_OFF (new_dh_ary [driver].drv_ptr);
             hdr_ptr->name_unit.int_ary [2] =
                 FP_SEG (new_dh_ary [driver].drv_ptr);
         }
         driver++;
     }
     hdr_ptr = hdr_ptr->next_hdr;
  }
}
```

```
/* - - - - - - - - - - - - - - - - - - - - - - - - - - - - - - - - -*/
/*                                                                   */
/* FUNCTION:   F i n d _ b l k _ d e v                               */
/*                                                                   */
/* REMARKS :   Find_blk_dev finds block device drivers in the        */
/*             device header chain and swaps them out for new        */
/*             device header elements.                               */
/*                                                                   */
/* - - - - - - - - - - - - - - - - - - - - - - - - - - - - - - - - -*/

void    Find_blk_dev (void)
{
    unsigned int               es_reg;
    unsigned int               bx_reg;
    struct DOS_struct          far *dos_ptr;
    struct DEVICE_HEADER_struct far *hdr_ptr;

    clrscr ();

    _AX = 0x5200;
    geninterrupt (0x21);
    bx_reg = _BX;
    es_reg = _ES;

    dos_ptr = MK_FP (es_reg, bx_reg);
    hdr_ptr =
        (struct DEVICE_HEADER_struct far *) &dos_ptr->ddh_ptr;

    Check_HDR (hdr_ptr);
}
```

```
/* - - - - - - - - - - - - - - - - - - - - - - - - - - - - - - - - -*/
/*                                                                   */
/*  FUNCTION:    m a i n                                             */
/*                                                                   */
/*  REMARKS :    Main is the main driver routine for visual.         */
/*               After it runs it Terminates and Stays Resident      */
/*               (TSR).                                              */
/*                                                                   */
/* - - - - - - - - - - - - - - - - - - - - - - - - - - - - - - - - -*/

void main (void)
{
    int i;

    Find_blk_dev ();

    printf ("\n\t\tBlock Device Headers\n");
    for (i = 0; i < driver; i++)
    {
        Print_HDR (&new_dh_ary [i].dh);
        Print_HDR (new_dh_ary [i].dh.next_hdr);
    }

    _heaplen = 0x10;
    _stklen = 0x1000;
    keep (0x0000, 0x2000);  /* terminate and stay resident     */
}
```

The file **dos_dd.h** appears in Appendix F. The only difference is that we modified DEVICE_HEADER_struct:

```
struct    DEVICE_HEADER_struct
{
    struct DEVICE_HEADER_struct      far *next_hdr;
    unsigned int  attribute;         /* Device Driver Attributes */
    unsigned int  dev_strat;         /* Pointer To Strategy Code */
    unsigned int  dev_int;           /* Pointer To Interrupt Code*/
    union
    {
        unsigned char char_ary [8];/* Name/Unit Field          */
        unsigned int  int_ary [4]; /* Integer Version Of Name  */
    } name_unit;
};
```

Appendix F

TEMPLATE Files

We discussed the template files in Chapter 4 and we showed some of them. Now we present the complete versions for **dos_dd.h**, **dos_env.c** (page 222), and **dos_drvr.c** (page 229).

Here is the source listing for **dos_dd.h**.

```
/* - - - - - - - - - - - - - - - - - - - - - - - - - - - - - -*/
/*                                                             */
/* PROGRAM :  D O S   D e v i c e   D r i v e r   H e a d e r  */
/*                                                             */
/* REMARKS :   This file contains the structures and manifests */
/*          required by a DOS Device Driver.                   */
/*                                                             */
/* - - - - - - - - - - - - - - - - - - - - - - - - - - - - - -*/


/* - - - - - - - - - - - - - - - - - - - - - - - - - - - - - -*/
/*                                                             */
/*   Miscellaneous Device Driver Symbolic Constants            */
/*                                                             */
/* - - - - - - - - - - - - - - - - - - - - - - - - - - - - - -*/


#define  DOS_CMDS      25        /* Number Of DOS Commands    */
#define  STK_SIZE      512       /* DOS Device Drive Stack    */
#define  DEVICES       1         /* Number Of Block Devices   */
#define  OP_COMPLETE   0x0000    /* No Errors Return Code     */
```

213

```
/* - - - - - - - - - - - - - - - - - - - - - - - - - - - - - - - -*/
/*                                                                 */
/*    Device Attribute Field Definitions                           */
/*                                                                 */
/* - - - - - - - - - - - - - - - - - - - - - - - - - - - - - - - -*/


#define  CHAR_DD       0x8000      /* Character Device Driver  */
#define  IOCTL_SUP     0x4000      /* IOCTL Supported          */
#define  NON_IBM       0x2000      /* Non-IBM Format (Block)   */
#define  REMOVABLE     0x0800      /* Removable Media (Block)  */
#define  GET_SET       0x0040      /* Get/Set Logical Device   */
#define  CLOCK_DD      0x0008      /* Current Clock Device     */
#define  NUL_DD        0x0004      /* Current NUL Device        */
#define  STDOUT_DD     0x0002      /* Current Standard Output  */
#define  STDIN_DD      0x0001      /* Current Standard Input   */
#define  GEN_IOCTL     0x0001      /* Generic IOCTL If Block DD*/


/* - - - - - - - - - - - - - - - - - - - - - - - - - - - - - - - -*/
/*                                                                 */
/*       Device Driver Structure For DOS Device Drivers            */
/*                                                                 */
/* - - - - - - - - - - - - - - - - - - - - - - - - - - - - - - - -*/

struct   DEVICE_HEADER_struct
{
     struct DEVICE_HEADER_struct      far *next_hdr;
     unsigned int  attribute;         /* Device Driver Attributes */
     unsigned int  dev_strat;         /* Pointer To Strategy Code */
     unsigned int  dev_int;           /* Pointer To Interrupt Code*/
     unsigned char name_unit [8];     /* Name/Unit Field          */
};
```

```
/* - - - - - - - - - - - - - - - - - - - - - - - - - - - - - - - -*/
/*                                                                 */
/*    Device Status Word Format                                    */
/*                                                                 */
/* - - - - - - - - - - - - - - - - - - - - - - - - - - - - - - - -*/

#define   ERROR_BIT       0x8000        /* Error Bit Mask            */
#define   ERROR_NUM       0x00FF        /* Error Number Mask         */
#define   DONE_BIT        0x0100        /* Device Operation Done     */
#define   BUSY_BIT        0x0200        /* Device Busy (Not Done)    */


/* - - - - - - - - - - - - - - - - - - - - - - - - - - - - - - - -*/
/*                                                                 */
/*    Device Error Codes Contained In The Device Status Word       */
/*                                                                 */
/* - - - - - - - - - - - - - - - - - - - - - - - - - - - - - - - -*/

#define   WRITE_PROTECT 0x00            /* Write Protect Violation  */
#define   UNKNOWN_UNIT  0x01            /* Unit Not Known By Driver */
#define   NOT_READY     0x02            /* Device Is Not Ready      */
#define   UNKNOWN_CMD   0x03            /* Unknown Device Command   */
#define   CRC_ERROR     0x04            /* Device CRC Error         */
#define   BAD_REQ_LEN   0x05            /* Bad Drive Req Struct Len */
#define   SEEK_ERROR    0x06            /* Device Seek Error        */
#define   UNKNOWN_MEDIA 0x07            /* Unknown Media In Drive   */
#define   NOT_FOUND     0x08            /* Sector Not Found         */
#define   OUT_OF_PAPER  0x09            /* Printer Out Of Paper     */
#define   WRITE_FAULT   0x0A            /* Device Write Fault       */
#define   READ_FAULT    0x0B            /* Device Read Fault        */
#define   GENERAL_FAIL  0x0C            /* General Device Failure   */
```

```
/* - - - - - - - - - - - - - - - - - - - - - - - - - - - - - - - -*/
/*                                                                 */
/*    Device Driver Command Codes                                  */
/*                                                                 */
/* - - - - - - - - - - - - - - - - - - - - - - - - - - - - - - - -*/

#define  INIT            0        /* Initialize Device          */
#define  MEDIA_CHECK     1        /* Check For Correct Media    */
#define  BUILD_BPB       2        /* Build A BIOS Parm Block    */
#define  IOCTL_INPUT     3        /* IOCTL Input Requested      */
#define  INPUT           4        /* Device Read Operation      */
#define  INPUT_NO_WAIT   5        /* No Wait Input (Char Only)  */
#define  INPUT_STATUS    6        /* Character Devices Only     */
#define  INPUT_FLUSH     7        /* Character Devices Only     */
#define  OUTPUT          8        /* Device Write Operation     */
#define  OUTPUT_VERIFY   9        /* Device Write/Verify Oper   */
#define  OUTPUT_STATUS   10       /* Character Devices Only     */
#define  OUTPUT_FLUSH    11       /* Character Devices Only     */
#define  IOCTL_OUTPUT    12       /* IOCTL Output Requested     */
#define  DEV_OPEN        13       /* Device Open Command        */
#define  DEV_CLOSE       14       /* Device Close Command       */
#define  REMOVE_MEDIA    15       /* Removable Media            */
#define  RESERVED_1      16       /* Reserved Command 1         */
#define  RESERVED_2      17       /* Reserved Command 2         */
#define  RESERVED_3      18       /* Reserved Command 3         */
#define  IOCTL           19       /* Generic IOCTL              */
#define  RESERVED_4      20       /* Reserved Command 4         */
#define  RESERVED_5      21       /* Reserved Command 5         */
#define  RESERVED_6      22       /* Reserved Command 6         */
#define  GET_L_D_MAP     23       /* Get Logical Drive Map      */
#define  SET_L_D_MAP     24       /* Set Logical Drive Map      */
```

```
/* - - - - - - - - - - - - - - - - - - - - - - - - - - - - - -*/
/*                                                             */
/*   INIT         Variable Portion Of Request Header     (0)  */
/*                                                             */
/* - - - - - - - - - - - - - - - - - - - - - - - - - - - - - -*/

struct   INIT_struct
{
    unsigned char num_of_units;     /* Number Of Units        */
    unsigned char far *end_ptr;     /* Ending Address Of Driver */
    unsigned char far *BPB_ptr;     /* Pointer To Init Arguments*/
                                    /* Set To BPB Array On Exit */
    unsigned char drive_num;        /* Driver Number          */
    unsigned int  config_err;       /* config.sys Error flag  */
};


/* - - - - - - - - - - - - - - - - - - - - - - - - - - - - - -*/
/*                                                             */
/*   MEDIA_CHECK   Variable Portion Of Request Header     (1)  */
/*                                                             */
/* - - - - - - - - - - - - - - - - - - - - - - - - - - - - - -*/

struct   MEDIA_CHECK_struct
{
    unsigned char media_byte;      /* Media Descriptor From DOS*/
    unsigned char return_info;     /* Return Information       */
    unsigned char far *return_ptr; /* Pointer To Previous VOLID*/
};


/* - - - - - - - - - - - - - - - - - - - - - - - - - - - - - -*/
/*                                                             */
/*   BUILD_BPB     Variable Portion Of Request Header     (2)  */
/*                                                             */
/* - - - - - - - - - - - - - - - - - - - - - - - - - - - - - -*/

struct   BUILD_BPB_struct
{
    unsigned char      media_byte;  /* Media Descriptor From DOS*/
    unsigned char      far *buffer_ptr; /* Pointer To Buffer    */
    struct BPB_struct far *BPB_table;  /* Pointer To BPB Table */
};
```

```
/* - - - - - - - - - - - - - - - - - - - - - - - - - - - - - -*/
/*                                                              */
/*   IOCTL_INPUT    Variable Portion Of Request Header    (3)   */
/*   INPUT          Variable Portion Of Request Header    (4)   */
/*   OUTPUT         Variable Portion Of Request Header    (8)   */
/*   OUTPUT_VERIFY  Variable Portion Of Request Header    (9)   */
/*   IOCTL_OUTPUT   Variable Portion Of Request Header    (12)  */
/*                                                              */
/* - - - - - - - - - - - - - - - - - - - - - - - - - - - - - -*/

struct I_O_struct
{
    unsigned char media_byte;      /* Media Descriptor From DOS*/
    unsigned char far *buffer_ptr; /* Pointer To Buffer        */
    unsigned int  count;           /* Byte/Sector Count        */
    unsigned int  start_sector;    /* Starting Sector Number   */
    unsigned char far *vol_id_ptr; /* Pointer To Volume ID     */
    unsigned long start_sector_32; /* 32-Bit Starting Sector   */
};


/* - - - - - - - - - - - - - - - - - - - - - - - - - - - - - -*/
/*                                                              */
/*   INPUT_NO_WAIT Variable Portion Of Request Header     (5)   */
/*                                                              */
/* - - - - - - - - - - - - - - - - - - - - - - - - - - - - - -*/

struct INPUT_NO_WAIT_struct
{
    unsigned char byte_read;       /* Byte Read From Device    */
};
```

```
/* - - - - - - - - - - - - - - - - - - - - - - - - - - - - - - -*/
/*                                                               */
/*    IOCTL          Variable Portion Of Request Header    (19) */
/*                                                               */
/* - - - - - - - - - - - - - - - - - - - - - - - - - - - - - - -*/

struct IOCTL_struct
{
     unsigned char major_func;      /* Function (Major)        */
     unsigned char minor_func;      /* Function (Minor)        */
     unsigned int  SI_reg;          /* Contents Of SI Register */
     unsigned int  DI_reg;          /* Contents Of DI Register */
                                    /* Pointer To Request Packet*/
     unsigned char far *ioctl_req_ptr;
};


/* - - - - - - - - - - - - - - - - - - - - - - - - - - - - - - -*/
/*                                                               */
/*    GET_L_D_MAP   Variable Portion Of Request Header    (23) */
/*                                                               */
/*    SET_L_D_MAP   Variable Portion Of Request Header    (24) */
/*                                                               */
/* - - - - - - - - - - - - - - - - - - - - - - - - - - - - - - -*/

struct   L_D_MAP_struct
{
     unsigned char    unit_code;      /* Input - Unit Code       */
                                      /* Output- Last Device Used */
     unsigned char    cmd_code;       /* Command Code            */
     unsigned int     status;         /* Status Word             */
     unsigned long    reserved;       /* DOS Reserved            */
};
```

```
/* - - - - - - - - - - - - - - - - - - - - - - - - - - - - - -*/
/*                                                             */
/*   Request Header Structure For Device Drivers              */
/*   (Static & Variable)                                       */
/*                                                             */
/* - - - - - - - - - - - - - - - - - - - - - - - - - - - - - -*/

struct REQ_struct
{
     unsigned char length;           /* Length In Bytes Of Req    */
     unsigned char unit;             /* Minor Device Unit Number */
     unsigned char command;          /* Device Command Code       */
     unsigned int  status;           /* Device Status Word        */
     unsigned char reserved [8];     /* Reserved For DOS          */
     union
     {
          struct   INIT_struct            init_req;
          struct   MEDIA_CHECK_struct     media_check_req;
          struct   BUILD_BPB_struct       build_bpb_req;
          struct   I_O_struct             i_o_req;
          struct   INPUT_NO_WAIT_struct   input_no_wait_req;
          struct   IOCTL_struct           ioctl_req;
          struct   L_D_MAP_struct         l_d_map_req;
     } req_type;
};
```

```
/* - - - - - - - - - - - - - - - - - - - - - - - - - - - - - -*/
/*                                                             */
/*    BIOS Parameter Block (BPB) For Fixed/Removable Disks     */
/*                                                             */
/* - - - - - - - - - - - - - - - - - - - - - - - - - - - - - -*/

struct    BPB_struct
{
    unsigned int  bps;               /* Bytes Per Sector       */
    unsigned char spau;              /* Sectors/Allocation Unit */
    unsigned int  rs;                /* Reserved Sectors       */
    unsigned char num_FATs;          /* Number Of FATS         */
    unsigned int  root_entries;      /* # Of Root Dir Entries  */
    unsigned int  num_sectors;       /* Number Of Sectors      */
    unsigned char media_descriptor;/* Media Descriptor         */
    unsigned int  spfat;             /* # Of Sectors Per FAT   */
    unsigned int  spt;               /* # Of Sectors Per Track */
    unsigned int  heads;             /* Number Of Heads        */
    unsigned long hidden;            /* Number Of Hidden Sectors */
    unsigned long num_sectors_32;    /* 32-Bit Number of Sectors */
};
```

Here is the source listing for **dos_env.c**.

```
/* - - - - - - - - - - - - - - - - - - - - - - - - - - - - - - - -*/
/*                                                                 */
/*  PROGRAM :       D O S    D e v i c e    D r i v e r            */
/*                                                                 */
/*  REMARKS :       This file contains the set of command         */
/*          routines specified by the DOS Technical Reference      */
/*          Manual.                                                */
/*                                                                 */
/*          The following include file is required to             */
/*          compile this file :                                    */
/*          DOS_DD.H                                               */
/*                                                                 */
/* - - - - - - - - - - - - - - - - - - - - - - - - - - - - - - - -*/

#include     <dos.h>
#include     "dos_dd.h"


/* - - - - - - - - - - - - - - - - - - - - - - - - - - - - - - - -*/
/*                                                                 */
/*      DOS  Device Driver Routine Declarations                    */
/*                                                                 */
/* - - - - - - - - - - - - - - - - - - - - - - - - - - - - - - - -*/

extern   unsigned Init_cmd ();              /* INIT Command          */
extern   unsigned Media_check_cmd ();       /* MEDIA_CHECK Command   */
extern   unsigned Build_bpb_cmd ();         /* BUILD_BPB Command     */
extern   unsigned Ioctl_input_cmd ();       /* IOCTL Input Command   */
extern   unsigned Input_cmd ();             /* INPUT Command         */
extern   unsigned Input_no_wait_cmd ();     /* INPUT No Wait Command*/
extern   unsigned Input_status_cmd ();      /* INPUT Status Command */
extern   unsigned Input_flush_cmd ();       /* INPUT Flush Command   */
extern   unsigned Output_cmd ();            /* OUTPUT Command        */
extern   unsigned Output_verify_cmd ();     /* OUTPUT Verify Command*/
extern   unsigned Output_status_cmd ();     /* OUTPUT Status Command*/
extern   unsigned Output_flush_cmd ();      /* OUTPUT Flush Command */
extern   unsigned Ioctl_output_cmd ();      /* IOCTL Output Command  */
extern   unsigned Dev_open_cmd ();          /* DEVICE Open Command   */
extern   unsigned Dev_close_cmd ();         /* DEVICE Close Command */
extern   unsigned Remove_media_cmd ();      /* REMOVABLE Media Com. */
extern   unsigned Ioctl_cmd ();           /* GENERIC IOCTL Command   */
```

```c
extern   unsigned Get_l_d_map_cmd ();/* GET Logical Device Map  */
extern   unsigned Set_l_d_map_cmd ();/* SET Logical Device Map  */
extern   unsigned Unknown_cmd ();    /* UNKNOWN Command Default */

/* - - - - - - - - - - - - - - - - - - - - - - - - - - - - - -*/
/*                                                             */
/*      DOS   Device Driver Global Data Region                 */
/*                                                             */
/* - - - - - - - - - - - - - - - - - - - - - - - - - - - - - -*/

extern   unsigned rc;                /* Function Return Code   */
extern   unsigned driver;            /* Global Driver Variable */
extern   unsigned SS_reg;            /* SS Register Variable   */
extern   unsigned SP_reg;            /* SP Register Variable   */
extern   unsigned ES_reg;            /* ES Register Variable   */
extern   unsigned AX_reg;            /* AX Register Variable   */
extern   unsigned BX_reg;            /* BX Register Variable   */
extern   unsigned CX_reg;            /* CX Register Variable   */
extern   unsigned DX_reg;            /* DX Register Variable   */
extern   unsigned DS_reg;            /* DS Register Variable   */
extern   unsigned SI_reg;            /* SI Register Variable   */

/* Local Device Driver Stack                                   */
extern unsigned local_stk [STK_SIZE];

/* DOS Request Packet Pointer                                  */
extern   struct REQ_struct far *r_ptr;
```

```
unsigned (*dos_cmd [DOS_CMDS]) (struct REQ_struct far *r_ptr) =
{
    Init_cmd,                       /* INIT Command               */
    Media_check_cmd,                /* MEDIA_CHECK Command        */
    Build_bpb_cmd,                  /* BUILD_BPB Command          */
    Ioctl_input_cmd,                /* IOCTL Input Command        */
    Input_cmd,                      /* INPUT Command              */
    Input_no_wait_cmd,              /* INPUT No Wait Command      */
    Input_status_cmd,               /* INPUT Status Command       */
    Input_flush_cmd,                /* INPUT Flush Command        */
    Output_cmd,                     /* OUTPUT Command             */
    Output_verify_cmd,              /* OUTPUT Verify Command      */
    Output_status_cmd,              /* OUTPUT Status Command      */
    Output_flush_cmd,               /* OUTPUT Flush Command       */
    Ioctl_output_cmd,               /* IOCTL Output Command       */
    Dev_open_cmd,                   /* DEVICE Open Command        */
    Dev_close_cmd,                  /* DEVICE Close Command       */
    Remove_media_cmd,               /* REMOVABLE Media Commmand   */
    Unknown_cmd,                    /* UNKNOWN Command Default    */
    Unknown_cmd,                    /* UNKNOWN Command Default    */
    Unknown_cmd,                    /* UNKNOWN Command Default    */
    Ioctl_cmd,                      /* GENERIC IOCTL Command      */
    Unknown_cmd,                    /* UNKNOWN Command Default    */
    Unknown_cmd,                    /* UNKNOWN Command Default    */
    Unknown_cmd,                    /* UNKNOWN Command Default    */
    Get_l_d_map_cmd,                /* GET Logical Device Map     */
    Set_l_d_map_cmd                 /* SET Logical Device Map     */
};
```

```
/* - - - - - - - - - - - - - - - - - - - - - - - - - - - - - - -*/
/*                                                               */
/*  FUNCTION:   D O S _ S e t u p                                */
/*                                                               */
/*  REMARKS :   DOS_Setup establishes a C environment prior to   */
/*          allowing the actual device driver routines to        */
/*          execute.                                             */
/*                                                               */
/*  INPUTS  :                                                    */
/*          which   0 : Strategy Entry; 1 : Interrupt Entry      */
/*          ES_tmp  Pointer To Request Packet                    */
/*          DS_tmp  Original DS Register Value                   */
/*          AX_tmp  Original AX Register Value                   */
/*                                                               */
/*  OUTPUTS :   Status  Must Be Set In The Request Packet        */
/*                                                               */
/*  NOTES   :   Register manipulations require this routine to   */
/*          be compiled with the TURBO C Compiler.               */
/*                                                               */
/* - - - - - - - - - - - - - - - - - - - - - - - - - - - - - - -*/

void DOS_Setup (unsigned int which,
                unsigned int ES_tmp,
                unsigned int DS_tmp,
                unsigned int AX_tmp)
{
    _AX = _CS;                  /* Obtain Code Segment       */
    _DS = _AX;                  /* Setup Data Segment        */

    BX_reg = _BX;               /* Save BX Register          */
    CX_reg = _CX;               /* Save CX Register          */
    DX_reg = _DX;               /* Save DX Register          */

    AX_reg = AX_tmp;            /* Save AX Register          */
    ES_reg = ES_tmp;            /* Save Request Pointer      */

    driver = which;             /* Move Value From Stack     */

    SS_reg = _SS;               /* Save Stack Segment        */
    SP_reg = _SP;               /* Save Stack Pointer        */

    disable ();                 /* Disable Interrupts        */
```

```
    _AX = _DS;                      /* Obtain Data Segment      */
    _SS = _AX;                      /* Setup New Stack          */
                                    /* Set Stack Ptr Value      */
    _SP = (unsigned int) &local_stk [STK_SIZE];
    enable ();                      /* Enable Interrupts        */

    if (driver)
    {                               /* Interrupt Entry Point    */
        rc = 0x0000;                /* Clear Return Code        */
                                    /* DOS Request Packet Ptr   */
        r_ptr = MK_FP (ES_reg, BX_reg);
        if (r_ptr->command >= DOS_CMDS)
        {
            rc = ERROR_BIT | UNKNOWN_CMD;
        }
        else
        {
            rc |= (*dos_cmd [r_ptr->command]) (r_ptr);
        }
                                    /* Set Driver Complete Bit  */
        r_ptr->status = rc | DONE_BIT;
    }
    else
    {                               /* Strategy Entry Point     */
        /* Don't Save ES:BX Because It's Passed To Interrupt!!  */
    }

    disable ();                     /* Disable Interrupts       */
    _SS = SS_reg;                   /* Restore Entry Stack      */
    _SP = SP_reg;                   /* Restore Entry Stack Ptr  */
    enable ();                      /* Enable Interrupts        */

    _DX = DX_reg;                   /* Restore DX Register      */
    _CX = CX_reg;                   /* Restore CX Register      */
    _BX = BX_reg;                   /* Restore BX Register      */
    _AX = AX_reg;                   /* Restore AX Register      */

    _ES = ES_tmp;                   /* Restore ES Register      */
    _DS = DS_tmp;                   /* Restore DS Register      */
}
```

```
/* - - - - - - - - - - - - - - - - - - - - - - - - - - - - - - -*/
/*                                                               */
/*  FUNCTION:    S t r a t e g y                                 */
/*                                                               */
/*  REMARKS :    Strategy is the routine that is called by the   */
/*               Operating System when this device is requested to */
/*               perform some activity (typically READs and WRITEs). */
/*                                                               */
/*  INPUTS  :    ES:BX    Pointer To Request Packet              */
/*                                                               */
/*  NOTES   :    Register manipulations require this routine to  */
/*               be compiled with the TURBO C Compiler.          */
/*                                                               */
/* - - - - - - - - - - - - - - - - - - - - - - - - - - - - - - -*/

void far Strategy (void)
{

#ifdef  DEBUG
    geninterrupt (0x03);
#endif

    DOS_Setup (0x00, _ES, _DS, _AX);
}
```

```
/* - - - - - - - - - - - - - - - - - - - - - - - - - - - - - - - -*/
/*                                                                 */
/*  FUNCTION:    I n t e r r u p t                                 */
/*                                                                 */
/*  REMARKS :    Interrupt is the routine that is called by the    */
/*               Operating System immediately after the Strategy   */
/*               routine has been called.  Interrupt is responsible */
/*               for performing the work required to accomplish the */
/*               requested operation.                              */
/*                                                                 */
/*  INPUTS  :    ES:BX   Pointer To Request Packet                 */
/*                                                                 */
/*  OUTPUTS :    Status  Must Be Set In The Request Packet         */
/*               RETF    Must Be Used To Return From Interrupt      */
/*                                                                 */
/*  NOTES   :    Register manipulations require this routine to     */
/*               be compiled with the TURBO C Compiler.            */
/*                                                                 */
/* - - - - - - - - - - - - - - - - - - - - - - - - - - - - - - - -*/

void far Interrupt (void)
{

#ifdef   DEBUG
    geninterrupt (0x03);
#endif

    DOS_Setup (0x01, _ES, _DS, _AX);
}
```

Here is the source listing for `dos_drvr.c`.

```
/* - - - - - - - - - - - - - - - - - - - - - - - - - - - - - - - - -*/
/*                                                                   */
/*  PROGRAM :        D O S    D e v i c e    D r i v e r             */
/*                                                                   */
/*  REMARKS :        This file contains the set of command          */
/*          routines specified by the DOS Technical Reference        */
/*          Manual.                                                  */
/*                                                                   */
/*              The following include file is required to            */
/*          compile this file :                                      */
/*          DOS_DD.H                                                 */
/*                                                                   */
/* - - - - - - - - - - - - - - - - - - - - - - - - - - - - - - - - -*/


/* - - - - - - - - - - - - - - - - - - - - - - - - - - - - - - - - -*/
/*                                                                   */
/*      DOS  Device Driver Required Includes / Constants             */
/*                                                                   */
/* - - - - - - - - - - - - - - - - - - - - - - - - - - - - - - - - -*/

#include    "dos_dd.h"          /* DOS  Command Structures      */
#include    <dos.h>             /* DOS Specific Definitions     */
#include    <string.h>          /* C String Library Prototypes  */

extern  void    End_code (void);
extern  struct  BPB_struct  bpb;
extern  struct  BPB_struct  *bpb_ary [DEVICES];
```

```
/* - - - - - - - - - - - - - - - - - - - - - - - - - - - - - -*/
/*                                                              */
/*  FUNCTION:    I n i t _ c m d                                */
/*                                                              */
/*  REMARKS :                                                   */
/*                                                              */
/*  INPUTS  :    r_ptr    Pointer To Request Packet             */
/*                                                              */
/*  OUTPUTS :    Status   Returned In Function Return Value     */
/*                                                              */
/* - - - - - - - - - - - - - - - - - - - - - - - - - - - - - -*/

unsigned int Init_cmd (struct REQ_struct far *r_ptr)
{
    r_ptr->req_type.init_req.num_of_units = 1;

    bpb_ary [0] = (unsigned int) &bpb;
    r_ptr->req_type.init_req.BPB_ptr =
                          MK_FP (_DS, (unsigned int) bpb_ary);

    r_ptr->req_type.init_req.end_ptr =
                          MK_FP (_DS, (unsigned int) End_code);

    return OP_COMPLETE;
}
```

```
/* - - - - - - - - - - - - - - - - - - - - - - - - - - - - - -*/
/*                                                             */
/*  FUNCTION:    M e d i a _ c h e c k _ c m d                 */
/*                                                             */
/*  REMARKS :                                                  */
/*                                                             */
/*  INPUTS  :    r_ptr    Pointer To Request Packet            */
/*                                                             */
/*  OUTPUTS :    Status   Returned In Function Return Value    */
/*                                                             */
/* - - - - - - - - - - - - - - - - - - - - - - - - - - - - - -*/

unsigned int Media_check_cmd (struct REQ_struct far *r_ptr)
{
    r_ptr->req_type.media_check_req.return_info = 1;

    return OP_COMPLETE;
}


/* - - - - - - - - - - - - - - - - - - - - - - - - - - - - - -*/
/*                                                             */
/*  FUNCTION:    B u i l d _ b p b _ c m d                     */
/*                                                             */
/*  REMARKS :                                                  */
/*                                                             */
/*  INPUTS  :    r_ptr    Pointer To Request Packet            */
/*                                                             */
/*  OUTPUTS :    Status   Returned In Function Return Value    */
/*                                                             */
/* - - - - - - - - - - - - - - - - - - - - - - - - - - - - - -*/

unsigned int Build_bpb_cmd (struct REQ_struct far *r_ptr)
{
    r_ptr->req_type.build_bpb_req.BPB_table = &bpb;

    return OP_COMPLETE;
}
```

```
/* - - - - - - - - - - - - - - - - - - - - - - - - - - - - - - -*/
/*                                                                */
/*  FUNCTION:    I o c t l _ i n p u t _ c m d                    */
/*                                                                */
/*  REMARKS :                                                     */
/*                                                                */
/*  INPUTS  :    r_ptr   Pointer To Request Packet                */
/*                                                                */
/*  OUTPUTS :    Status  Returned In Function Return Value        */
/*                                                                */
/* - - - - - - - - - - - - - - - - - - - - - - - - - - - - - - -*/

unsigned int    Ioctl_input_cmd (struct REQ_struct  far *r_ptr)
{
    return UNKNOWN_CMD;
}


/* - - - - - - - - - - - - - - - - - - - - - - - - - - - - - - -*/
/*                                                                */
/*  FUNCTION:    I n p u t _ c m d                                */
/*                                                                */
/*  REMARKS :                                                     */
/*                                                                */
/*  INPUTS  :    r_ptr   Pointer To Request Packet                */
/*                                                                */
/*  OUTPUTS :    Status  Returned In Function Return Value        */
/*                                                                */
/* - - - - - - - - - - - - - - - - - - - - - - - - - - - - - - -*/

unsigned int Input_cmd (struct REQ_struct far *r_ptr)
{
    r_ptr->req_type.i_o_req.count = 0;

    return OP_COMPLETE;
}
```

```
/* - - - - - - - - - - - - - - - - - - - - - - - - - - - - - - -*/
/*                                                               */
/*  FUNCTION:    I n p u t _ n o _ w a i t _ c m d               */
/*                                                               */
/*  REMARKS :                                                    */
/*                                                               */
/*  INPUTS  :   r_ptr   Pointer To Request Packet                */
/*                                                               */
/*  OUTPUTS :   Status  Returned In Function Return Value        */
/*                                                               */
/* - - - - - - - - - - - - - - - - - - - - - - - - - - - - - - -*/

unsigned int Input_no_wait_cmd (struct REQ_struct far *r_ptr)
{
    return UNKNOWN_CMD;
}


/* - - - - - - - - - - - - - - - - - - - - - - - - - - - - - - -*/
/*                                                               */
/*  FUNCTION:    I n p u t _ s t a t u s _ c m d                 */
/*                                                               */
/*  REMARKS :                                                    */
/*                                                               */
/*  INPUTS  :   r_ptr   Pointer To Request Packet                */
/*                                                               */
/*  OUTPUTS :   Status  Returned In Function Return Value        */
/*                                                               */
/* - - - - - - - - - - - - - - - - - - - - - - - - - - - - - - -*/

unsigned int Input_status_cmd (struct REQ_struct far *r_ptr)
{
    return UNKNOWN_CMD;
}
```

```
/* - - - - - - - - - - - - - - - - - - - - - - - - - - - - - - - -*/
/*                                                                 */
/*  FUNCTION:    I n p u t _ f l u s h _ c m d                      */
/*                                                                 */
/*  REMARKS :                                                      */
/*                                                                 */
/*  INPUTS  :    r_ptr    Pointer To Request Packet                */
/*                                                                 */
/*  OUTPUTS :    Status   Returned In Function Return Value         */
/*                                                                 */
/* - - - - - - - - - - - - - - - - - - - - - - - - - - - - - - - -*/

unsigned int Input_flush_cmd (struct REQ_struct far *r_ptr)
{
    return OP_COMPLETE;
}


/* - - - - - - - - - - - - - - - - - - - - - - - - - - - - - - - -*/
/*                                                                 */
/*  FUNCTION:    O u t p u t _ c m d                               */
/*                                                                 */
/*  REMARKS :                                                      */
/*                                                                 */
/*  INPUTS  :    r_ptr    Pointer To Request Packet                */
/*                                                                 */
/*  OUTPUTS :    Status   Returned In Function Return Value         */
/*                                                                 */
/* - - - - - - - - - - - - - - - - - - - - - - - - - - - - - - - -*/

unsigned int Output_cmd (struct REQ_struct far *r_ptr)
{
    r_ptr->req_type.i_o_req.count = 0;

    return OP_COMPLETE;
}
```

```
/* - - - - - - - - - - - - - - - - - - - - - - - - - - - - - - - -*/
/*                                                                 */
/*  FUNCTION:   O u t p u t _ v e r i f y _ c m d                   */
/*                                                                 */
/*  REMARKS :                                                      */
/*                                                                 */
/*  INPUTS  :   r_ptr   Pointer To Request Packet                  */
/*                                                                 */
/*  OUTPUTS :   Status  Returned In Function Return Value          */
/*                                                                 */
/* - - - - - - - - - - - - - - - - - - - - - - - - - - - - - - - -*/

unsigned int Output_verify_cmd (struct REQ_struct far *r_ptr)
{
    r_ptr->req_type.i_o_req.count = 0;

    return OP_COMPLETE;
}


/* - - - - - - - - - - - - - - - - - - - - - - - - - - - - - - - -*/
/*                                                                 */
/*  FUNCTION:   O u t p u t _ s t a t u s _ c m d                   */
/*                                                                 */
/*  REMARKS :                                                      */
/*                                                                 */
/*  INPUTS  :   r_ptr   Pointer To Request Packet                  */
/*                                                                 */
/*  OUTPUTS :   Status  Returned In Function Return Value          */
/*                                                                 */
/* - - - - - - - - - - - - - - - - - - - - - - - - - - - - - - - -*/

unsigned int Output_status_cmd (struct REQ_struct far *r_ptr)
{
    return UNKNOWN_CMD;
}
```

```
/* - - - - - - - - - - - - - - - - - - - - - - - - - - - - - - -*/
/*                                                               */
/*  FUNCTION:    O u t p u t _ f l u s h _ c m d                 */
/*                                                               */
/*  REMARKS :                                                    */
/*                                                               */
/*  INPUTS  :   r_ptr   Pointer To Request Packet               */
/*                                                               */
/*  OUTPUTS :   Status  Returned In Function Return Value        */
/*                                                               */
/* - - - - - - - - - - - - - - - - - - - - - - - - - - - - - - -*/

unsigned int Output_flush_cmd (struct REQ_struct far *r_ptr)
{
    return OP_COMPLETE;
}


/* - - - - - - - - - - - - - - - - - - - - - - - - - - - - - - -*/
/*                                                               */
/*  FUNCTION:    I o c t l _ o u t p u t _ c m d                 */
/*                                                               */
/*  REMARKS :                                                    */
/*                                                               */
/*  INPUTS  :   r_ptr   Pointer To Request Packet               */
/*                                                               */
/*  OUTPUTS :   Status  Returned In Function Return Value        */
/*                                                               */
/* - - - - - - - - - - - - - - - - - - - - - - - - - - - - - - -*/

unsigned int Ioctl_output_cmd (struct REQ_struct far *r_ptr)
{
    return UNKNOWN_CMD;
}
```

```
/* - - - - - - - - - - - - - - - - - - - - - - - - - - - - - - -*/
/*                                                                */
/* FUNCTION:   D e v _ o p e n _ c m d                            */
/*                                                                */
/* REMARKS :                                                      */
/*                                                                */
/* INPUTS  :   r_ptr   Pointer To Request Packet                  */
/*                                                                */
/* OUTPUTS :   Status  Returned In Function Return Value          */
/*                                                                */
/* - - - - - - - - - - - - - - - - - - - - - - - - - - - - - - -*/

unsigned int Dev_open_cmd (struct REQ_struct far *r_ptr)
{
    return OP_COMPLETE;
}


/* - - - - - - - - - - - - - - - - - - - - - - - - - - - - - - -*/
/*                                                                */
/* FUNCTION:   D e v _ c l o s e _ c m d                          */
/*                                                                */
/* REMARKS :                                                      */
/*                                                                */
/* INPUTS  :   r_ptr   Pointer To Request Packet                  */
/*                                                                */
/* OUTPUTS :   Status  Returned In Function Return Value          */
/*                                                                */
/* - - - - - - - - - - - - - - - - - - - - - - - - - - - - - - -*/

unsigned int Dev_close_cmd (struct REQ_struct far *r_ptr)
{
    return OP_COMPLETE;
}
```

```
/* - - - - - - - - - - - - - - - - - - - - - - - - - - - - - -*/
/*                                                             */
/*  FUNCTION:    R e m o v e _ m e d i a _ c m d               */
/*                                                             */
/*  REMARKS :                                                  */
/*                                                             */
/*  INPUTS  :   r_ptr   Pointer To Request Packet              */
/*                                                             */
/*  OUTPUTS :   Status  Returned In Function Return Value      */
/*                                                             */
/* - - - - - - - - - - - - - - - - - - - - - - - - - - - - - -*/

unsigned int Remove_media_cmd (struct REQ_struct far *r_ptr)
{
    return UNKNOWN_CMD;
}


/* - - - - - - - - - - - - - - - - - - - - - - - - - - - - - -*/
/*                                                             */
/*  FUNCTION:    I o c t l _ c m d                             */
/*                                                             */
/*  REMARKS :                                                  */
/*                                                             */
/*  INPUTS  :   r_ptr   Pointer To Request Packet              */
/*                                                             */
/*  OUTPUTS :   Status  Returned In Function Return Value      */
/*                                                             */
/* - - - - - - - - - - - - - - - - - - - - - - - - - - - - - -*/

unsigned int Ioctl_cmd (struct REQ_struct far *r_ptr)
{
    return UNKNOWN_CMD;
}
```

```
/* - - - - - - - - - - - - - - - - - - - - - - - - - - - - - - - -*/
/*                                                                 */
/*  FUNCTION:    G e t _ l _ d _ m a p _ c m d                     */
/*                                                                 */
/*  REMARKS :                                                      */
/*                                                                 */
/*  INPUTS  :    r_ptr    Pointer To Request Packet                */
/*                                                                 */
/*  OUTPUTS :    Status   Returned In Function Return Value        */
/*                                                                 */
/* - - - - - - - - - - - - - - - - - - - - - - - - - - - - - - - -*/

unsigned int Get_l_d_map_cmd (struct REQ_struct far *r_ptr)
{
    r_ptr->req_type.l_d_map_req.unit_code = 0;

    return OP_COMPLETE;
}


/* - - - - - - - - - - - - - - - - - - - - - - - - - - - - - - - -*/
/*                                                                 */
/*  FUNCTION:    S e t _ l _ d _ m a p _ c m d                     */
/*                                                                 */
/*  REMARKS :                                                      */
/*                                                                 */
/*  INPUTS  :    r_ptr    Pointer To Request Packet                */
/*                                                                 */
/*  OUTPUTS :    Status   Returned In Function Return Value        */
/*                                                                 */
/* - - - - - - - - - - - - - - - - - - - - - - - - - - - - - - - -*/

unsigned int Set_l_d_map_cmd (struct REQ_struct far *r_ptr)
{
    r_ptr->req_type.l_d_map_req.unit_code = 0;

    return OP_COMPLETE;
}
```

```
/* - - - - - - - - - - - - - - - - - - - - - - - - - - - - - -*/
/*                                                              */
/* FUNCTION:    U n k n o w n _ c m d                           */
/*                                                              */
/* REMARKS :                                                    */
/*                                                              */
/* INPUTS   :   r_ptr    Pointer To Request Packet              */
/*                                                              */
/* OUTPUTS :    Status   Returned In Function Return Value      */
/*                                                              */
/* - - - - - - - - - - - - - - - - - - - - - - - - - - - - - -*/

unsigned int Unknown_cmd (struct REQ_struct far *r_ptr)
{
    return UNKNOWN_CMD;
}
```

Appendix G

CONSOLE Files

We discussed the CONSOLE device driver in Chapter 6 where we have showed some of the files. Now we present the complete versions for `console` (the makefile for the device driver); `console.h` (page 245); `dos_data.c` (page 246); `dos_env.c` (page 248); and `dos_drvr.c` (page 255). The remaining files we use in the `console` makefile have not changed — they remain as they appear in Chapter 4 and Appendix F.

Here is the source listing for the `console` makefile.

```
#
#    Makefile For DOS Device Driver Template Written In C
#

#
#    Assembler Definitions
#

ASM     = \turbo\asm\tasm
AFLAGS  =

#
#    TURBO C Compiler Definitions
#
#    -c      Do Not Perform Link Step
#    -M      Produce Link/Load Map
#    -mt     Produce TINY Model Output
#    -S      Produce Assembler Module
#    -y      Produce Line Number Information
```

241

```
#   -Idir   Place To Search For Include Files

TURBO   = \turbo\c\tcc
TFLAGS  = -c -M -mt -S -y -I\turbo\c\include

#
#   Linker Definitions
#

LINK    = \turbo\c\tlink
LFLAGS  =

#
#   List Of Required Libraries
#

LIBS    = \turbo\c\lib\cs.lib

#
#   List Of Required Include Files
#
#   DOS_DD.H    DOS Device Driver Command Include File

INCS    = dos_dd.h

#
#   List Of Required Object Files
#
#   M1.OBJ      TURBO C Version Assembler Header For TINY Model
#   M2.OBJ      Modified C Assembler For DOS_DATA.C
#   M3.OBJ      Modified C Assembler For DOS_ENV.C
#   M4.OBJ      Modified C Assembler For DOS_DRVR.C
#   M5.OBJ      Modified C Assembler For DOS_END.C
#   VID.OBJ     BIOS interface routines

OBJS    = m1.obj  m2.obj  m3.obj  m4.obj  m5.obj  video.obj

#
#   Perform DOS Device Driver Linkage
#

console.sys:    $(OBJS)  $(INCS)
```

```
                    $(LINK) $(LFLAGS) m1+m2+m3+m4+m5+video, \
                                     console.exe,,$(LIBS);
                    erase  m3.*
                    exe2bin  console.exe  console.sys


#
#    Perform DOS_HDR Assembly
#

m1.obj:      dos_hdr.asm
             copy  dos_hdr.asm  m1.asm
             $(ASM) $(AFLAGS)  m1.asm;


#
#    Perform DOS_DATA Compilation
#

m2.obj:      $(INCS)  dos_data.c
             $(TURBO) $(TFLAGS)  dos_data.c
             arrange  dos.arr  dos_data.asm  m2.asm
             erase  dos_data.asm
             $(ASM) $(AFLAGS)  m2.asm;


#
#    Perform DOS_ENV Compilation
#

m3.obj:      $(INCS)  dos_env.c
             $(TURBO) $(TFLAGS)  dos_env.c
             arrange  dos.arr  dos_env.asm  m3.asm
             erase  dos_env.asm
             $(ASM) $(AFLAGS)  m3.asm;


#
#    Perform DOS_DRVR Compilation
#

m4.obj:      $(INCS)  dos_drvr.c
             $(TURBO) $(TFLAGS)  dos_drvr.c
             arrange  dos.arr  dos_drvr.asm  m4.asm
             erase  dos_drvr.asm
             $(ASM) $(AFLAGS)  m4.asm;
```

```
#
#    Perform DOS_END Compilation
#

m5.obj:     $(INCS)  dos_end.c
            $(TURBO) $(TFLAGS) dos_end.c
            arrange  dos.arr  dos_end.asm  m5.asm
            erase  dos_end.asm
            $(ASM) $(AFLAGS)  m5.asm;

video.obj:  video.c
            $(TURBO) $(TFLAGS) video.c
            arrange  dos.arr  video.asm  tmp.asm
            erase    video.asm
            rename   tmp.asm  video.asm
            $(ASM) $(AFLAGS)  video.asm;
```

Here is the source listing for `console.h`.

```
/* - - - - - - - - - - - - - - - - - - - - - - - - - - - - - -*/
/*                                                             */
/*   PROGRAM :      C O N S O L E   D D   H E A D E R   F I L E */
/*                                                             */
/*   REMARKS :      This file contains the local structures and */
/*           defines required by the new CONSOLE Device Driver. */
/*                                                             */
/* - - - - - - - - - - - - - - - - - - - - - - - - - - - - - -*/

#define BIOS_DATA    0x40               /* BIOS Data Segment Value  */
#define KBD_HEAD     0x1A               /* KBD Buffer Head Offset   */
#define KBD_TAIL     0x1C               /* KBD Buffer Tail Offset   */
```

Here is the source listing for dos_data.c.

```
/* - - - - - - - - - - - - - - - - - - - - - - - - - - - - - -*/
/*                                                             */
/*  PROGRAM :      D O S    D e v i c e    D r i v e r         */
/*                                                             */
/*  REMARKS :       This file contains the set of command      */
/*          action routines specified by the DOS Technical      */
/*          Reference Manual.                                   */
/*                                                             */
/*          The following include files are required to        */
/*          compile this file :                                 */
/*          DOS_DD.H                                            */
/*          CONSOLE.H                                           */
/*                                                             */
/* - - - - - - - - - - - - - - - - - - - - - - - - - - - - - -*/

#include   "dos_dd.h"              /* DOS  Command Structures */
#include   "console.h"             /* Local Defines           */

extern void far Strategy ();       /* Strategy Routine        */
extern void far Interrupt ();      /* Interrupt Routine       */


/* - - - - - - - - - - - - - - - - - - - - - - - - - - - - - -*/
/*                                                             */
/*      Allocate And Initialize DOS Device Header              */
/*                                                             */
/* - - - - - - - - - - - - - - - - - - - - - - - - - - - - - -*/

/* DOS   Device Header                                         */
struct DEVICE_HEADER_struct dos_header =
{
    (struct DEVICE_HEADER_struct far *) 0xFFFFFFFFL,
    0x8003,                         /* CHR, STDIN, STDOUT      */
    (unsigned int) Strategy,        /* Strategy Function       */
    (unsigned int) Interrupt,       /* Interrupt Function      */
    {                               /* Unit/Name Field         */
        'C',                        /* "CON      "             */
        'O',
        'N',
        ' ',
        ' ',
```

```
        , ,,
        , ,,
        , ,
    }
};


/* - - - - - - - - - - - - - - - - - - - - - - - - - - - - - -*/
/*                                                             */
/*      DOS  Device Driver Global Data Region                  */
/*                                                             */
/* - - - - - - - - - - - - - - - - - - - - - - - - - - - - - -*/

unsigned int        rc;          /* Function Return Code       */
unsigned int        driver;      /* Global Driver Variable     */
unsigned int        SS_reg;      /* SS Register Variable       */
unsigned int        SP_reg;      /* SP Register Variable       */
unsigned int        ES_reg;      /* ES Register Variable       */
unsigned int        AX_reg;      /* AX Register Variable       */
unsigned int        BX_reg;      /* BX Register Variable       */
unsigned int        CX_reg;      /* CX Register Variable       */
unsigned int        DX_reg;      /* DX Register Variable       */
unsigned int        DS_reg;      /* DS Register Variable       */
unsigned int        SI_reg;      /* SI Register Variable       */

/* Local Device Driver Stack                                   */
unsigned int        local_stk [STK_SIZE];

struct REQ_struct  far *r_ptr;  /* DOS Request Packet Pointer  */
```

Here is the source listing for `dos_env.c`.

```
/* - - - - - - - - - - - - - - - - - - - - - - - - - - - - - - - -*/
/*                                                                 */
/*  PROGRAM :       D O S   D e v i c e   D r i v e r             */
/*                                                                 */
/*  REMARKS :       This file contains the set of command          */
/*         action routines specified by the DOS Technical          */
/*         Reference Manual.                                        */
/*                                                                 */
/*         The following include files are required to             */
/*         compile this file :                                     */
/*         DOS_DD.H                                                 */
/*         CONSOLE.H                                                */
/*                                                                 */
/* - - - - - - - - - - - - - - - - - - - - - - - - - - - - - - - -*/

#include    "dos_dd.h"              /* DOS  Command Structures */
#include    "console.h"             /* Local Defines           */

/* - - - - - - - - - - - - - - - - - - - - - - - - - - - - - - - -*/
/*                                                                 */
/*      DOS  Device Driver Required Includes / Constants           */
/*                                                                 */
/* - - - - - - - - - - - - - - - - - - - - - - - - - - - - - - - -*/

#include    <dos.h>                 /* DOS Specific Definitions */
```

```
/* - - - - - - - - - - - - - - - - - - - - - - - - - - - - - -*/
/*                                                             */
/*      DOS  Device Driver Routine Declarations                */
/*                                                             */
/* - - - - - - - - - - - - - - - - - - - - - - - - - - - - - -*/

extern  unsigned Init_cmd ();            /* INIT Command          */
extern  unsigned Input_cmd ();           /* INPUT Command         */
extern  unsigned Input_no_wait_cmd ();   /* INPUT No Wait Command*/
extern  unsigned Input_flush_cmd ();     /* INPUT Flush Command   */
extern  unsigned Output_cmd ();          /* OUTPUT Command        */
extern  unsigned Output_verify_cmd ();   /* OUTPUT Verify Command*/
extern  unsigned Unknown_cmd ();       /* UNKNOWN Command Default */


/* - - - - - - - - - - - - - - - - - - - - - - - - - - - - - -*/
/*                                                             */
/*      DOS  Device Driver Global Data Region                  */
/*                                                             */
/* - - - - - - - - - - - - - - - - - - - - - - - - - - - - - -*/

extern  unsigned rc;                 /* Function Return Code    */
extern  unsigned driver;             /* Global Driver Variable  */
extern  unsigned SS_reg;             /* SS Register Variable    */
extern  unsigned SP_reg;             /* SP Register Variable    */
extern  unsigned ES_reg;             /* ES Register Variable    */
extern  unsigned AX_reg;             /* AX Register Variable    */
extern  unsigned BX_reg;             /* BX Register Variable    */
extern  unsigned CX_reg;             /* CX Register Variable    */
extern  unsigned DX_reg;             /* DX Register Variable    */
extern  unsigned DS_reg;             /* DS Register Variable    */
extern  unsigned SI_reg;             /* SI Register Variable    */

/* Local Device Driver Stack                                   */
extern unsigned local_stk [STK_SIZE];

/* DOS Request Packet Pointer                                  */
extern  struct REQ_struct far *r_ptr;
```

```
unsigned (*dos_cmd [DOS_CMDS]) (struct REQ_struct far *r_ptr) =
{
    Init_cmd,                           /* INIT Command             */
    Unknown_cmd,                        /* MEDIA_CHECK Command      */
    Unknown_cmd,                        /* BUILD_BPB Command        */
    Unknown_cmd,                        /* IOCTL Input Command      */
    Input_cmd,                          /* INPUT Command            */
    Input_no_wait_cmd,                  /* INPUT No Wait Command    */
    Unknown_cmd,                        /* INPUT Status Command     */
    Input_flush_cmd,                    /* INPUT Flush Command      */
    Output_cmd,                         /* OUTPUT Command           */
    Output_verify_cmd,                  /* OUTPUT Verify Command    */
    Unknown_cmd,                        /* OUTPUT Status Command    */
    Unknown_cmd,                        /* OUTPUT Flush Command     */
    Unknown_cmd,                        /* IOCTL Output Command     */
    Unknown_cmd,                        /* DEVICE Open Command      */
    Unknown_cmd,                        /* DEVICE Close Command     */
    Unknown_cmd,                        /* REMOVABLE Media Commmand */
    Unknown_cmd,                        /* UNKNOWN Command Default  */
    Unknown_cmd,                        /* UNKNOWN Command Default  */
    Unknown_cmd,                        /* UNKNOWN Command Default  */
    Unknown_cmd,                        /* GENERIC IOCTL Command    */
    Unknown_cmd,                        /* UNKNOWN Command Default  */
    Unknown_cmd,                        /* UNKNOWN Command Default  */
    Unknown_cmd,                        /* UNKNOWN Command Default  */
    Unknown_cmd,                        /* GET Logical Device Map   */
    Unknown_cmd                         /* SET Logical Device Map   */
};
```

```
/* - - - - - - - - - - - - - - - - - - - - - - - - - - - - - - -*/
/*                                                               */
/*  FUNCTION:    D O S _ S e t u p                               */
/*                                                               */
/*  REMARKS :   DOS_Setup establishes a C environment prior to   */
/*          allowing the actual device driver routines to        */
/*          execute.                                             */
/*                                                               */
/*  INPUTS  :                                                    */
/*          which   0 : Strategy Entry; 1 : Interrupt Entry      */
/*          ES_tmp  Pointer To Request Packet                    */
/*          DS_tmp  Original DS Register Value                   */
/*          AX_tmp  Original AX Register Value                   */
/*                                                               */
/*  OUTPUTS :   Status  Must Be Set In The Request Packet        */
/*                                                               */
/*  NOTES   :   Register manipulations require this routine to   */
/*          be compiled with the TURBO C Compiler.               */
/*                                                               */
/* - - - - - - - - - - - - - - - - - - - - - - - - - - - - - - -*/

void DOS_Setup (unsigned int which,
                unsigned int ES_tmp,
                unsigned int DS_tmp,
                unsigned int AX_tmp)
{
    _AX = _CS;                      /* Obtain Code Segment       */
    _DS = _AX;                      /* Setup Data Segment        */

    BX_reg = _BX;                   /* Save BX Register          */
    CX_reg = _CX;                   /* Save CX Register          */
    DX_reg = _DX;                   /* Save DX Register          */

    AX_reg = AX_tmp;                /* Save AX Register          */
    ES_reg = ES_tmp;                /* Save Request Pointer      */

    driver = which;                 /* Move Value From Stack     */

    SS_reg = _SS;                   /* Save Stack Segment        */
    SP_reg = _SP;                   /* Save Stack Pointer        */

    disable ();                     /* Disable Interrupts        */
```

```
_AX = _DS;                      /* Obtain Data Segment          */
_SS = _AX;                      /* Setup New Stack              */
                                /* Set Stack Ptr Value          */
_SP = (unsigned int) &local_stk [STK_SIZE];
enable ();                      /* Enable Interrupts            */

if (driver)
{                               /* Interrupt Entry Point        */
    rc = 0x0000;                /* Clear Return Code            */
                                /* DOS Request Packet Ptr       */
    r_ptr = MK_FP (ES_reg, BX_reg);
    if (r_ptr->command >= DOS_CMDS)
    {
        rc = ERROR_BIT | UNKNOWN_CMD;
    }
    else
    {
        rc |= (*dos_cmd [r_ptr->command]) (r_ptr);
    }
                                /* Set Driver Complete Bit      */
    r_ptr->status = rc | DONE_BIT;
}
else
{                               /* Strategy Entry Point         */
    /* Don't Save ES:BX Because It's Passed To Interrupt!!      */
}

disable ();                     /* Disable Interrupts           */
_SS = SS_reg;                   /* Restore Entry Stack          */
_SP = SP_reg;                   /* Restore Entry Stack Ptr      */
enable ();                      /* Enable Interrupts            */

_DX = DX_reg;                   /* Restore DX Register          */
_CX = CX_reg;                   /* Restore CX Register          */
_BX = BX_reg;                   /* Restore BX Register          */
_AX = AX_reg;                   /* Restore AX Register          */

_ES = ES_tmp;                   /* Restore ES Register          */
_DS = DS_tmp;                   /* Restore DS Register          */
}
```

```
/* - - - - - - - - - - - - - - - - - - - - - - - - - - - - - - - -*/
/*                                                                 */
/*  FUNCTION:    S t r a t e g y                                   */
/*                                                                 */
/*  REMARKS :   Strategy is the routine that is called by the      */
/*       Operating System when this device is requested to         */
/*       perform some activity (typically READs and WRITEs).       */
/*                                                                 */
/*  INPUTS  :   ES:BX   Pointer To Request Packet                  */
/*                                                                 */
/*  NOTES   :   Register manipulations require this routine to     */
/*       be compiled with the TURBO C Compiler.                    */
/*                                                                 */
/* - - - - - - - - - - - - - - - - - - - - - - - - - - - - - - - -*/

void far Strategy (void)
{

#ifdef  DEBUG
    geninterrupt (0x03);
#endif

    DOS_Setup (0x00, _ES, _DS, _AX);
}
```

```
/* - - - - - - - - - - - - - - - - - - - - - - - - - - - - - - -*/
/*                                                                */
/*  FUNCTION:    I n t e r r u p t                                */
/*                                                                */
/*  REMARKS :    Interrupt is the routine that is called by the   */
/*               Operating System immediately after the Strategy  */
/*               routine has been called.  Interrupt is responsible */
/*               for performing the work required to accomplish the */
/*               requested operation.                             */
/*                                                                */
/*  INPUTS  :    ES:BX    Pointer To Request Packet               */
/*                                                                */
/*  OUTPUTS :    Status  Must Be Set In The Request Packet        */
/*               RETF    Must Be Used To Return From Interrupt     */
/*                                                                */
/*  NOTES   :    Register manipulations require this routine to    */
/*          be compiled with the TURBO C Compiler.                */
/*                                                                */
/* - - - - - - - - - - - - - - - - - - - - - - - - - - - - - - -*/

void far Interrupt (void)
{

#ifdef   DEBUG
    geninterrupt (0x03);
#endif

    DOS_Setup (0x01, _ES, _DS, _AX);
}
```

Here is the source listing for dos_drvr.c.

```
/* - - - - - - - - - - - - - - - - - - - - - - - - - - - - - -*/
/*                                                             */
/*  PROGRAM :      D O S   D e v i c e   D r i v e r           */
/*                                                             */
/*  REMARKS :      This file contains the set of command       */
/*          action routines specified by the DOS Technical     */
/*          Reference Manual.                                  */
/*                                                             */
/*          The following include files are required to        */
/*          compile this file :                                */
/*          DOS_DD.H                                           */
/*          CONSOLE.H                                          */
/*                                                             */
/* - - - - - - - - - - - - - - - - - - - - - - - - - - - - - -*/

#include    "dos_dd.h"           /* DOS  Command Structures  */
#include    "console.h"          /* Local Defines            */

/* - - - - - - - - - - - - - - - - - - - - - - - - - - - - - -*/
/*                                                             */
/*      DOS  Device Driver Required Includes / Constants       */
/*                                                             */
/* - - - - - - - - - - - - - - - - - - - - - - - - - - - - - -*/

#include    <dos.h>              /* DOS Specific Definitions */
#include    <bios.h>             /* C BIOS I/O Definitions   */
#include    <string.h>           /* C String Library Protos  */

extern  void    End_code ();
```

```
/* - - - - - - - - - - - - - - - - - - - - - - - - - - - - - -*/
/*                                                             */
/*  FUNCTION:    I n i t _ c m d                               */
/*                                                             */
/*  REMARKS :                                                  */
/*                                                             */
/*  INPUTS  :   r_ptr   Pointer To Request Packet              */
/*                                                             */
/*  OUTPUTS :   Status  Returned In Function Return Value      */
/*                                                             */
/* - - - - - - - - - - - - - - - - - - - - - - - - - - - - - -*/

unsigned int Init_cmd (struct REQ_struct far *r_ptr)
{
    unsigned int    save_x;
    unsigned int    save_y;

    save_x = Get_X ();
    save_y = Get_Y ();

    Clear_screen ();
    Goto_XY (5, 5);
    Write_tty ("New Console Device Driver (CON:) Installed ...");
    Goto_XY (save_x, save_y);

    r_ptr->req_type.init_req.end_ptr =
                        MK_FP (_DS, (unsigned int) End_code);

    return OP_COMPLETE;
}
```

```
/* - - - - - - - - - - - - - - - - - - - - - - - - - - - - - - -*/
/*                                                               */
/*  FUNCTION:    I n p u t _ c m d                               */
/*                                                               */
/*  REMARKS :                                                    */
/*                                                               */
/*  INPUTS  :   r_ptr    Pointer To Request Packet               */
/*                                                               */
/*  OUTPUTS :   Status  Returned In Function Return Value         */
/*                                                               */
/* - - - - - - - - - - - - - - - - - - - - - - - - - - - - - - -*/

unsigned int Input_cmd (struct REQ_struct far *r_ptr)
{
    unsigned int    i;
    unsigned int    key;
    unsigned char   chr;
    unsigned int    save_x;
    unsigned int    save_y;

    for (i = 0; i < r_ptr->req_type.i_o_req.count; i++)
    {
        key = Get_key (0);   /* Obtain Next Key Stroke         */

        if (key & 0xFF)      /* Normal Mode Key Strokes        */
        {
            chr = key & 0xFF;
        }
        else                 /* Extended Function Key Strokes  */
        {
            chr = key >> 8;
        }
        *r_ptr->req_type.i_o_req.buffer_ptr++ = chr;
        save_x = Get_X ();
        save_y = Get_Y ();
        Goto_XY (78, 1);
        Write_chr (chr);
        Goto_XY (save_x, save_y);
    }


    return OP_COMPLETE;
}
```

```
/* - - - - - - - - - - - - - - - - - - - - - - - - - - - - - - -*/
/*                                                               */
/*  FUNCTION:    I n p u t _ n o _ w a i t _ c m d              */
/*                                                               */
/*  REMARKS :                                                    */
/*                                                               */
/*  INPUTS  :   r_ptr    Pointer To Request Packet              */
/*                                                               */
/*  OUTPUTS :   Status  Returned In Function Return Value        */
/*                                                               */
/* - - - - - - - - - - - - - - - - - - - - - - - - - - - - - - -*/

unsigned int Input_no_wait_cmd (struct REQ_struct far *r_ptr)
{
    unsigned int    rc;
    unsigned int    key;
    unsigned char   chr;
    unsigned int    far *head_ptr;
    unsigned int    far *tail_ptr;

    head_ptr = MK_FP (BIOS_DATA, KBD_HEAD);
    tail_ptr = MK_FP (BIOS_DATA, KBD_TAIL);

    if (*head_ptr == *tail_ptr)
    {                           /* Keyboard Buffer Empty         */
        rc = BUSY_BIT;          /* Indicate Buffer Empty         */
    }
    else
    {                           /* Characters In KBD Buffer      */
        rc = OP_COMPLETE;       /* Indicate Characters In Buffer */
        key = Get_key (1);      /* Obtain Next Key Stroke        */

        if (key & 0xFF)         /* Normal Mode Key Strokes       */
        {
            chr = key & 0xFF;
        }
        else                    /* Extended Function Key Strokes */
        {
            chr = key >> 8;
        }

        r_ptr->req_type.input_no_wait_req.byte_read = chr;
```

```
    }

    return rc;
}



/* - - - - - - - - - - - - - - - - - - - - - - - - - - - - - -*/
/*                                                             */
/*  FUNCTION:    I n p u t _ f l u s h _ c m d                 */
/*                                                             */
/*  REMARKS :                                                  */
/*                                                             */
/*  INPUTS  :    r_ptr    Pointer To Request Packet            */
/*                                                             */
/*  OUTPUTS :    Status  Returned In Function Return Value     */
/*                                                             */
/* - - - - - - - - - - - - - - - - - - - - - - - - - - - - - -*/

unsigned int Input_flush_cmd (struct REQ_struct far *r_ptr)
{
    unsigned int    far *head_ptr;
    unsigned int    far *tail_ptr;

    head_ptr = MK_FP (BIOS_DATA, KBD_HEAD);
    tail_ptr = MK_FP (BIOS_DATA, KBD_TAIL);

    *tail_ptr = *head_ptr;

    return OP_COMPLETE;
}
```

```
/* - - - - - - - - - - - - - - - - - - - - - - - - - - - - - -*/
/*                                                             */
/*  FUNCTION:    O u t p u t _ c m d                           */
/*                                                             */
/*  REMARKS :                                                  */
/*                                                             */
/*  INPUTS  :    r_ptr    Pointer To Request Packet            */
/*                                                             */
/*  OUTPUTS :    Status   Returned In Function Return Value    */
/*                                                             */
/* - - - - - - - - - - - - - - - - - - - - - - - - - - - - - -*/

unsigned int Output_cmd (struct REQ_struct far *r_ptr)
{
    unsigned int    i;
    unsigned char   chr;

    for (i = 0; i < r_ptr->req_type.i_o_req.count; i++)
    {
        chr = *r_ptr->req_type.i_o_req.buffer_ptr++;

        Write_chr (chr);
    }

    return OP_COMPLETE;
}
```

```
/* - - - - - - - - - - - - - - - - - - - - - - - - - - - - - -*/
/*                                                             */
/*  FUNCTION:   O u t p u t _ v e r i f y _ c m d             */
/*                                                             */
/*  REMARKS :                                                  */
/*                                                             */
/*  INPUTS  :   r_ptr   Pointer To Request Packet              */
/*                                                             */
/*  OUTPUTS :   Status  Returned In Function Return Value      */
/*                                                             */
/* - - - - - - - - - - - - - - - - - - - - - - - - - - - - - -*/

unsigned int Output_verify_cmd (struct REQ_struct far *r_ptr)
{
    Output_cmd (r_ptr);

    return OP_COMPLETE;
}




/* - - - - - - - - - - - - - - - - - - - - - - - - - - - - - -*/
/*                                                             */
/*  FUNCTION:   U n k n o w n _ c m d                         */
/*                                                             */
/*  REMARKS :                                                  */
/*                                                             */
/*  INPUTS  :   r_ptr   Pointer To Request Packet              */
/*                                                             */
/*  OUTPUTS :   Status  Returned In Function Return Value      */
/*                                                             */
/* - - - - - - - - - - - - - - - - - - - - - - - - - - - - - -*/

unsigned int Unknown_cmd (struct REQ_struct far *r_ptr)
{
    return UNKNOWN_CMD;
}
```

Appendix H

ROM BIOS

This is a summary of ROM BIOS. The numbers, interrupt numbers, and values for AH (in parentheses) are in hexadecimal.

Consult your hardware technical reference manual for details.

Interrupt Number	Input Registers	Output Registers	Description
5			print screen
8			time of day
9			keyboard services
10			video services
	AH		set video mode (00)
	AL		video type
10			video services
	AH		set cursor size (01)
	CH		start row
	CL		end row
10			video services
	AH		set cursor position (02)
	DH		row
	DL		column
	BH		video page

263

Interrupt Number	Input Registers	Output Registers	Description
10			video services
	AH		read cursor position (03)
	BH		video page
		DH	current row
		DL	current column
		CH	start row for cursor size
		CL	end row for cursor size
10			video services
	AH		read light pen position (04)
		AH	light pen state
		DH	row number in text mode
		DL	column number in text mode
		CH	raster line in graphics mode
		BX	pixel column in graphics mode
10			video services
	AH		set display page (05)
	BH		display page desired
10			video services
	AH		scroll page up (06)
	AL		number of lines to scroll
	CH		row number upper left window
	CL		column number upper left window
	DH		row number lower right window
	DL		column number lower right window
	BH		display attributes for window
10			video services
	AH		scroll page down (07)
	AL		number of lines to scroll
	CH		row number upper left window
	CL		column number upper left window
	DH		row number lower right window
	DL		column number lower right window
	BH		display attributes for window
10			video services
	AH		read character and attribute (08)
	BH		display page desired
		AL	character read
		AH	attribute for character read

Interrupt Number	Input Registers	Output Registers	Description
10			video services
	AH		write character and attribute (09)
	BH		display page desired
	AL		character
	BL		attribute
	CX		times to write character and attribute
10			video services
	AH		write character (0A)
	BH		display page desired
	AL		character
	BL		foreground color
	CX		times to write character
10			video services
	AH		set color palette (0B)
	BH		background or border or palette
	BL		color or palette
10			video services
	AH		write pixel (0C)
	AL		palette color
	DX		raster line desired
	CX		pixel column desired
10			video services
	AH		read pixel (0D)
	DX		raster line desired
	CX		pixel column desired
		AL	palette color
10			video services
	AH		write character as tty (0E)
	AL		character
	BL		foreground color
10			video services
	AH		get video mode (0F)
		AH	characters per line
		AL	current video mode
		BH	current display page

Interrupt Number	Input Registers	Output Registers	Description
10			video services
	AH		write string (13)
	AL		attribute/color/cursor position
	ES		segment for character string
	BX		offset for character string
	CX		number of characters in the string
	BH		display page desired
	BL		attribute or color
	DH		start row
	DL		start column
11			equipment check
		AX	equipment information
12			memory available
		AX	memory available in 1K units
13			disk services
	AH		reset disk (00)
	DL		drive number
		AH	error number if carry flag is set
13			disk services
	AH		get disk status (01)
	DL		drive number
		AL	status returned
13			disk services
	AH		read disk sectors (02)
	AL		number of sectors to read
	DL		drive number
	DH		head number
	CH		lower 8 bits of cylinder number
	CL		upper 2 bits of cylinder number
	ES		segment for data transfer area
	BX		offset for data transfer area
		AH	status returned

Interrupt Number	Input Registers	Output Registers	Description
13			disk services
	AH		write disk sectors (03)
	AL		number of sectors to write
	DL		drive number
	DH		head number
	CH		lower 8 bits of cylinder number
	CL		upper 2 bits of cylinder number
	ES		segment for data transfer area
	BX		offset for data transfer area
		AH	status returned
13			disk services
	AH		verify disk sectors (04)
	AL		number of sectors to verify
	DL		drive number
	DH		head number
	CH		lower 8 bits of cylinder number
	CL		upper 2 bits of cylinder number
		AH	status returned
13			disk services
	AH		format tracks (05)
	DL		drive number
	DH		head number
	CH		lower 8 bits of cylinder number
	CL		upper 2 bits of cylinder number
	ES		segment for format table
	BX		offset for format table
		AH	status returned
13			disk services
	AH		get drive parameters (08)
	DL		drive number
		DL	highest drive number
		DH	highest head number
		CH	lower 8 bits of cylinder number
		CL	upper 2 bits of cylinder number
13			disk services
	AH		initialize drive characteristics (09)

Interrupt Number	Input Registers	Output Registers	Description
13			disk services
	AH		read (long) sectors (0A)
	AL		number of sectors to read
	DL		drive number
	DH		head number
	CH		lower 8 bits of cylinder number
	CL		upper 2 bits of cylinder number
	ES		segment for data transfer area
	BX		offset for data transfer area
		AH	status returned
13			disk services
	AH		write (long) sectors (0B)
	DL		drive number
	DH		head number
	CH		lower 8 bits of cylinder number
	CL		upper 2 bits of cylinder number
	ES		segment for data transfer area
	BX		offset for data transfer area
		AH	status returned
13			disk services
	AH		seek (0C)
	DL		drive number
	DH		head number
	CH		lower 8 bits of cylinder number
	CL		upper 2 bits of cylinder number
		AH	status returned
13			disk services
	AH		reset disk (0D)
	DL		drive number
		AH	status returned
13			disk services
	AH		drive ready test (10)
	DL		drive number
		AH	status returned
13			disk services
	AH		recalibrate disk (11)
	DL		drive number
		AH	status returned

Interrupt Number	Input Registers	Output Registers	Description
13			disk services
	AH		diagnostics (14)
		AH	status returned
13			disk services
	AH		get disk type (15)
	DL		drive number
		AH	status returned
		CX	total sectors in fixed disk
		DX	total sectors in fixed disk
13			disk services
	AH		disk status (16)
	DL		drive number
		AH	status returned
13			disk services
	AH		set disk type (17)
	DL		drive number
	AL		diskette type
		AH	status returned
14			serial port services
	AH		initialize serial port (00)
	AL		serial port parameter
	DX		serial port desired
		AH	line status returned
		AL	modem status returned
14			serial port services
	AH		send one character (01)
	AL		character
	DX		serial port desired
		AH	status returned
14			serial port services
	AH		receive one character (02)
	DX		serial port desired
		AL	character received
		AH	line status returned
14			serial port services
	AH		get serial port status (03)
	DX		serial port desired
		AL	status returned
		AH	serial port parameter

Interrupt Number	Input Registers	Output Registers	Description
16			keyboard services
	AH		read for next character (00)
		AL	character
		AH	scan code for character
16			keyboard services
	AH		check next character (01)
		AL	character
		AH	scan code for character
16			keyboard services
	AH		get shift status (02)
		AL	shift status
17			printer services
	AH		print a character (00)
	AL		character
	DX		printer number
		AH	printer status
17			printer services
	AH		initialize printer (01)
	DX		printer number
		AH	printer status
17			printer services
	AH		get printer status (02)
	DX		printer number
		AH	printer status
18			activate ROM BASIC
19			reboot from disk
1A			time of day services
	AH		read system clock (00)
		AL	new day indicator
		CX	high-order word of clock value
		DX	low-order word of clock value
1A			time of day services
	AH		set system clock (01)
	CX		high-order word of clock value
	DX		low-order word of clock value
1C			timer tick

Appendix I

dos_fat Program

We mentioned the `dos_fat` program in Chapter 7. Now we present the complete source for the program. It consists of two files: `dos_fat.h` and `dos_fat.c` (page 277). The main program appears at the end of `dos_fat.c`.

Here is the source listing for the `dos_fat.h`.

```
/* - - - - - - - - - - - - - - - - - - - - - - - - - - - - - - -*/
/*                                                              */
/* PROGRAM :   D O S   F A T   H e a d e r   F i l e            */
/*                                                              */
/* REMARKS :   This file contains all of the DOS FAT           */
/*         program structure definitions used in the           */
/*         DOS_FAT.C program.                                   */
/*                                                              */
/*                                                              */
/* - - - - - - - - - - - - - - - - - - - - - - - - - - - - - - -*/


/* - - - - - - - - - - - - - - - - - - - - - - - - - - - - - - -*/
/*                                                              */
/* DOS Application Programming Interface Constants              */
/*                                                              */
/* - - - - - - - - - - - - - - - - - - - - - - - - - - - - - - -*/

#define TMP_BUF_SIZE    512 /* Buffer Size Required For API     */
#define FAT_BUF_SIZE    512 /* Buffer Size Required For FATs     */
```

271

```
#define BYTE      unsigned char   /* Define Unsigned Character   */
#define WORD      unsigned int    /* Define Unsigned Word        */
#define DWORD     unsigned long   /* Define Unsigned Double-Word */

#define TRUE    1
#define FALSE   0
#define MAXPART 4                  /* Maximum Partitions On A Disk */

#define SECSIZE     512            /* # Of Bytes Per Sector       */
#define DIRESIZE    sizeof (struct d_entry)
#define DIRSPSEC    (SECSIZE/DIRESIZE) /* # Dir. Entries/Sector */

#define DIREND          0x00   /* DOS Filename Status         */
#define ROOTDIR         0      /* Root Directory Cluster      */
#define FIRSTCLUSTER    2      /* First Data Cluster In File  */

#define VOLUME      0x08   /* Volume Bit In Attribute Field   */
#define NULL        0x0000 /* Null Pointer Value              */

#define DOS_UNUSED  0      /* System ID - Unused Partition    */
#define DOS_FAT12   1      /* System ID - 12-bit FATs         */
#define DOS_FAT16   4      /* System ID - 16-bit FATs         */
#define DOS_EXTPAR  5      /* System ID - Extended DOS Partitn */
#define DOS_40PAR   6      /* System ID - 4.0 >32Mb Partition */

#define FATENTRY    union FAT_union

/* - - - - - - - - - - - - - - - - - - - - - - - - - - - - -*/
/*                                                          */
/*   File Attributes And State Definitions                  */
/*                                                          */
/* - - - - - - - - - - - - - - - - - - - - - - - - - - - - -*/

#define R_O          0x01      /* Read Only File Attribute       */
#define HIDDEN       0x02      /* Hidden File Attribute          */
#define SYSTEM       0x04      /* System File Attribute          */
#define VOLUME       0x08      /* Volume Entry Attribute         */
#define SUBDIRECTORY 0x10      /* Subdirectory Entry Attribute   */
#define ARCHIVE      0x20      /* Archive Entry Attribute Bit    */
#define UNUSED       0x00      /* Directory Entry Never Used     */
#define ERASED       0xE5      /* Directory Was Used But Erased  */
#define DIRECTORY    0x2E      /* Directory Entry Is A Direct.   */
```

```
/* - - - - - - - - - - - - - - - - - - - - - - - - - - - - - - - -*/
/*                                                                  */
/*  Hardware Specific Disk Device Parameters                        */
/*                                                                  */
/* - - - - - - - - - - - - - - - - - - - - - - - - - - - - - - - -*/

struct   device_info
{
    BYTE     drives;          /* Number Of Drives On System       */
    WORD     heads;           /* Number Of Heads On Device        */
    WORD     cylinders;       /* Number Of Cylinders On Device    */
    WORD     sectors;         /* Number Of Sectors On Device      */
};


/* - - - - - - - - - - - - - - - - - - - - - - - - - - - - - - - -*/
/*                                                                  */
/*  DOS Boot Record Layout Or Structure Definition                 */
/*                                                                  */
/* - - - - - - - - - - - - - - - - - - - - - - - - - - - - - - - -*/

struct  BOOT_struct
{
    BYTE     entry_point [3];/* Jump To Beginning Of Boot Code     */
    BYTE     oem [8];         /* OEM Name And Version              */
    WORD     bps;             /* Bytes Per Sector                  */
    BYTE     spau;            /* Sectors Per Allocation Unit       */
    WORD     res_sectors;     /* Number Of Reserved Sectors        */
    BYTE     num_FATs;        /* Number Of FATs                    */
    WORD     root_files;      /* Number Of Files In Root Directry  */
    WORD     volume_size;     /* Number Of Sectors On Volume       */
    BYTE     media_byte;      /* Media Descriptor Byte             */
    WORD     spf;             /* Number Of Sectors Per FAT         */
    WORD     spt;             /* Number Of Sectors Per Track       */
    WORD     hpc;             /* Number Of Heads Per Cylinder      */
    DWORD    hidden;          /* Number Of Hidden Sectors          */
    DWORD    volume_size_32;  /* 32-Bit Volume Size                */
};
```

```
/* - - - - - - - - - - - - - - - - - - - - - - - - - - - - - - - -*/
/*                                                                 */
/*  DOS Fixed Disk Partition Table Entry Structure                */
/*                                                                 */
/* - - - - - - - - - - - - - - - - - - - - - - - - - - - - - - - -*/

struct  p_entry
{
    BYTE     boot_ID;              /* Boot Indicator             */
    BYTE     boot_HSC [3];         /* Head, Sec, Cyl Of Boot Record*/
    BYTE     system_ID;            /* Owning System ID           */
    BYTE     end_HSC [3];          /* Head, Sec, Cyl Of Last Sector*/
    DWORD    sector_offset;        /* Sector Offset From Phys 0   */
    DWORD    sector_length;        /* Sector Length Of Partition  */
};


/* - - - - - - - - - - - - - - - - - - - - - - - - - - - - - - - -*/
/*                                                                 */
/*  DOS Fixed Disk Partition Table Structure                      */
/*                                                                 */
/* - - - - - - - - - - - - - - - - - - - - - - - - - - - - - - - -*/

struct  partition
{
    BYTE             code [446]; /* Boot Code For Device (Disk)  */
    struct p_entry   p_tbl [MAXPART];/* Partition Table Entries  */
    WORD             signature;  /* Valid Part. Signature 0xAA55 */
};
```

```
/* - - - - - - - - - - - - - - - - - - - - - - - - - - - - - -*/
/*                                                              */
/*  File Allocation Table (FAT) Structure/Union                */
/*                                                              */
/* - - - - - - - - - - - - - - - - - - - - - - - - - - - - - -*/

union   FAT_union
{
    struct
    {
        unsigned int    _16 : 16;
    } fat_16;

    struct
    {
        unsigned int    _12 : 12;
        unsigned int    xxx : 4;
    } fat_12_lo;

    struct
    {
        unsigned int    xxx : 4;
        unsigned int    _12 : 12;
    } fat_12_hi;

};

/* - - - - - - - - - - - - - - - - - - - - - - - - - - - - - -*/
/*                                                              */
/*  DOS File System Directory Structure Definition             */
/*                                                              */
/* - - - - - - - - - - - - - - - - - - - - - - - - - - - - - -*/

struct  d_entry
{
    BYTE    f_name [8];     /* File's Name              */
    BYTE    f_ext [3];      /* File's Extension         */
    BYTE    f_attribute;    /* File's Attribute         */
    BYTE    f_res [10];     /* DOS Reserved Region      */
    WORD    f_time;         /* Time Last Changed        */
    WORD    f_date;         /* Date Last Changed        */
    WORD    f_FAT;          /* Starting FAT Entry       */
```

```
    DWORD    f_size;                 /* File's Size (In Bytes)              */
};



/* - - - - - - - - - - - - - - - - - - - - - - - - - - - - - - -*/
/*                                                               */
/*  Miscellaneous DOS File System Structure                      */
/*                                                               */
/* - - - - - - - - - - - - - - - - - - - - - - - - - - - - - - -*/

struct  file_system
{
    BYTE     drive;                 /* Physical Drive Of File System    */
    BYTE     partition;             /* Partition Of File System         */
    DWORD    start;                 /* Sector # Of Partition Start       */
    DWORD    base;                  /* Base Sector # Of Master Boot      */
    BYTE     bpFAT;                 /* # Of Bits Per FAT Number          */
    BYTE     spau;                  /* Sectors Per Allocation Unit       */
    WORD     res_sectors;           /* Number Of Reserved Sectors        */
    BYTE     num_FATs;              /* Number Of FATs                    */
    WORD     root_files;            /* Number Of Files In Root Directory*/
    WORD     spf;                   /* Number Of Sectors Per FAT         */
    DWORD    hidden;                /* Number Of Hidden Sectors          */

    WORD     fps;                   /* Number Of FATs Per Sector         */
    DWORD    FAT_rba;               /* RBA Of First FAT Sector           */
    DWORD    DIR_rba;               /* RBA Of First Directory Sector     */
    DWORD    DATA_rba;              /* RBA Of First Data Sector          */

    DWORD    FAT_loaded;            /* Currently Loaded RBA Of FAT       */

    WORD     FAT_size;              /* Number Of Sectors For FATs        */
    WORD     DIR_size;              /* Number Of Sectors For DIR         */
    DWORD    VOL_size;              /* Number Of Sectors For Volume      */

    BYTE     *FAT_ptr;             /* Pointer To The Buffered FAT        */
};
```

Here is the source listing for `dos_fat.c`.

```
/* - - - - - - - - - - - - - - - - - - - - - - - - - - - - - - -*/
/*                                                               */
/*  PROGRAM :   D O S   F A T   F i l e   S y s t e m            */
/*                                                               */
/* - - - - - - - - - - - - - - - - - - - - - - - - - - - - - - -*/

#include    "dos_fat.h"
#include    <dos.h>
#include    <bios.h>
#include    <conio.h>
#include    <stdio.h>
#include    <string.h>

struct device_info  d_i;
struct file_system  f_s;
struct d_entry      entry;
unsigned char       *tmp_buf;
unsigned char       boot_device;
unsigned char       filename [80];
unsigned char       big_buf [2048];
```

```
/* - - - - - - - - - - - - - - - - - - - - - - - - - - - - - -*/
/*                                                              */
/*  FUNCTION:    P r o c e s s _ L B A                          */
/*                                                              */
/*  REMARKS :    Process_LBA performs a read or write operation */
/*               from/to the specific logical sector of a DOS   */
/*               FAT-based file system.                         */
/*                                                              */
/*  INPUTS  :    cmd      Disk Command                          */
/*               drive       Disk Drive Number                  */
/*               count       Number Of Sectors                  */
/*               b_ptr       Buffer Pointer                     */
/*               rba       Relative Block Address               */
/*                                                              */
/*  OUTPUTS :    status       Return Status                     */
/*                                                              */
/* - - - - - - - - - - - - - - - - - - - - - - - - - - - - - -*/

unsigned int    Process_LBA (unsigned int    cmd,
                    unsigned int    drive,
                    unsigned int    count,
                    void        *b_ptr,
                    unsigned long  rba)
{
    unsigned int    rc;
    unsigned int    cyl;
    unsigned int    head;
    unsigned int    sector;

    cyl = ((rba / d_i.sectors) / d_i.heads);
    head = ((rba / d_i.sectors) % d_i.heads);
    sector = ((rba % d_i.sectors) + 1);
#ifdef  PRINT_DATA
    printf ("Process_LBA - RBA : %08lx\n", rba);
#endif
    rc = biosdisk (cmd, drive, head, cyl, sector, count, b_ptr);
    if (rc != 0x0000)
    {
        rc = 0xFFFF;          /* Recalibration Of Diskette Here  */
    }
    return rc;
}
```

```
/* - - - - - - - - - - - - - - - - - - - - - - - - - - - - -*/
/*                                                           */
/*  FUNCTION:    I n i t _ F S                               */
/*                                                           */
/*  REMARKS :   Init_FS reads the boot sector and establishes */
/*          various values in the file system structure (f_s). */
/*                                                           */
/*  INPUTS  :   none                                         */
/*                                                           */
/*  OUTPUTS :   f_s File System Structure Initialized        */
/*                                                           */
/* - - - - - - - - - - - - - - - - - - - - - - - - - - - - -*/

unsigned int    Init_FS (unsigned int   c,
                         unsigned int   h,
                         unsigned int   s)
{
    unsigned int        rc;
    unsigned long       vol_size;
    struct BOOT_struct  *b_ptr;

    rc = biosdisk (0x02, f_s.drive, h, c, s, 1, tmp_buf);
    if (rc != 0x00)
    {
        rc = biosdisk (0x02, f_s.drive, h, c, s, 1, tmp_buf);
        if (rc != 0x00)
        {
#ifdef  PRINT_DATA
    printf ("Init_FS - biosdisk Failed (rc) : %x\n", rc);
#endif
            return 0xFFFF;
        }
    }

    (unsigned char *) b_ptr = tmp_buf;

    d_i.drives = 1;
    d_i.heads = b_ptr->hpc;
    vol_size = ((b_ptr->volume_size == 0) ? b_ptr->volume_size_32
                        : b_ptr->volume_size);
```

```
        d_i.cylinders = (((vol_size / b_ptr->spt) / b_ptr->hpc) + 1);
        d_i.sectors = b_ptr->spt;

#ifdef  PRINT_DATA
    printf ("Drives : %02x\tHeads : %02x\t"
            "Cyls : %02x\tSecs : %02x\n",
                d_i.drives, d_i.heads, d_i.cylinders, d_i.sectors);
#endif

        f_s.spau = b_ptr->spau;
        f_s.res_sectors = b_ptr->res_sectors;
        f_s.num_FATs = b_ptr->num_FATs;
        f_s.root_files = b_ptr->root_files;
        f_s.spf = b_ptr->spf;
        f_s.hidden = b_ptr->hidden;

        f_s.FAT_rba = (f_s.base + f_s.hidden + f_s.res_sectors);
        f_s.DIR_rba = (f_s.FAT_rba + (f_s.num_FATs * f_s.spf));
        f_s.DATA_rba = (f_s.DIR_rba + ((f_s.root_files+DIRSPSEC-1) /
                        DIRSPSEC));
        f_s.VOL_size = vol_size;
        f_s.FAT_size = f_s.DIR_rba - f_s.FAT_rba;
        f_s.DIR_size = f_s.DATA_rba - f_s.DIR_rba;

#ifdef  PRINT_DATA
    printf ("f_s.spau : %02x\t\tf_s.res_sectors : %04x\n",
        f_s.spau, f_s.res_sectors);
    printf ("f_s.num_FATs : %02x\tf_s.root_files : %04x\n",
        f_s.num_FATs, f_s.root_files);
    printf ("f_s.spf : %04x\t\tf_s.hidden : %08lx\n",
        f_s.spf, f_s.hidden);
    printf ("f_s.FAT_rba : %08lx\tf_s.DIR_rba : %08lx\n",
        f_s.FAT_rba, f_s.DIR_rba);
    printf ("f_s.DATA_rba : %08lx\n\n",
        f_s.DATA_rba);
    printf ("f_s.VOL_size : %08lx\tf_s.FAT_size : %04x\t"
            "f_s.DIR_size : %04x\n",
            f_s.VOL_size, f_s.FAT_size, f_s.DIR_size);
#endif

    return 0x00;
}
```

```
/* - - - - - - - - - - - - - - - - - - - - - - - - - - - - - - -*/
/*                                                                */
/*  FUNCTION:    G e t _ F i l e _ S y s t e m                    */
/*                                                                */
/*  REMARKS :    Get_File_System checks for a valid file system.  */
/*                                                                */
/*  INPUTS  :    drive    Device File System Is On                */
/*               rba      Sector Offset Of File System            */
/*               p_base   Partition's Base Sector Location         */
/*                                                                */
/*  OUTPUTS :    0x00     If Successful                           */
/*               0xFF     If Otherwise                            */
/*                                                                */
/*                                                                */
/* - - - - - - - - - - - - - - - - - - - - - - - - - - - - - - -*/

unsigned int    Get_File_System (unsigned int   drive,
                                 unsigned long  rba,
                                 unsigned int   p_base)
{
    unsigned int        rc;
    unsigned int        p_num;
    unsigned int        cyl;
    unsigned int        head;
    unsigned int        sec;
    unsigned char       *c_ptr;
    unsigned long       ep_off;
    struct partition    *p_ptr;
    struct p_entry      *pe_ptr;

    if (drive & 0x80)
    {
        rc = biosdisk (0x02, drive, 0x00, 0x00, 0x01, 0x01,
                    tmp_buf);
        if (rc != 0x00)
        {
            return 0xFFFF;
        }
```

```
(unsigned char *) p_ptr = tmp_buf;
if (p_ptr->signature != 0xAA55)
{
    return 0xFFFF;
}

for (p_num = 0; p_num < MAXPART; p_num++)
{
    pe_ptr = &(p_ptr->p_tbl [p_num]);
    if (pe_ptr->boot_ID == 0x80)
    {
        break;
    }
}
if (p_num == MAXPART)
{
    return 0xFFFF;
}
switch (pe_ptr->system_ID)
{
    case DOS_UNUSED :
    case DOS_EXTPAR :
    {
        return 0xFFFF;
    }

    case DOS_FAT12 :
    case DOS_FAT16 :
    case DOS_40PAR :
    {
        f_s.drive = drive;
        f_s.partition = p_base + p_num;
        f_s.start = rba + pe_ptr->sector_offset;
        f_s.base = rba;
        if (pe_ptr->system_ID == DOS_FAT12)
        {
            f_s.bpFAT = 12;
            f_s.fps = 342;
        }
```

```
                else
                {
                    f_s.bpFAT = 16;
                    f_s.fps = 256;
                }

                c_ptr = &(pe_ptr->boot_HSC [0]);
                head = *c_ptr;
                sec = (*(c_ptr + 1) & 0x3F);
                cyl = (*(c_ptr + 1) & 0xC0);
                cyl = (*(c_ptr + 2) | (cyl << 2));

                if (Init_FS (cyl, head, sec))
                {
                    return 0xFFFF;
                }
                break;
            }

            default :
            {
                return 0xFFFF;
            }

        }
    }
    else
    {
        f_s.drive = 0x00;
        f_s.partition = 0;
        f_s.start = 0x00000000L;
        f_s.base = 0x00000000L;
        f_s.bpFAT = 12;
        f_s.fps = 342;

        cyl = 0;
        head = 0;
        sec = 1;
        if (Init_FS (cyl, head, sec))
        {
            return 0xFFFF;
        }
```

```
    }


#ifdef  PRINT_DATA
    printf ("f_s.drive : %02x\t\tf_s.partition : %02x\n",
        f_s.drive, f_s.partition);
    printf ("f_s.start : %08lx\tf_s.base : %08lx\n",
        f_s.start, f_s.base);
    printf ("f_s.bpFAT : %02x\t\tf_s.fps : %04x\n",
        f_s.bpFAT, f_s.fps);
#endif

    return 0x00;
}
```

```
/* - - - - - - - - - - - - - - - - - - - - - - - - - - - - - - - -*/
/*                                                                 */
/*  FUNCTION:    G o o d _ C l u s t e r                           */
/*                                                                 */
/*  REMARKS :    Good_Cluster returns an indication whether the    */
/*               cluster is valid.                                 */
/*                                                                 */
/*  INPUTS  :    cluster The Allocation Unit Number                */
/*                                                                 */
/*  OUTPUTS :    TRUE    If Cluster Is Valid                       */
/*               FALSE   If Cluster Is Invalide                    */
/*                                                                 */
/* - - - - - - - - - - - - - - - - - - - - - - - - - - - - - - - -*/

unsigned int    Good_Cluster (unsigned int  cluster)
{
    if ((cluster < FIRSTCLUSTER)                        ||
        ((f_s.bpFAT == 16) && (cluster > 0xFFF8))       ||
        ((f_s.bpFAT == 12) && (cluster > 0x0FF8)))
    {
        return FALSE;
    }
    else
    {
        return TRUE;
    }
}
```

```
/* - - - - - - - - - - - - - - - - - - - - - - - - - - - - - - -*/
/*                                                                */
/*  FUNCTION:    N e x t _ C l u s t e r                          */
/*                                                                */
/*  REMARKS :    Next_Cluster returns the next cluster number in  */
/*               the file allocation chain indicated by the       */
/*               specified cluster.                               */
/*                                                                */
/*  INPUTS  :    cluster Current File Allocation Cluster          */
/*                                                                */
/*  OUTPUTS :    next    Next File Allocation Cluster             */
/*                                                                */
/* - - - - - - - - - - - - - - - - - - - - - - - - - - - - - - -*/

unsigned int     Next_Cluster (unsigned int   cluster)
{
    unsigned int        rc;
    unsigned int        n_cluster;
    unsigned int        fat_pos;
    unsigned long       fat_rba;
    unsigned long       l_cluster;
    union FAT_union     *f_ptr;

    l_cluster = cluster;
    if (f_s.bpFAT == 12)
    {
        l_cluster = ((l_cluster * 3) / 2);
        fat_pos = (l_cluster % SECSIZE);
        fat_rba = (f_s.FAT_rba + (l_cluster / SECSIZE));
        if (f_s.FAT_loaded != fat_rba)
        {
            f_s.FAT_loaded = fat_rba;
            rc = Process_LBA (0x02, boot_device, 1,
                    f_s.FAT_ptr, fat_rba);
        }

        f_ptr = (union FAT_union *) (f_s.FAT_ptr + fat_pos);

        if (cluster & 1)
        {
            n_cluster = f_ptr->fat_12_hi._12;
        }
```

```
        else
        {
            n_cluster = f_ptr->fat_12_lo._12;
        }
    }
    else
    {
        l_cluster = (l_cluster * 2);
        fat_pos = (l_cluster % SECSIZE);
        fat_rba = (f_s.FAT_rba + (l_cluster / SECSIZE));
        if (f_s.FAT_loaded != fat_rba)
        {
            f_s.FAT_loaded = fat_rba;
            rc = Process_LBA (0x02, boot_device, 1,
                        f_s.FAT_ptr, fat_rba);
        }

        f_ptr = (union FAT_union *) (f_s.FAT_ptr + fat_pos);

        n_cluster = f_ptr->fat_16._16;
    }

    if (!Good_Cluster (n_cluster))
    {
        n_cluster = 0xFFFF;
    }

#ifdef  PRINT_DATA
    printf ("Next_Cluster - cluster : %04x %d\tnext : %04x %d\n",
            cluster, cluster, n_cluster, n_cluster);
#endif

    return n_cluster;
}
```

```
/* - - - - - - - - - - - - - - - - - - - - - - - - - - - - - - - - -*/
/*                                                                    */
/*  FUNCTION:    R e a d _ C l u s t e r                              */
/*                                                                    */
/*  REMARKS :    Read_Cluster reads the file data indicated by        */
/*               the specified cluster number into the supplied       */
/*               buffer.                                              */
/*                                                                    */
/*  INPUTS  :    cluster Current File Allocation Cluster              */
/*               b_ptr   Buffer Address                               */
/*                                                                    */
/*  OUTPUTS :    status  Indicator Of Function Success                */
/*                                                                    */
/* - - - - - - - - - - - - - - - - - - - - - - - - - - - - - - - - -*/

unsigned int    Read_Cluster (unsigned int  cluster,
                              unsigned char *b_ptr,
                              unsigned char clstr_sec,
                              unsigned char count)
{
    unsigned int    rc;
    unsigned long   rba;
    unsigned long   l_cluster;

    l_cluster = cluster;
    if (Good_Cluster (cluster))
    {
        rba = (((l_cluster - FIRSTCLUSTER) * f_s.spau) +
                                        f_s.DATA_rba);
        rba += clstr_sec;
        rc = Process_LBA (0x02, boot_device, count, b_ptr, rba);
        if (rc)
        {
            rc = 0xFFFF;
        }
    }
    else
    {
        rc = 0xFFFF;
    }
```

```
#ifdef  PRINT_DATA
    printf ("Read_Cluster - cluster : %04x %d\trba : %08lx %ld\n",
            cluster, cluster, rba, rba);
#endif

    return rc;
}
```

```
/* - - - - - - - - - - - - - - - - - - - - - - - - - - - - - -*/
/*                                                             */
/*  FUNCTION:    P r i n t _ D I R                             */
/*                                                             */
/*  REMARKS :    Print_DIR prints the directory entry          */
/*            information that is pointed to by the parameter. */
/*                                                             */
/*  INPUTS  :    entry   Print_DIR Caller's ID (Location)      */
/*               d_ptr   Pointer To Directory Entry            */
/*                                                             */
/*  OUTPUTS :    None    No Status Returned                    */
/*                                                             */
/* - - - - - - - - - - - - - - - - - - - - - - - - - - - - - -*/

unsigned int    Print_DIR (unsigned int    entry,
                           struct d_entry   *d_ptr)
{
    unsigned int    i;

    printf ("Print_DIR : %02d\n", entry);
    printf ("\tFilename : ");
    for (i = 0; i < 8; i++)
    {
        printf ("%c", d_ptr->f_name [i]);
    }
    printf ("\tExtension: ");
    for (i = 0; i < 3; i++)
    {
        printf ("%c", d_ptr->f_ext [i]);
    }
    printf ("\n\tAttribute: %02x\tFile FAT : %04x\n",
        d_ptr->f_attribute, d_ptr->f_FAT);
    printf ("\tFile Size : %08lx\n", d_ptr->f_size);
}
```

```
/* - - - - - - - - - - - - - - - - - - - - - - - - - - - - - -*/
/*                                                             */
/*  FUNCTION:    F i n d _ E n t r y                           */
/*                                                             */
/*  REMARKS :    Find_Entry finds the directory entry for the  */
/*           specified filename.                               */
/*                                                             */
/*  INPUTS  :    cluster Current File Allocation Cluster       */
/*               d_ptr   Pointer To Directory Entry            */
/*                                                             */
/*  OUTPUTS :    status  Indicator Of Function Success         */
/*               d_ptr   Updated Contents Of Directory         */
/*                                                             */
/* - - - - - - - - - - - - - - - - - - - - - - - - - - - - - -*/

unsigned int    Find_Entry (unsigned int    cluster,
                            struct d_entry  *d_ptr)
{
    unsigned int    rc;
    unsigned int    i;
    unsigned int    j;
    unsigned int    k;
    unsigned int    found;
    unsigned char   *src;
    unsigned char   *dst;
    unsigned char   *fc_ptr;
    struct d_entry  *fd_ptr;

#ifdef  PRINT_DATA
    Print_DIR (1, d_ptr);
#endif

    if (cluster == ROOTDIR)
    {
        for (i = 0; i < f_s.DIR_size; i++)
        {
            rc = Process_LBA (0x02, boot_device, 1, tmp_buf,
                    (f_s.DIR_rba + i));
            if (rc)
            {
                return 0xFFFF;
            }
```

```
            for (fc_ptr = tmp_buf;
                 fc_ptr < tmp_buf + SECSIZE;
                 fc_ptr += DIRESIZE)
            {
                if (*fc_ptr == DIREND)
                {
                    return 0xFFFF;
                }
                fd_ptr = (struct d_entry *) fc_ptr;

#ifdef  PRINT_DATA
    Print_DIR (2, fd_ptr);
#endif

                if (!(fd_ptr->f_attribute & VOLUME))
                {
                    src = fd_ptr->f_name;
                    dst = d_ptr->f_name;
                    for (j = 0, found = TRUE;
                         j < 11; j++)
                    {
                        if (*(src + j) != *(dst + j))
                        {
                            found = FALSE;
                            break;
                        }
                    }
                    if (found)
                    {
                        for (j = 0;
                             j < sizeof(struct d_entry);
                             *(dst + j) = *(src + j++));

                        return cluster;
                    }
                }
            }
        }
    }
}
```

```
    else
    {
        while (Good_Cluster (cluster))
        {
            for (k = 0; k < f_s.spau; k++)
            {
            rc = Read_Cluster (cluster, tmp_buf, k, 1);
            if (rc != 0x0000)
            {
                return 0xFFFF;
            }

            for (fc_ptr = tmp_buf;
                 fc_ptr < (tmp_buf + SECSIZE);
                 fc_ptr += DIRESIZE)
            {
                if (*fc_ptr == DIREND)
                {
                    return 0xFFFF;
                }
                fd_ptr = (struct d_entry *) fc_ptr;

#ifdef  PRINT_DATA
    Print_DIR (3, fd_ptr);
#endif
```

```
            if (!(fd_ptr->f_attribute & VOLUME))
            {
                src = fd_ptr->f_name;
                dst = d_ptr->f_name;
                for (j = 0, found = TRUE;
                     j < 11; j++)
                {
                    if (*(src + j) != *(dst + j))
                    {
                        found = FALSE;
                        break;
                    }
                }
                if (found)
                {
                    for (j = 0;
                         j < sizeof(struct d_entry);
                         *(dst + j) = *(src + j++));

                    return cluster;
                }
            }
        }
    }
    cluster = Next_Cluster (cluster);
    }
}
return 0xFFFF;
}
```

```
/* - - - - - - - - - - - - - - - - - - - - - - - - - - - - - -*/
/*                                                             */
/*  FUNCTION:    F i n d _ F i l e n a m e                     */
/*                                                             */
/*  REMARKS :    Find_Filename parses the specified filename   */
/*               and the repeated invocation of Find_Entry descends */
/*               the file hierarchy.                           */
/*                                                             */
/*  INPUTS  :    name     Pointer To Desired Filename          */
/*                                                             */
/*  OUTPUTS :    cluster Cluster Number Of The Filename        */
/*                                                             */
/* - - - - - - - - - - - - - - - - - - - - - - - - - - - - - -*/

unsigned int    Find_Filename (unsigned char   *n_ptr,
                               struct d_entry  *d_ptr)
{
    unsigned int    i;
    unsigned int    rc;
    unsigned int    cl;
    unsigned char   *ptr;
    unsigned char   *c_ptr;

    for (c_ptr = n_ptr; *c_ptr;
        *c_ptr++ = (((*c_ptr >= 'a') && (*c_ptr <= 'z')) ?
                            (*c_ptr - 'a' + 'A') : (*c_ptr)))
        ;

    for (ptr = n_ptr, cl = ROOTDIR, i = 0; *ptr; i++)
    {
        for ( ; *ptr == '\\'; ptr++)
            ;
        for (c_ptr = d_ptr->f_name; c_ptr < (d_ptr->f_name + 8);
                            *c_ptr++ = ' ')
            ;
        for (c_ptr = d_ptr->f_ext; c_ptr < (d_ptr->f_ext + 3);
                            *c_ptr++ = ' ')
            ;

        for (c_ptr = d_ptr->f_name;
            ((*ptr != '.') && (*ptr != '\\') && *ptr);
            *c_ptr++ = *ptr++);
```

```
        if (*ptr == '.')
        {
            ptr++;
            for (c_ptr = d_ptr->f_ext; ((*ptr != '\\') && *ptr);
                                    *c_ptr++ = *ptr++)
                ;
        }

        rc = Find_Entry (cl, d_ptr);
        if (rc == 0xFFFF)
        {

#ifdef  PRINT_DATA
    printf ("Find_Filename - Entry Not Found\n");
#endif

            break;
        }

        cl = d_ptr->f_FAT;
    }

    rc = ((i == 0) ? 0xFFFF : rc);

    return rc;
}
```

```
/* - - - - - - - - - - - - - - - - - - - - - - - - - - - - -*/
/*                                                           */
/*  FUNCTION:    I n i t i a l i z e                         */
/*                                                           */
/*  REMARKS :    Initialize initializes the variables required */
/*          for execution.                                   */
/*                                                           */
/*  INPUTS  :    None                                        */
/*                                                           */
/*  OUTPUTS :    Zero    If Operation Successful             */
/*               Not     If Operation Fails                  */
/*                                                           */
/* - - - - - - - - - - - - - - - - - - - - - - - - - - - - -*/

unsigned int    Initialize (void)
{
    unsigned int rc;

    tmp_buf = big_buf;
    f_s.FAT_ptr = (big_buf + TMP_BUF_SIZE);

    boot_device = 0x80;
    Get_File_System (boot_device, 0x0L, 0x0);

    f_s.FAT_loaded = f_s.FAT_rba;
    rc = Process_LBA (0x02, boot_device, 1, f_s.FAT_ptr,
                                            f_s.FAT_rba);

    return rc;
}
```

```
/* - - - - - - - - - - - - - - - - - - - - - - - - - - - - - - -*/
/*                                                              */
/*  FUNCTION:    M a i n                                        */
/*                                                              */
/*  REMARKS  :   Main controls the overall operation of the     */
/*          DOS_FAT file system program.                        */
/*                                                              */
/*  INPUTS   :   None                                           */
/*                                                              */
/*  OUTPUTS  :   Various DOS FAT Tracing Is Displayed           */
/*                                                              */
/* - - - - - - - - - - - - - - - - - - - - - - - - - - - - - - -*/

void main (void)
{
    Initialize ();

    do
    {
        printf ("Enter Filename : ");
        gets (filename);
        Find_Filename (filename, &entry);
        Print_DIR (0, &entry);
    }
    while (strlen (filename) > 0);
}
```

Appendix J

RAM_DISK Files

We discussed the RAM_DISK device driver in Chapter 8 where we have showed parts of the files. Now we present the complete versions for **ram_disk** (the makefile for the device driver); **dos_data.c** (page 303); **dos_env.c** (page 306); and **dos_drvr.c** (page 313). The remaining files we use in the **ram_disk** makefile have not changed — they remain as they appear in Chapter 4 and Appendix F.

Here is the source listing for the **ram_disk** makefile.

```
#
#   Makefile For DOS Device Driver Template Written In C
#


#
#   Assembler Definitions
#

ASM     = \turbo\asm\tasm
AFLAGS  =


#
#   TURBO C Compiler Definitions
#
#   -c      Do Not Perform Link Step
#   -M      Produce Link/Load Map
#   -mt     Produce TINY Model Output
#   -S      Produce Assembler Module
#   -y      Produce Line Number Information
#   -Idir   Place To Search For Include Files
```

```
TURBO   = \turbo\c\tcc
TFLAGS  = -c -M -mt -S -y -I\turbo\c\include

#
#   Linker Definitions
#

LINK    = \turbo\c\tlink
LFLAGS  =

#
#   List Of Required Libraries
#

LIBS    = \turbo\c\lib\cs.lib

#
#   List Of Required Include Files
#
#   DOS_DD.H    DOS Device Driver Command Include File

INCS    = dos_dd.h

#
#   List Of Required Object Files
#
#   M1.OBJ      TURBO C Version Assembler Header For TINY Model
#   M2.OBJ      Modified C Assembler For DOS_DATA.C
#   M3.OBJ      Modified C Assembler For DOS_ENV.C
#   M4.OBJ      Modified C Assembler For DOS_DRVR.C
#   M5.OBJ      Modified C Assembler For DOS_END.C

OBJS    = m1.obj  m2.obj  m3.obj  m4.obj  m5.obj

#
#   Perform DOS Device Driver Linkage
#

ram_disk.sys:   $(OBJS) $(INCS)
        $(LINK) $(LFLAGS) m1+m2+m3+m4+m5,          \
                            ram_disk.exe,,$(LIBS);
```

```
            erase  m3.*
            exe2bin  ram_disk.exe  ram_disk.sys

#
#    Perform DOS_HDR Assembly
#

m1.obj:     dos_hdr.asm
            copy  dos_hdr.asm  m1.asm
            $(ASM) $(AFLAGS)  m1.asm;

#
#    Perform DOS_DATA Compilation
#

m2.obj:     $(INCS)  dos_data.c
            $(TURBO) $(TFLAGS)  dos_data.c
            arrange  dos.arr  dos_data.asm  m2.asm
            erase  dos_data.asm
            $(ASM) $(AFLAGS)  m2.asm;

#
#    Perform DOS_ENV Compilation
#

m3.obj:     $(INCS)  dos_env.c
            $(TURBO) $(TFLAGS)  dos_env.c
            arrange  dos.arr  dos_env.asm  m3.asm
            erase  dos_env.asm
            $(ASM) $(AFLAGS)  m3.asm;

#
#    Perform DOS_DRVR Compilation
#

m4.obj:     $(INCS)  dos_drvr.c
            $(TURBO) $(TFLAGS)  dos_drvr.c
            arrange  dos.arr  dos_drvr.asm  m4.asm
            erase  dos_drvr.asm
            $(ASM) $(AFLAGS)  m4.asm;

#
```

```
#    Perform DOS_END Compilation
#

m5.obj:      $(INCS)  dos_end.c
             $(TURBO) $(TFLAGS) dos_end.c
             arrange  dos.arr  dos_end.asm  m5.asm
             erase  dos_end.asm
             $(ASM) $(AFLAGS)  m5.asm;
```

Here is the source listing for dos_data.c.

```
/* - - - - - - - - - - - - - - - - - - - - - - - - - - - - -*/
/*                                                          */
/*   PROGRAM :      D O S   D e v i c e   D r i v e r       */
/*                                                          */
/*   REMARKS :      This file contains the set of command   */
/*          routines specified by the DOS Technical Reference */
/*          Manual.                                         */
/*                                                          */
/*            The following include file is required to     */
/*          compile this file :                             */
/*          DOS_DD.H                                        */
/*                                                          */
/* - - - - - - - - - - - - - - - - - - - - - - - - - - - - -*/

#include    "dos_dd.h"              /* DOS  Command Structures */

extern      void    far Strategy ();    /* Strategy Routine   */
extern      void    far Interrupt ();   /* Interrupt Routine  */

/* - - - - - - - - - - - - - - - - - - - - - - - - - - - - -*/
/*                                                          */
/*       Allocate And Initialize DOS Device Header          */
/*                                                          */
/* - - - - - - - - - - - - - - - - - - - - - - - - - - - - -*/

/* DOS  Device  Header                                      */
struct  DEVICE_HEADER_struct  dos_header =
{
    (struct DEVICE_HEADER_struct far *) 0xFFFFFFFFL,
    0x2000,                         /* Non-IBM Format        */
    (unsigned int) Strategy,        /* Strategy Function     */
    (unsigned int) Interrupt,       /* Interrupt Function    */
    {                               /* Unit/Name Field       */
        0x01,                       /* Initial Number Of Units */
        0x00,                       /* Zero Remaining Entries */
        0x00,                       /* Zero Remaining Entries */
        0x00,                       /* Zero Remaining Entries */
        0x00,                       /* Zero Remaining Entries */
        0x00,                       /* Zero Remaining Entries */
        0x00,                       /* Zero Remaining Entries */
```

```
        0x00                          /* Zero Remaining Entries  */
    }
};



/* - - - - - - - - - - - - - - - - - - - - - - - - - - - - - -*/
/*                                                             */
/*      DOS   Device Driver Global Data Region                 */
/*                                                             */
/* - - - - - - - - - - - - - - - - - - - - - - - - - - - - - -*/

struct  BPB_struct  bpb =
{
    0
};

struct  BPB_struct  *bpb_ary [DEVICES] = { 0 };

unsigned int        rc;           /* Function Return Code       */
unsigned int        driver;       /* Global Driver Variable     */
unsigned int        SS_reg;       /* SS Register Variable       */
unsigned int        SP_reg;       /* SP Register Variable       */
unsigned int        ES_reg;       /* ES Register Variable       */
unsigned int        AX_reg;       /* AX Register Variable       */
unsigned int        BX_reg;       /* BX Register Variable       */
unsigned int        CX_reg;       /* CX Register Variable       */
unsigned int        DX_reg;       /* DX Register Variable       */
unsigned int        DS_reg;       /* DS Register Variable       */
unsigned int        SI_reg;       /* SI Register Variable       */

/* Local Device Driver Stack                                   */
unsigned int        local_stk [STK_SIZE];

struct REQ_struct  far *r_ptr;  /* DOS Request Packet Pointer  */
```

```
/* - - - - - - - - - - - - - - - - - - - - - - - - - - - - - -*/
/*                                                              */
/*       RAM_DISK variables                                     */
/*                                                              */
/* - - - - - - - - - - - - - - - - - - - - - - - - - - - - - -*/

void                           (far *v_call) (void);
struct REQ_struct              tmp_req = { 0 };
struct DEVICE_HEADER_struct far *vdisk = { 0 };

unsigned char   vdisk_str [ ] = "VDISK";
unsigned char   found_msg [ ] = "\r\nVDISK Found\r\n"
                                "Driver Installed\r\n\r\n$";
unsigned char   error_msg [ ] = "\r\nVDISK Not Found\r\n"
                                "Driver Not Installed\r\n\r\n$";
```

Here is the source listing for `dos_env.c`.

```
/* - - - - - - - - - - - - - - - - - - - - - - - - - - - - - - -*/
/*                                                               */
/*  PROGRAM :       D O S   D e v i c e   D r i v e r            */
/*                                                               */
/*  REMARKS :        This file contains the set of command       */
/*          routines specified by the DOS Technical Reference    */
/*          Manual.                                              */
/*                                                               */
/*          The following include file is required to            */
/*          compile this file :                                  */
/*          DOS_DD.H                                             */
/*                                                               */
/* - - - - - - - - - - - - - - - - - - - - - - - - - - - - - - -*/

#include    <dos.h>
#include    "dos_dd.h"

/* - - - - - - - - - - - - - - - - - - - - - - - - - - - - - - -*/
/*                                                               */
/*      DOS  Device Driver Routine Declarations                  */
/*                                                               */
/* - - - - - - - - - - - - - - - - - - - - - - - - - - - - - - -*/

extern  unsigned Init_cmd ();       /* INIT Command             */
extern  unsigned Unknown_cmd ();    /* UNKNOWN Command Default   */
```

```
/* - - - - - - - - - - - - - - - - - - - - - - - - - - - - - -*/
/*                                                             */
/*       DOS   Device Driver Global Data Region                */
/*                                                             */
/* - - - - - - - - - - - - - - - - - - - - - - - - - - - - - -*/

extern   unsigned rc;                /* Function Return Code    */
extern   unsigned driver;            /* Global Driver Variable  */
extern   unsigned SS_reg;            /* SS Register Variable    */
extern   unsigned SP_reg;            /* SP Register Variable    */
extern   unsigned ES_reg;            /* ES Register Variable    */
extern   unsigned AX_reg;            /* AX Register Variable    */
extern   unsigned BX_reg;            /* BX Register Variable    */
extern   unsigned CX_reg;            /* CX Register Variable    */
extern   unsigned DX_reg;            /* DX Register Variable    */
extern   unsigned DS_reg;            /* DS Register Variable    */
extern   unsigned SI_reg;            /* SI Register Variable    */

/* Local Device Driver Stack                                   */
extern unsigned local_stk [STK_SIZE];

/* DOS Request Packet Pointer                                  */
extern   struct REQ_struct far *r_ptr;
```

```
unsigned (*dos_cmd [DOS_CMDS]) (struct REQ_struct far *r_ptr) =
{
    Init_cmd,                          /* INIT Command                */
    Unknown_cmd,                       /* MEDIA_CHECK Command         */
    Unknown_cmd,                       /* BUILD_BPB Command           */
    Unknown_cmd,                       /* IOCTL Input Command         */
    Unknown_cmd,                       /* INPUT Command               */
    Unknown_cmd,                       /* INPUT No Wait Command       */
    Unknown_cmd,                       /* INPUT Status Command        */
    Unknown_cmd,                       /* INPUT Flush Command         */
    Unknown_cmd,                       /* OUTPUT Command              */
    Unknown_cmd,                       /* OUTPUT Verify Command       */
    Unknown_cmd,                       /* OUTPUT Status Command       */
    Unknown_cmd,                       /* OUTPUT Flush Command        */
    Unknown_cmd,                       /* IOCTL Output Command        */
    Unknown_cmd,                       /* DEVICE Open Command         */
    Unknown_cmd,                       /* DEVICE Close Command        */
    Unknown_cmd,                       /* REMOVABLE Media Commmand    */
    Unknown_cmd,                       /* UNKNOWN Command Default     */
    Unknown_cmd,                       /* UNKNOWN Command Default     */
    Unknown_cmd,                       /* UNKNOWN Command Default     */
    Unknown_cmd,                       /* GENERIC IOCTL Command       */
    Unknown_cmd,                       /* UNKNOWN Command Default     */
    Unknown_cmd,                       /* UNKNOWN Command Default     */
    Unknown_cmd,                       /* UNKNOWN Command Default     */
    Unknown_cmd,                       /* GET Logical Device Map      */
    Unknown_cmd                        /* SET Logical Device Map      */
};
```

```
/* - - - - - - - - - - - - - - - - - - - - - - - - - - - - - - - -*/
/*                                                                 */
/*  FUNCTION:    D O S _ S e t u p                                 */
/*                                                                 */
/*  REMARKS  :   DOS_Setup establishes a C environment prior to    */
/*          allowing the actual device driver routines to          */
/*          execute.                                               */
/*                                                                 */
/*  INPUTS  :                                                      */
/*          which   0 : Strategy Entry; 1 : Interrupt Entry        */
/*          ES_tmp  Pointer To Request Packet                      */
/*          DS_tmp  Original DS Register Value                     */
/*          AX_tmp  Original AX Register Value                     */
/*                                                                 */
/*  OUTPUTS :   Status  Must Be Set In The Request Packet          */
/*                                                                 */
/*  NOTES   :   Register manipulations require this routine to     */
/*          be compiled with the TURBO C Compiler.                 */
/*                                                                 */
/* - - - - - - - - - - - - - - - - - - - - - - - - - - - - - - - -*/

void DOS_Setup (unsigned int which,
                unsigned int ES_tmp,
                unsigned int DS_tmp,
                unsigned int AX_tmp)
{
    _AX = _CS;                    /* Obtain Code Segment      */
    _DS = _AX;                    /* Setup Data Segment       */

    BX_reg = _BX;                 /* Save BX Register         */
    CX_reg = _CX;                 /* Save CX Register         */
    DX_reg = _DX;                 /* Save DX Register         */

    AX_reg = AX_tmp;              /* Save AX Register         */
    ES_reg = ES_tmp;              /* Save Request Pointer     */

    driver = which;              /* Move Value From Stack    */

    SS_reg = _SS;                 /* Save Stack Segment       */
    SP_reg = _SP;                 /* Save Stack Pointer       */

    disable ();                   /* Disable Interrupts       */
```

```
    _AX = _DS;                      /* Obtain Data Segment          */
    _SS = _AX;                      /* Setup New Stack              */
                                    /* Set Stack Ptr Value          */
    _SP = (unsigned int) &local_stk [STK_SIZE];
    enable ();                      /* Enable Interrupts            */

    if (driver)
    {                               /* Interrupt Entry Point        */
        rc = 0x0000;                /* Clear Return Code            */
                                    /* DOS Request Packet Ptr       */
        r_ptr = MK_FP (ES_reg, BX_reg);
        if (r_ptr->command >= DOS_CMDS)
        {
            rc = ERROR_BIT | UNKNOWN_CMD;
        }
        else
        {
            rc |= (*dos_cmd [r_ptr->command]) (r_ptr);
        }
                                    /* Set Driver Complete Bit      */
        r_ptr->status = rc | DONE_BIT;
    }
    else
    {                               /* Strategy Entry Point         */
        /* Don't Save ES:BX Because It's Passed To Interrupt!!  */
    }

    disable ();                     /* Disable Interrupts           */
    _SS = SS_reg;                   /* Restore Entry Stack          */
    _SP = SP_reg;                   /* Restore Entry Stack Ptr      */
    enable ();                      /* Enable Interrupts            */

    _DX = DX_reg;                   /* Restore DX Register          */
    _CX = CX_reg;                   /* Restore CX Register          */
    _BX = BX_reg;                   /* Restore BX Register          */
    _AX = AX_reg;                   /* Restore AX Register          */

    _ES = ES_tmp;                   /* Restore ES Register          */
    _DS = DS_tmp;                   /* Restore DS Register          */
}
```

```
/* - - - - - - - - - - - - - - - - - - - - - - - - - - - - - - - -*/
/*                                                                 */
/*  FUNCTION:    S t r a t e g y                                   */
/*                                                                 */
/*  REMARKS :    Strategy is the routine that is called by the     */
/*         Operating System when this device is requested to       */
/*         perform some activity (typically READs and WRITEs).     */
/*                                                                 */
/*  INPUTS  :    ES:BX   Pointer To Request Packet                 */
/*                                                                 */
/*  NOTES   :    Register manipulations require this routine to    */
/*         be compiled with the TURBO C Compiler.                  */
/*                                                                 */
/* - - - - - - - - - - - - - - - - - - - - - - - - - - - - - - - -*/

void far Strategy (void)
{

#ifdef  DEBUG
    geninterrupt (0x03);
#endif

    DOS_Setup (0x00, _ES, _DS, _AX);
}
```

```
/* - - - - - - - - - - - - - - - - - - - - - - - - - - - - - -*/
/*                                                             */
/*  FUNCTION:    I n t e r r u p t                             */
/*                                                             */
/*  REMARKS :    Interrupt is the routine that is called by the */
/*               Operating System immediately after the Strategy */
/*               routine has been called.  Interrupt is responsible */
/*               for performing the work required to accomplish the */
/*               requested operation.                          */
/*                                                             */
/*  INPUTS  :    ES:BX   Pointer To Request Packet             */
/*                                                             */
/*  OUTPUTS :    Status  Must Be Set In The Request Packet     */
/*               RETF    Must Be Used To Return From Interrupt */
/*                                                             */
/*  NOTES   :    Register manipulations require this routine to */
/*         be compiled with the TURBO C Compiler.              */
/*                                                             */
/* - - - - - - - - - - - - - - - - - - - - - - - - - - - - - -*/

void far Interrupt (void)
{

#ifdef  DEBUG
    geninterrupt (0x03);
#endif

    DOS_Setup (0x01, _ES, _DS, _AX);
}
```

Here is the source listing for `dos_drvr.c`.

```
/* - - - - - - - - - - - - - - - - - - - - - - - - - - - - - - -*/
/*                                                               */
/*  PROGRAM :        D O S   D e v i c e   D r i v e r           */
/*                                                               */
/*  REMARKS :        This file contains the set of command       */
/*          routines specified by the DOS Technical Reference    */
/*          Manual.                                              */
/*                                                               */
/*              The following include file is required to        */
/*          compile this file :                                  */
/*          DOS_DD.H                                             */
/*                                                               */
/* - - - - - - - - - - - - - - - - - - - - - - - - - - - - - - -*/


/* - - - - - - - - - - - - - - - - - - - - - - - - - - - - - - -*/
/*                                                               */
/*      DOS  Device Driver Required Includes / Constants         */
/*                                                               */
/* - - - - - - - - - - - - - - - - - - - - - - - - - - - - - - -*/

#include    "dos_dd.h"              /* DOS  Command Structures    */
#include    <dos.h>                 /* DOS Specific Definitions   */
#include    <string.h>              /* C String Library Prototypes */

extern  void    End_code (void);
extern  struct  BPB_struct  bpb;
extern  struct  BPB_struct  *bpb_ary [DEVICES];
```

```
#define END_OF_CHAIN      0xFFFF   /* End Of D.D.H. List          */
#define SEARCH_SIZE       30       /* Search Length For VDISK     */
#define TRUE              1        /* Value Of Logical TRUE       */
#define FALSE             0        /* Value Of Logical FALSE      */


extern  void                          (far *v_call) (void);
extern  unsigned char                 vdisk_str [];
extern  unsigned char                 found_msg [];
extern  unsigned char                 error_msg [];
extern  struct REQ_struct             tmp_req;
extern  struct DEVICE_HEADER_struct far *vdisk;


/* - - - - - - - - - - - - - - - - - - - - - - - - - - - - - - -*/
/*                                                              */
/*      DOS Internal Variables Block Structure                  */
/*                                                              */
/* - - - - - - - - - - - - - - - - - - - - - - - - - - - - - - -*/


struct  DOS_struct
{
    unsigned char                 reserved [34];
    struct  DEVICE_HEADER_struct  far *ddh_ptr;
};
```

```
/* - - - - - - - - - - - - - - - - - - - - - - - - - - - - - - - -*/
/*                                                                 */
/*  FUNCTION:    U n k n o w n _ c m d                             */
/*                                                                 */
/*  REMARKS :                                                      */
/*                                                                 */
/*  INPUTS  :   r_ptr    Pointer To Request Packet                */
/*                                                                 */
/*  OUTPUTS :   Status   Returned In Function Return Value        */
/*                                                                 */
/* - - - - - - - - - - - - - - - - - - - - - - - - - - - - - - - -*/

unsigned int Unknown_cmd (struct REQ_struct far *r_ptr)
{
    v_call = MK_FP (FP_SEG (vdisk), vdisk->dev_strat);
    _ES = FP_SEG (r_ptr);
    _BX = FP_OFF (r_ptr);
    v_call ();

    v_call = MK_FP (FP_SEG (vdisk), vdisk->dev_int);
    _ES = FP_SEG (r_ptr);
    _BX = FP_OFF (r_ptr);
    v_call ();
}
```

```
/* - - - - - - - - - - - - - - - - - - - - - - - - - - - - - - - -*/
/*                                                                 */
/*  FUNCTION:    I n i t _ c m d                                   */
/*                                                                 */
/*  REMARKS :                                                      */
/*                                                                 */
/*  INPUTS  :   r_ptr    Pointer To Request Packet                 */
/*                                                                 */
/*  OUTPUTS :   Status   Returned In Function Return Value         */
/*                                                                 */
/* - - - - - - - - - - - - - - - - - - - - - - - - - - - - - - - -*/

unsigned int Init_cmd (struct REQ_struct far *r_ptr)
{
    unsigned char                    i;
    unsigned char                    found;
    unsigned char                    far *c_ptr;
    unsigned char                    far *s_ptr;
    unsigned char                    far *t_ptr;
    unsigned int                     es_reg;
    unsigned int                     bx_reg;
    struct  DOS_struct          far *dos_ptr;
    struct DEVICE_HEADER_struct far *v_ptr;

    _AX = 0x5200;
    geninterrupt (0x21);
    bx_reg = _BX;
    es_reg = _ES;

    dos_ptr = MK_FP (es_reg, bx_reg);
    v_ptr = (struct DEVICE_HEADER_struct far *)
            &dos_ptr->ddh_ptr;

    for (found = FALSE;
        ((!found) && (FP_OFF (v_ptr) != END_OF_CHAIN));
        v_ptr = v_ptr->next_hdr)
    {
        for (i = 0, c_ptr = (v_ptr->name_unit + 8);
            ((!found) && (i < SEARCH_SIZE));
            i++, c_ptr++)
        {
            if (*c_ptr == 'V')
```

```
            {
                for (s_ptr = vdisk_str, t_ptr = c_ptr;
                    ((*s_ptr) && (*s_ptr == *t_ptr));
                    s_ptr++, t_ptr++);
                if (!(*s_ptr))
                {
                    found = TRUE;
                    vdisk = v_ptr;
                }
            }
        }
    }

    if (found)
    {                               /*  Send Command On To VDISK   */
        tmp_req.length = sizeof (struct BUILD_BPB_struct);
        tmp_req.unit = 0;
        tmp_req.command = BUILD_BPB;
        tmp_req.status = 0;
        tmp_req.req_type.build_bpb_req.media_byte = 0xFE;

        Unknown_cmd ((struct REQ_struct far *) &tmp_req);

        for (i = 0, t_ptr = (unsigned char far *) &bpb,
            (struct BPB_struct far *) s_ptr =
                tmp_req.req_type.build_bpb_req.BPB_table;
            i < sizeof (struct BPB_struct);
            *t_ptr++ = *s_ptr++, i++);

        bpb_ary [0] = (unsigned int) &bpb;
        r_ptr->req_type.init_req.num_of_units = 1;
        r_ptr->req_type.init_req.end_ptr =
                MK_FP (_CS, (unsigned int) End_code);
        r_ptr->req_type.init_req.BPB_ptr =
                MK_FP (_CS, (unsigned int) bpb_ary);

        _DX = (unsigned int) found_msg;
        _AH = 9;
        geninterrupt (0x21);
    }
    else
    {                               /*  VDISK Not Installed   */
```

```
                                    /*  Do Not Install Driver      */
        _DX = (unsigned int) error_msg;
        _AH = 9;
        geninterrupt (0x21);

        r_ptr->req_type.init_req.num_of_units = 0;
        r_ptr->req_type.init_req.BPB_ptr = MK_FP (0, 0);
        r_ptr->req_type.init_req.end_ptr = MK_FP (_CS, 0);
    }
    return OP_COMPLETE;
}
```

Appendix K

SHADOW Files

We discussed the SHADOW device driver in Chapter 8 where we have showed parts of the files. Now we present the complete versions for **shadow** (the makefile for the device driver); **dos_data.c** (page 323); **dos_env.c** (page 326); and **dos_drvr.c** (page 333). The remaining files that we use in the **shadow** makefile have not changed — they remain as they appear in Chapter 4 and Appendix F.

Here is the source listing for the **shadow** makefile.

```
#
#    Makefile For DOS Device Driver Template Written In C
#


#
#    Assembler Definitions
#

ASM     = \turbo\asm\tasm
AFLAGS  =


#
#    TURBO C Compiler Definitions
#
#    -c      Do Not Perform Link Step
#    -M      Produce Link/Load Map
#    -mt     Produce TINY Model Output
#    -S      Produce Assembler Module
#    -y      Produce Line Number Information
#    -Idir   Place To Search For Include Files
```

```
TURBO   = \turbo\c\tcc
TFLAGS  = -c -M -mt -S -y -I\turbo\c\include


#
#   Linker Definitions
#


LINK    = \turbo\c\tlink
LFLAGS  =


#
#   List Of Required Libraries
#


LIBS    = \turbo\c\lib\cs.lib


#
#   List Of Required Include Files
#
#   DOS_DD.H    DOS Device Driver Command Include File


INCS    = dos_dd.h


#
#   List Of Required Object Files
#
#   M1.OBJ      TURBO C Version Assembler Header For TINY Model
#   M2.OBJ      Modified C Assembler For DOS_DATA.C
#   M3.OBJ      Modified C Assembler For DOS_ENV.C
#   M4.OBJ      Modified C Assembler For DOS_DRVR.C
#   M5.OBJ      Modified C Assembler For DOS_END.C


OBJS    = m1.obj  m2.obj  m3.obj  m4.obj  m5.obj


#
#   Perform DOS Device Driver Linkage
#


shadow.sys: $(OBJS) $(INCS)
            $(LINK) $(LFLAGS) m1+m2+m3+m4+m5,         \
```

```
                              shadow.exe,,$(LIBS);
            erase  m3.*
            exe2bin  shadow.exe  shadow.sys

#
#     Perform DOS_HDR Assembly
#

m1.obj:     dos_hdr.asm
            copy  dos_hdr.asm  m1.asm
            $(ASM) $(AFLAGS)  m1.asm;

#
#     Perform DOS_DATA Compilation
#

m2.obj:     $(INCS)  dos_data.c
            $(TURBO) $(TFLAGS)  dos_data.c
            arrange  dos.arr  dos_data.asm  m2.asm
            erase  dos_data.asm
            $(ASM) $(AFLAGS)  m2.asm;

#
#     Perform DOS_ENV Compilation
#

m3.obj:     $(INCS)  dos_env.c
            $(TURBO) $(TFLAGS)  dos_env.c
            arrange  dos.arr  dos_env.asm  m3.asm
            erase  dos_env.asm
            $(ASM) $(AFLAGS)  m3.asm;

#
#     Perform DOS_DRVR Compilation
#

m4.obj:     $(INCS)  dos_drvr.c
            $(TURBO) $(TFLAGS)  dos_drvr.c
            arrange  dos.arr  dos_drvr.asm  m4.asm
            erase  dos_drvr.asm
            $(ASM) $(AFLAGS)  m4.asm;
```

```
#
#   Perform DOS_END Compilation
#

m5.obj:       $(INCS)  dos_end.c
              $(TURBO) $(TFLAGS) dos_end.c
              arrange  dos.arr  dos_end.asm  m5.asm
              erase  dos_end.asm
              $(ASM) $(AFLAGS)  m5.asm;
```

Here is the source listing for `dos_data.c`.

```c
/* - - - - - - - - - - - - - - - - - - - - - - - - - - - - - - - -*/
/*                                                                 */
/*  PROGRAM :       D O S    D e v i c e    D r i v e r            */
/*                                                                 */
/*  REMARKS :       This file contains the set of command         */
/*          routines specified by the DOS Technical Reference      */
/*          Manual.                                                 */
/*                                                                 */
/*          The following include file is required to             */
/*          compile this file :                                    */
/*          DOS_DD.H                                               */
/*                                                                 */
/* - - - - - - - - - - - - - - - - - - - - - - - - - - - - - - - -*/

#include    "dos_dd.h"                  /* DOS  Command Structures */

extern      void    far Strategy ();    /* Strategy Routine        */
extern      void    far Interrupt ();   /* Interrupt Routine       */

/* - - - - - - - - - - - - - - - - - - - - - - - - - - - - - - - -*/
/*                                                                 */
/*       Allocate And Initialize DOS Device Header                 */
/*                                                                 */
/* - - - - - - - - - - - - - - - - - - - - - - - - - - - - - - - -*/

/* DOS  Device  Header                                             */
struct  DEVICE_HEADER_struct  dos_header =
{
    (struct DEVICE_HEADER_struct far *) 0xFFFFFFFFL,
    0x2000,                             /* Non-IBM Format          */
    (unsigned int) Strategy,            /* Strategy Function       */
    (unsigned int) Interrupt,           /* Interrupt Function      */
    {                                   /* Unit/Name Field         */
        0x01,                           /* Initial Number Of Units */
        0x00,                           /* Zero Remaining Entries  */
        0x00,                           /* Zero Remaining Entries  */
        0x00,                           /* Zero Remaining Entries  */
        0x00,                           /* Zero Remaining Entries  */
        0x00,                           /* Zero Remaining Entries  */
        0x00,                           /* Zero Remaining Entries  */
```

```
        0x00                            /* Zero Remaining Entries    */
    }
};



/* - - - - - - - - - - - - - - - - - - - - - - - - - - - - - - - -*/
/*                                                                  */
/*       DOS  Device Driver Global Data Region                     */
/*                                                                  */
/* - - - - - - - - - - - - - - - - - - - - - - - - - - - - - - - -*/

struct  BPB_struct  bpb =
{
    0
};

struct  BPB_struct  *bpb_ary [DEVICES] = { 0 };

unsigned int         rc;          /* Function Return Code        */
unsigned int         driver;      /* Global Driver Variable      */
unsigned int         SS_reg;      /* SS Register Variable        */
unsigned int         SP_reg;      /* SP Register Variable        */
unsigned int         ES_reg;      /* ES Register Variable        */
unsigned int         AX_reg;      /* AX Register Variable        */
unsigned int         BX_reg;      /* BX Register Variable        */
unsigned int         CX_reg;      /* CX Register Variable        */
unsigned int         DX_reg;      /* DX Register Variable        */
unsigned int         DS_reg;      /* DS Register Variable        */
unsigned int         SI_reg;      /* SI Register Variable        */

/* Local Device Driver Stack                                      */
unsigned int         local_stk [STK_SIZE];

struct REQ_struct  far *r_ptr;  /* DOS Request Packet Pointer   */
```

```
/* - - - - - - - - - - - - - - - - - - - - - - - - - - - - - - -*/
/*                                                               */
/*        SHADOW variables                                       */
/*                                                               */
/* - - - - - - - - - - - - - - - - - - - - - - - - - - - - - - -*/

void                        (far *v_call) (void);
struct REQ_struct           tmp_req = { 0 };
struct DEVICE_HEADER_struct far *ddh_ptr = { 0 };

unsigned char   com_str [ ]   = "COM1    ";
unsigned char   found_msg [ ] = "\r\nDDH Found\r\n"
                                "Driver Installed\r\n\r\n$";
unsigned char   error_msg [ ] = "\r\nDDH Not Found\r\n"
                                "Driver Not Installed\r\n\r\n$";
```

Here is the source listing for `dos_env.c`.

```
/* - - - - - - - - - - - - - - - - - - - - - - - - - - - - - - - - -*/
/*                                                                   */
/*   PROGRAM :       D O S    D e v i c e    D r i v e r             */
/*                                                                   */
/*   REMARKS :       This file contains the set of command          */
/*           routines specified by the DOS Technical Reference       */
/*           Manual.                                                 */
/*                                                                   */
/*           The following include file is required to              */
/*           compile this file :                                     */
/*           DOS_DD.H                                                */
/*                                                                   */
/* - - - - - - - - - - - - - - - - - - - - - - - - - - - - - - - - -*/

#include    <dos.h>
#include    "dos_dd.h"

/* - - - - - - - - - - - - - - - - - - - - - - - - - - - - - - - - -*/
/*                                                                   */
/*      DOS   Device Driver Routine Declarations                     */
/*                                                                   */
/* - - - - - - - - - - - - - - - - - - - - - - - - - - - - - - - - -*/

extern  unsigned Init_cmd ();        /* INIT Command                 */
extern  unsigned Output_cmd ();      /* OUTPUT Command Function      */
extern  unsigned Unknown_cmd ();     /* UNKNOWN Command Default      */
```

```
/* - - - - - - - - - - - - - - - - - - - - - - - - - - - - - -*/
/*                                                             */
/*      DOS  Device Driver Global Data Region                  */
/*                                                             */
/* - - - - - - - - - - - - - - - - - - - - - - - - - - - - - -*/

extern  unsigned rc;              /* Function Return Code    */
extern  unsigned driver;          /* Global Driver Variable  */
extern  unsigned SS_reg;          /* SS Register Variable    */
extern  unsigned SP_reg;          /* SP Register Variable    */
extern  unsigned ES_reg;          /* ES Register Variable    */
extern  unsigned AX_reg;          /* AX Register Variable    */
extern  unsigned BX_reg;          /* BX Register Variable    */
extern  unsigned CX_reg;          /* CX Register Variable    */
extern  unsigned DX_reg;          /* DX Register Variable    */
extern  unsigned DS_reg;          /* DS Register Variable    */
extern  unsigned SI_reg;          /* SI Register Variable    */

/* Local Device Driver Stack                                 */
extern unsigned local_stk [STK_SIZE];

/* DOS Request Packet Pointer                                */
extern  struct REQ_struct far *r_ptr;
```

```
unsigned (*dos_cmd [DOS_CMDS]) (struct REQ_struct far *r_ptr) =
{
    Init_cmd,                       /* INIT Command              */
    Unknown_cmd,                    /* MEDIA_CHECK Command       */
    Unknown_cmd,                    /* BUILD_BPB Command         */
    Unknown_cmd,                    /* IOCTL Input Command       */
    Unknown_cmd,                    /* INPUT Command             */
    Unknown_cmd,                    /* INPUT No Wait Command     */
    Unknown_cmd,                    /* INPUT Status Command      */
    Unknown_cmd,                    /* INPUT Flush Command       */
    Output_cmd,                     /* OUTPUT Command            */
    Output_cmd,                     /* OUTPUT Verify Command     */
    Unknown_cmd,                    /* OUTPUT Status Command     */
    Unknown_cmd,                    /* OUTPUT Flush Command      */
    Unknown_cmd,                    /* IOCTL Output Command      */
    Unknown_cmd,                    /* DEVICE Open Command       */
    Unknown_cmd,                    /* DEVICE Close Command      */
    Unknown_cmd,                    /* REMOVABLE Media Commmand  */
    Unknown_cmd,                    /* UNKNOWN Command Default   */
    Unknown_cmd,                    /* UNKNOWN Command Default   */
    Unknown_cmd,                    /* UNKNOWN Command Default   */
    Unknown_cmd,                    /* GENERIC IOCTL Command     */
    Unknown_cmd,                    /* UNKNOWN Command Default   */
    Unknown_cmd,                    /* UNKNOWN Command Default   */
    Unknown_cmd,                    /* UNKNOWN Command Default   */
    Unknown_cmd,                    /* GET Logical Device Map    */
    Unknown_cmd                     /* SET Logical Device Map    */
};
```

```
/* - - - - - - - - - - - - - - - - - - - - - - - - - - - - - - -*/
/*                                                               */
/*  FUNCTION:   D O S _ S e t u p                                */
/*                                                               */
/*  REMARKS :   DOS_Setup establishes a C environment prior to   */
/*          allowing the actual device driver routines to        */
/*          execute.                                             */
/*                                                               */
/*  INPUTS  :                                                     */
/*          which   0 : Strategy Entry; 1 : Interrupt Entry      */
/*          ES_tmp  Pointer To Request Packet                    */
/*          DS_tmp  Original DS Register Value                   */
/*          AX_tmp  Original AX Register Value                   */
/*                                                               */
/*  OUTPUTS :   Status  Must Be Set In The Request Packet         */
/*                                                               */
/*  NOTES   :   Register manipulations require this routine to    */
/*          be compiled with the TURBO C Compiler.              */
/*                                                               */
/* - - - - - - - - - - - - - - - - - - - - - - - - - - - - - - -*/

void DOS_Setup (unsigned int which,
                unsigned int ES_tmp,
                unsigned int DS_tmp,
                unsigned int AX_tmp)
{
    _AX = _CS;                      /* Obtain Code Segment     */
    _DS = _AX;                      /* Setup Data Segment      */

    BX_reg = _BX;                   /* Save BX Register        */
    CX_reg = _CX;                   /* Save CX Register        */
    DX_reg = _DX;                   /* Save DX Register        */

    AX_reg = AX_tmp;                /* Save AX Register        */
    ES_reg = ES_tmp;                /* Save Request Pointer    */

    driver = which;                 /* Move Value From Stack   */

    SS_reg = _SS;                   /* Save Stack Segment      */
    SP_reg = _SP;                   /* Save Stack Pointer      */

    disable ();                     /* Disable Interrupts      */
```

```
    _AX = _DS;                      /* Obtain Data Segment      */
    _SS = _AX;                      /* Setup New Stack          */
                                    /* Set Stack Ptr Value      */
    _SP = (unsigned int) &local_stk [STK_SIZE];
    enable ();                      /* Enable Interrupts        */

    if (driver)
    {                               /* Interrupt Entry Point    */
        rc = 0x0000;                /* Clear Return Code        */
                                    /* DOS Request Packet Ptr   */
        r_ptr = MK_FP (ES_reg, BX_reg);
        if (r_ptr->command >= DOS_CMDS)
        {
            rc = ERROR_BIT | UNKNOWN_CMD;
        }
        else
        {
            rc |= (*dos_cmd [r_ptr->command]) (r_ptr);
        }
                                    /* Set Driver Complete Bit  */
        r_ptr->status = rc | DONE_BIT;
    }
    else
    {                               /* Strategy Entry Point     */
        /* Don't Save ES:BX Because It's Passed To Interrupt!! */
    }

    disable ();                     /* Disable Interrupts       */
    _SS = SS_reg;                   /* Restore Entry Stack      */
    _SP = SP_reg;                   /* Restore Entry Stack Ptr  */
    enable ();                      /* Enable Interrupts        */

    _DX = DX_reg;                   /* Restore DX Register      */
    _CX = CX_reg;                   /* Restore CX Register      */
    _BX = BX_reg;                   /* Restore BX Register      */
    _AX = AX_reg;                   /* Restore AX Register      */

    _ES = ES_tmp;                   /* Restore ES Register      */
    _DS = DS_tmp;                   /* Restore DS Register      */
}
```

```
/* - - - - - - - - - - - - - - - - - - - - - - - - - - - - - - -*/
/*                                                               */
/*  FUNCTION:     S t r a t e g y                                */
/*                                                               */
/*  REMARKS :    Strategy is the routine that is called by the   */
/*               Operating System when this device is requested to */
/*               perform some activity (typically READs and WRITEs). */
/*                                                               */
/*  INPUTS  :    ES:BX    Pointer To Request Packet              */
/*                                                               */
/*  NOTES   :    Register manipulations require this routine to  */
/*               be compiled with the TURBO C Compiler.          */
/*                                                               */
/* - - - - - - - - - - - - - - - - - - - - - - - - - - - - - - -*/

void far Strategy (void)
{

#ifdef   DEBUG
    geninterrupt (0x03);
#endif

    DOS_Setup (0x00, _ES, _DS, _AX);
}
```

```
/* - - - - - - - - - - - - - - - - - - - - - - - - - - - - - - - -*/
/*                                                                 */
/*  FUNCTION:    I n t e r r u p t                                 */
/*                                                                 */
/*  REMARKS :    Interrupt is the routine that is called by the    */
/*               Operating System immediately after the Strategy   */
/*               routine has been called.  Interrupt is responsible*/
/*               for performing the work required to accomplish the*/
/*               requested operation.                              */
/*                                                                 */
/*  INPUTS   :   ES:BX   Pointer To Request Packet                 */
/*                                                                 */
/*  OUTPUTS  :   Status  Must Be Set In The Request Packet         */
/*               RETF    Must Be Used To Return From Interrupt      */
/*                                                                 */
/*  NOTES    :   Register manipulations require this routine to     */
/*               be compiled with the TURBO C Compiler.            */
/*                                                                 */
/* - - - - - - - - - - - - - - - - - - - - - - - - - - - - - - - -*/

void far Interrupt (void)
{

#ifdef   DEBUG
    geninterrupt (0x03);
#endif

    DOS_Setup (0x01, _ES, _DS, _AX);
}
```

Here is the source listing for `dos_drvr.c`.

```
/* - - - - - - - - - - - - - - - - - - - - - - - - - - - - - - - -*/
/*                                                                 */
/*  PROGRAM :      D O S   D e v i c e   D r i v e r              */
/*                                                                 */
/*  REMARKS :      This file contains the set of command          */
/*          routines specified by the DOS Technical Reference     */
/*          Manual.                                                */
/*                                                                 */
/*             The following include file is required to          */
/*          compile this file :                                   */
/*          DOS_DD.H                                               */
/*                                                                 */
/* - - - - - - - - - - - - - - - - - - - - - - - - - - - - - - - -*/


/* - - - - - - - - - - - - - - - - - - - - - - - - - - - - - - - -*/
/*                                                                 */
/*      DOS  Device Driver Required Includes / Constants           */
/*                                                                 */
/* - - - - - - - - - - - - - - - - - - - - - - - - - - - - - - - -*/

#include    "dos_dd.h"           /* DOS  Command Structures    */
#include    <dos.h>              /* DOS Specific Definitions   */
#include    <string.h>           /* C String Library Prototypes */

extern  void    End_code (void);
extern  struct  BPB_struct  bpb;
extern  struct  BPB_struct  *bpb_ary [DEVICES];
```

```
#define END_OF_CHAIN      0xFFFF  /* End Of D.D.H. List           */
#define TRUE              1       /* Value Of Logical TRUE        */
#define FALSE             0       /* Value Of Logical FALSE       */
#define DRIVE_A           0       /* Unit Value For Drive A:      */
#define DRIVE_B           1       /* Unit Value For Drive B:      */

extern  void                              (far *v_call) (void);
extern  unsigned char                     com_str [];
extern  unsigned char                     found_msg [];
extern  unsigned char                     error_msg [];
extern  struct REQ_struct                 tmp_req;
extern  struct DEVICE_HEADER_struct far   *ddh_ptr;

/* - - - - - - - - - - - - - - - - - - - - - - - - - - - - - - -*/
/*                                                               */
/*      DOS Internal Variables Block Structure                   */
/*                                                               */
/* - - - - - - - - - - - - - - - - - - - - - - - - - - - - - - -*/

struct  DOS_struct
{
    unsigned char                 reserved [34];
    struct  DEVICE_HEADER_struct  far *ddh_ptr;
};
```

```
/* - - - - - - - - - - - - - - - - - - - - - - - - - - - - - - - -*/
/*                                                                  */
/*  FUNCTION:    U n k n o w n _ c m d                              */
/*                                                                  */
/*  REMARKS :                                                       */
/*                                                                  */
/*  INPUTS  :    r_ptr    Pointer To Request Packet                 */
/*                                                                  */
/*  OUTPUTS :    Status   Returned In Function Return Value         */
/*                                                                  */
/* - - - - - - - - - - - - - - - - - - - - - - - - - - - - - - - -*/

unsigned int Unknown_cmd (struct REQ_struct far *r_ptr)
{
    v_call = MK_FP (FP_SEG (ddh_ptr), ddh_ptr->dev_strat);
    _ES = FP_SEG (r_ptr);
    _BX = FP_OFF (r_ptr);
    v_call ();

    v_call = MK_FP (FP_SEG (ddh_ptr), ddh_ptr->dev_int);
    _ES = FP_SEG (r_ptr);
    _BX = FP_OFF (r_ptr);
    v_call ();
}
```

```
/* - - - - - - - - - - - - - - - - - - - - - - - - - - - - - - -*/
/*                                                                */
/*  FUNCTION:    O u t p u t _ c m d                              */
/*                                                                */
/*  REMARKS :    Output_cmd performs a shadow or duplex write to */
/*               drives A: and B:.  This command is used to process */
/*               both the OUTPUT command as well as the           */
/*               OUTPUT_VERIFY command.                           */
/*                                                                */
/*  INPUTS  :    r_ptr    Pointer To Request Packet               */
/*                                                                */
/*  OUTPUTS :    Status   Returned In Function Return Value       */
/*                                                                */
/* - - - - - - - - - - - - - - - - - - - - - - - - - - - - - - -*/

unsigned int Output_cmd (struct REQ_struct far *r_ptr)
{
    unsigned char   unit;

    unit = r_ptr->unit;
    r_ptr->unit = DRIVE_A;
    r_ptr->status = OP_COMPLETE;

    Unknown_cmd (r_ptr);            /* Initial Write To A Drive*/

    if (!(r_ptr->status & ERROR_BIT))
    {
        r_ptr->unit = DRIVE_B;
        r_ptr->status = OP_COMPLETE;

        Unknown_cmd (r_ptr);        /* Shadow Write To B Drive */
    }

    r_ptr->unit = unit;
}
```

```
/* - - - - - - - - - - - - - - - - - - - - - - - - - - - - - - -*/
/*                                                               */
/*  FUNCTION:    I n i t _ c m d                                 */
/*                                                               */
/*  REMARKS :                                                    */
/*                                                               */
/*  INPUTS  :    r_ptr    Pointer To Request Packet              */
/*                                                               */
/*  OUTPUTS :    Status  Returned In Function Return Value       */
/*                                                               */
/* - - - - - - - - - - - - - - - - - - - - - - - - - - - - - - -*/

unsigned int Init_cmd (struct REQ_struct far *r_ptr)
{
    unsigned char                i;
    unsigned char                found;
    unsigned char                far *s_ptr;
    unsigned char                far *t_ptr;
    unsigned int                 es_reg;
    unsigned int                 bx_reg;
    unsigned int                 com_seg;
    struct DOS_struct        far *dos_ptr;
    struct DEVICE_HEADER_struct far *v_ptr;
    struct DEVICE_HEADER_struct far *com_ptr;

    _AX = 0x5200;
    geninterrupt (0x21);
    bx_reg = _BX;
    es_reg = _ES;

    dos_ptr = MK_FP (es_reg, bx_reg);
    v_ptr = (struct DEVICE_HEADER_struct far *) &dos_ptr->ddh_ptr;
    com_ptr = v_ptr;
```

```
for (found = FALSE;
     ((!found) && (FP_OFF (com_ptr) != END_OF_CHAIN));
     com_ptr = com_ptr->next_hdr)
{
    for (s_ptr = com_ptr->name_unit, t_ptr = com_str;
         ((*t_ptr) && (*s_ptr == *t_ptr));
         s_ptr++, t_ptr++);

    if (!(*t_ptr))
    {
        found = TRUE;
        com_seg = FP_SEG (com_ptr);
    }
}


for (found = FALSE;
     ((!found) && (FP_OFF (v_ptr) != END_OF_CHAIN));
     v_ptr = v_ptr->next_hdr)
{
    if (((!(v_ptr->attribute & CHAR_DD)) &&
        (FP_SEG (v_ptr) == com_seg))
    {
        found = TRUE;
        ddh_ptr = v_ptr;
    }
}
```

```
if (found)
{                                    /*  Send Command On To VDISK  */
                                     /*  Original Device Driver    */

    bpb_ary [0] = (unsigned int) &bpb;
    r_ptr->req_type.init_req.num_of_units = 1;
    r_ptr->req_type.init_req.end_ptr =
            MK_FP (_CS, (unsigned int) End_code);
    r_ptr->req_type.init_req.BPB_ptr =
            MK_FP (_CS, (unsigned int) bpb_ary);

    _DX = (unsigned int) found_msg;
    _AH = 9;
    geninterrupt (0x21);
}
else
{                                    /*  DDH  Not  Found          */
                                     /*  Do Not Install Driver    */

    _DX = (unsigned int) error_msg;
    _AH = 9;
    geninterrupt (0x21);

    r_ptr->req_type.init_req.num_of_units = 0;
    r_ptr->req_type.init_req.BPB_ptr = MK_FP (0, 0);
    r_ptr->req_type.init_req.end_ptr = MK_FP (_CS, 0);
}
return (OP_COMPLETE);
}
```

Appendix L

WORM BIOS

This is a summary of the WORM BIOS. The values for AH (in parentheses) are in hexadecimal. All other values are in decimal. You can access the WORM BIOS with a far call to 0x04B0.

Consult your *IBM 3363 Optical Disk Drive* hardware technical reference manual for details.

Input Registers	Output Registers	Description
AH		selective drive reset (20)
DL		drive address 0 – 7
	AH	status returned
	AL	adapter status
AH		read sense (21)
DL		drive address 0 – 7
	AH	status returned
	AL	adapter status
AH		read attribute data (22)
DL		drive address 0 – 7
	AH	status returned
	AL	adapter status
AH		read verify normal ECC correction (23)
DL		drive address 0 – 7
DH		sector address 0 – 22
CX		track address 0 – 17099
AL		block count 1 – 128
	AH	status returned
	AL	adapter status

Input Registers	Output Registers	Description
AH		sector recovery (24) - 1 sector
AL		block count - must be set to 1
AH		sector recovery (25) - 2 sectors
AL		block count - must be set to 1
AH		no retry (26)
AL		maximum block count is 128
AH		no retry with sector recovery (27)
AL		block count - must be set to 1
AH		no retry with sector recovery (28)
AL		block count - must be set to 1
AH		read normal (29)
DL		drive address 0 – 7
DH		sector address 0 – 22
CX		track address 0 – 17099
AL		block count 1 – 128
ES		segment for read/write area
BX		offset for read/write area
	AH	status returned
	AL	adapter status
AH		sector recovery (2A) - 1 sector
AL		block count - must be set to 1
AH		sector recovery (2B) - 2 sectors
AL		block count - must be set to 1
AH		no ECC correction (2C)
AL		maximum block count is 128
AH		no ECC correction with sector recovery (2D)
AL		block count - must be set to 1
AH		no ECC correction with sector recovery (2E)
AL		block count - must be set to 1
AH		no retry (2F)
AL		maximum block count is 128
AH		no retry with sector recovery (30)
AL		block count - must be set to 1
AH		no retry with sector recovery (31)
AL		block count - must be set to 1

Input Registers	Output Registers	Description
AH		write normal (32)
DL		drive address 0 – 7
DH		sector address 0 – 22
CX		track address 0 – 17099
AL		block count 1 – 128
ES		segment for read/write area
BX		offset for read/write area
	AH	status returned
	AL	adapter status
AH		seek normal (33)
DL		drive address 0 – 7
CX		track address 0 – 17099
	AH	status returned
	AL	adapter status
AH		test seek (34)
AH		run diagnostic command (35)
DL		drive address 0 – 7
	AH	status returned
	AL	adapter status
AH		read suppress normal (36)
DL		drive address 0 – 7
DH		sector address 0 – 22
CX		track address 0 – 17099
AL		block count 1 – 128
ES		segment for read/write area
BX		offset for read/write area
	AH	status returned
	AL	adapter status
AH		sector recovery (37) - 1 sector
AL		block count - must be set to 1
AH		sector recovery (38) - 2 sectors
AL		block count - must be set to 1
AH		normal demark command (39)
DL		drive address 0 – 7
DH		sector address 0 – 22
CX		track address 0 – 17099
AL		block count 1 – 128
	AH	status returned
	AL	adapter status

Input Registers	Output Registers	Description
AH		demark recovery (3A)
AL		maximum block count is 128
AH		sector recovery (3B) - 1 sector
AL		block count - must be set to 1
AH		sector recovery (3D) - 2 sectors
AL		block count - must be set to 1
AH		demark recovery with sector recovery (3E)
AL		block count - must be set to 1
AH		read track address (3F)
DL		drive address 0 – 7
	AH	status returned
	AL	adapter status
	CX	track address
AH		adapter reset (40)
DL		drive address 0 – 7
AH		read adapter status (41)
DL		drive address 0 – 7
	AH	status returned
	AL	adapter status
AH		read scan (42)
DL		drive address 0 – 7
DH		sector address 0 – 22
CX		track address 0 – 17099
AL		block count 1 – 128
	AH	status returned
	AL	adapter status
AH		sector recovery (43) - 1 sector
AL		block count - must be set to 1
AH		sector recovery (44) - 2 sectors
AL		block count - must be set to 1

Appendix M

WORM Files

We discussed the WORM device driver in Chapter 13 where we have shown parts of the files. Now we present the complete versions for **worm** (the makefile for the device driver); **dos_data.c** (page 349); **dos_env.c** (page 352); **dos_drvr.c** (page 359); and **worm.h**, a new include file (page 376). The remaining files we use in the **worm** makefile have not changed — they remain as they appear in Chapter 4 and Appendix F.

Here is the source listing for the **worm** makefile.

```
#
#   Makefile For DOS Device Driver Template Written In C
#


#
#   Assembler Definitions
#

ASM     = \turbo\asm\tasm
AFLAGS  =


#
#   TURBO C Compiler Definitions
#
#   -c      Do Not Perform Link Step
#   -M      Produce Link/Load Map
#   -mt     Produce TINY Model Output
#   -S      Produce Assembler Module
#   -y      Produce Line Number Information
```

```
#    -Idir    Place To Search For Include Files

TURBO   = \turbo\c\tcc
TFLAGS  = -c -M -mt -S -y -I\turbo\c\include


#
#   Linker Definitions
#

LINK    = \turbo\c\tlink
LFLAGS  =


#
#   List Of Required Libraries
#

LIBS    = \turbo\c\lib\cs.lib


#
#   List Of Required Include Files
#
#   DOS_DD.H    DOS Device Driver Command Include File
#   WORM.H      DOS WORM Device Driver Include File

INCS    = dos_dd.h  worm.h


#
#   List Of Required Object Files
#
#   M1.OBJ      TURBO C Version Assembler Header For TINY Model
#   M2.OBJ      Modified C Assembler For DOS_DATA.C
#   M3.OBJ      Modified C Assembler For DOS_ENV.C
#   M4.OBJ      Modified C Assembler For DOS_DRVR.C
#   M5.OBJ      Modified C Assembler For DOS_END.C

OBJS    = m1.obj  m2.obj  m3.obj  m4.obj  m5.obj


#
#   Perform DOS Device Driver Linkage
#

worm.sys:    $(OBJS) $(INCS)
```

```
            $(LINK) $(LFLAGS) m1+m2+m3+m4+m5,worm.exe,,$(LIBS);
            erase  m3.*
            exe2bin  worm.exe  worm.sys

#
#    Perform DOS_HDR Assembly
#

m1.obj:     dos_hdr.asm
            copy  dos_hdr.asm  m1.asm
            $(ASM) $(AFLAGS)  m1.asm;

#
#    Perform DOS_DATA Compilation
#

m2.obj:     $(INCS)  dos_data.c
            $(TURBO) $(TFLAGS) dos_data.c
            arrange  dos.arr  dos_data.asm  m2.asm
            erase  dos_data.asm
            $(ASM) $(AFLAGS)  m2.asm;

#
#    Perform DOS_ENV Compilation
#

m3.obj:     $(INCS)  dos_env.c
            $(TURBO) $(TFLAGS)  dos_env.c
            arrange  dos.arr  dos_env.asm  m3.asm
            erase  dos_env.asm
            $(ASM) $(AFLAGS)  m3.asm;

#
#    Perform DOS_DRVR Compilation
#

m4.obj:     $(INCS)  dos_drvr.c
            $(TURBO) $(TFLAGS) dos_drvr.c
            arrange  dos.arr  dos_drvr.asm  m4.asm
            erase  dos_drvr.asm
            $(ASM) $(AFLAGS)  m4.asm;
```

```
#
#    Perform DOS_END Compilation
#

m5.obj:        $(INCS)  dos_end.c
               $(TURBO) $(TFLAGS) dos_end.c
               arrange  dos.arr  dos_end.asm  m5.asm
               erase  dos_end.asm
               $(ASM) $(AFLAGS)  m5.asm;
```

Here is the source listing for `dos_data.c`.

```
/* - - - - - - - - - - - - - - - - - - - - - - - - - - - - - -*/
/*                                                             */
/*  PROGRAM :       D O S    D e v i c e    D r i v e r        */
/*                                                             */
/*  REMARKS :      This file contains the set of command       */
/*          routines specified by the DOS Technical Reference  */
/*          Manual.                                            */
/*                                                             */
/*          The following include files are required to        */
/*          compile this file :                                */
/*          DOS_DD.H                                           */
/*          WORM.H                                             */
/*                                                             */
/* - - - - - - - - - - - - - - - - - - - - - - - - - - - - - -*/

#include    "dos_dd.h"              /* DOS  Command Structures */
#include    "worm.h"               /* WORM Header File        */

extern      void    far Strategy ();   /* Strategy Routine     */
extern      void    far Interrupt ();  /* Interrupt Routine    */
```

```
/* - - - - - - - - - - - - - - - - - - - - - - - - - - - - - - - -*/
/*                                                                 */
/*      Allocate And Initialize DOS Device Header                  */
/*                                                                 */
/* - - - - - - - - - - - - - - - - - - - - - - - - - - - - - - - -*/

/* DOS  Device  Header                                             */
struct  DEVICE_HEADER_struct  dos_header =
{
    (struct DEVICE_HEADER_struct far *) 0xFFFFFFFFL,
    0x2000,                         /* Non-IBM Format            */
    (unsigned int) Strategy,        /* Strategy Function         */
    (unsigned int) Interrupt,       /* Interrupt Function        */
    {                               /* Unit/Name Field           */
        0x01,                       /* Initial Number Of Units   */
        0x00,                       /* Zero Remaining Entries    */
        0x00,                       /* Zero Remaining Entries    */
        0x00,                       /* Zero Remaining Entries    */
        0x00,                       /* Zero Remaining Entries    */
        0x00,                       /* Zero Remaining Entries    */
        0x00,                       /* Zero Remaining Entries    */
        0x00                        /* Zero Remaining Entries    */
    }
};


/* - - - - - - - - - - - - - - - - - - - - - - - - - - - - - - - -*/
/*                                                                 */
/*      DOS  Device Driver Global Data Region                      */
/*                                                                 */
/* - - - - - - - - - - - - - - - - - - - - - - - - - - - - - - - -*/

struct  BPB_struct  bpb =
{
    0x200,                          /* Bytes Per Sector          */
    0x01,                           /* Sectors Per Allocation Unit */
    0x01,                           /* Reserved Sectors          */
    0x01,                           /* Number Of FATS            */
    0x0100,                         /* Number Of Root Dir Entries */
    0xF000,                         /* Number Of Sectors         */
    0xF0,                           /* Media Descriptor          */
    0x0100,                         /* Number Of Sectors Per FAT */
    1,                              /* Number Of Sectors Per Track */
```

```
        1,                      /* Number Of Heads          */
        1L,                     /* Number Of Hidden Sectors */
        0L                      /* 32-Bit Number of Sectors */
};


struct  BPB_struct  *bpb_ary [DEVICES] = { 0 };

unsigned int        rc;         /* Function Return Code     */
unsigned int        driver;     /* Global Driver Variable   */
unsigned int        SS_reg;     /* SS Register Variable     */
unsigned int        SP_reg;     /* SP Register Variable     */
unsigned int        ES_reg;     /* ES Register Variable     */
unsigned int        AX_reg;     /* AX Register Variable     */
unsigned int        BX_reg;     /* BX Register Variable     */
unsigned int        CX_reg;     /* CX Register Variable     */
unsigned int        DX_reg;     /* DX Register Variable     */
unsigned int        DS_reg;     /* DS Register Variable     */
unsigned int        SI_reg;     /* SI Register Variable     */

/* Local Device Driver Stack                                */
unsigned int        local_stk [STK_SIZE];

struct REQ_struct  far *r_ptr;  /* DOS Request Packet Pointer */

unsigned char       reg_ah;     /* AH Register - Command      */
unsigned char       reg_al;     /* AL Register - Block Count  */
unsigned char       reg_dh;     /* DH Register - Sector Number */
unsigned char       reg_dl;     /* DL Register - Drive Number */

unsigned int        reg_cx;     /* CX Register - Track Number  */
unsigned int        reg_es;     /* ES Register - Buffer Segment */
unsigned int        reg_bx;     /* BX Register - Buffer Offset */

unsigned char       mag_buf [512];    /* Temp. Sector Buffer  */
struct  INFO_struct disk_info = { 0 };  /* Disk Information    */
```

Here is the source listing for **dos_env.c**.

```
/* - - - - - - - - - - - - - - - - - - - - - - - - - - - - - - -*/
/*                                                               */
/*   PROGRAM :       D O S   D e v i c e   D r i v e r           */
/*                                                               */
/*   REMARKS :        This file contains the set of command      */
/*          routines specified by the DOS Technical Reference    */
/*          Manual.                                              */
/*                                                               */
/*            The following include file is required to          */
/*          compile this file :                                  */
/*          DOS_DD.H                                             */
/*                                                               */
/* - - - - - - - - - - - - - - - - - - - - - - - - - - - - - - -*/


#include    <dos.h>
#include    "dos_dd.h"


/* - - - - - - - - - - - - - - - - - - - - - - - - - - - - - - -*/
/*                                                               */
/*      DOS   Device Driver Routine Declarations                 */
/*                                                               */
/* - - - - - - - - - - - - - - - - - - - - - - - - - - - - - - -*/


extern   unsigned Init_cmd ();            /* INIT Command          */
extern   unsigned Media_check_cmd ();     /* MEDIA_CHECK Command   */
extern   unsigned Build_bpb_cmd ();       /* BUILD_BPB Command     */
extern   unsigned Input_cmd ();           /* INPUT Command         */
extern   unsigned Output_cmd ();          /* OUTPUT Command        */
extern   unsigned Unknown_cmd ();         /* UNKNOWN Command Default */
```

```
/* - - - - - - - - - - - - - - - - - - - - - - - - - - - - - -*/
/*                                                             */
/*       DOS   Device Driver Global Data Region                */
/*                                                             */
/* - - - - - - - - - - - - - - - - - - - - - - - - - - - - - -*/

extern   unsigned rc;               /* Function Return Code    */
extern   unsigned driver;           /* Global Driver Variable  */
extern   unsigned SS_reg;           /* SS Register Variable    */
extern   unsigned SP_reg;           /* SP Register Variable    */
extern   unsigned ES_reg;           /* ES Register Variable    */
extern   unsigned AX_reg;           /* AX Register Variable    */
extern   unsigned BX_reg;           /* BX Register Variable    */
extern   unsigned CX_reg;           /* CX Register Variable    */
extern   unsigned DX_reg;           /* DX Register Variable    */
extern   unsigned DS_reg;           /* DS Register Variable    */
extern   unsigned SI_reg;           /* SI Register Variable    */

/* Local Device Driver Stack                                   */
extern unsigned local_stk [STK_SIZE];

/* DOS Request Packet Pointer                                  */
extern   struct REQ_struct far *r_ptr;
```

```
unsigned (*dos_cmd [DOS_CMDS]) (struct REQ_struct far *r_ptr) =
{
    Init_cmd,                       /* INIT Command            */
    Media_check_cmd,                /* MEDIA_CHECK Command     */
    Build_bpb_cmd,                  /* BUILD_BPB Command       */
    Unknown_cmd,                    /* IOCTL Input Command     */
    Input_cmd,                      /* INPUT Command           */
    Unknown_cmd,                    /* INPUT No Wait Command   */
    Unknown_cmd,                    /* INPUT Status Command    */
    Unknown_cmd,                    /* INPUT Flush Command     */
    Output_cmd,                     /* OUTPUT Command          */
    Output_cmd,                     /* OUTPUT Verify Command   */
    Unknown_cmd,                    /* OUTPUT Status Command   */
    Unknown_cmd,                    /* OUTPUT Flush Command    */
    Unknown_cmd,                    /* IOCTL Output Command    */
    Unknown_cmd,                    /* DEVICE Open Command     */
    Unknown_cmd,                    /* DEVICE Close Command    */
    Unknown_cmd,                    /* REMOVABLE Media Command */
    Unknown_cmd,                    /* UNKNOWN Command Default */
    Unknown_cmd,                    /* UNKNOWN Command Default */
    Unknown_cmd,                    /* UNKNOWN Command Default */
    Unknown_cmd,                    /* GENERIC IOCTL Command   */
    Unknown_cmd,                    /* UNKNOWN Command Default */
    Unknown_cmd,                    /* UNKNOWN Command Default */
    Unknown_cmd,                    /* UNKNOWN Command Default */
    Unknown_cmd,                    /* GET Logical Device Map  */
    Unknown_cmd                     /* SET Logical Device Map  */
};
```

```
/* - - - - - - - - - - - - - - - - - - - - - - - - - - - - - - - -*/
/*                                                                 */
/*   FUNCTION:    D O S _ S e t u p                                */
/*                                                                 */
/*   REMARKS :   DOS_Setup establishes a C environment prior to    */
/*         allowing the actual device driver routines to           */
/*         execute.                                                */
/*                                                                 */
/*   INPUTS  :                                                     */
/*         which   0 : Strategy Entry; 1 : Interrupt Entry         */
/*         ES_tmp  Pointer To Request Packet                       */
/*         DS_tmp  Original DS Register Value                      */
/*         AX_tmp  Original AX Register Value                      */
/*                                                                 */
/*   OUTPUTS :   Status  Must Be Set In The Request Packet         */
/*                                                                 */
/*   NOTES   :   Register manipulations require this routine to    */
/*         be compiled with the TURBO C Compiler.                  */
/*                                                                 */
/* - - - - - - - - - - - - - - - - - - - - - - - - - - - - - - - -*/

void DOS_Setup (unsigned int which,
                unsigned int ES_tmp,
                unsigned int DS_tmp,
                unsigned int AX_tmp)
{
    _AX = _CS;                   /* Obtain Code Segment        */
    _DS = _AX;                   /* Setup Data Segment         */

    BX_reg = _BX;                /* Save BX Register           */
    CX_reg = _CX;                /* Save CX Register           */
    DX_reg = _DX;                /* Save DX Register           */

    AX_reg = AX_tmp;             /* Save AX Register           */
    ES_reg = ES_tmp;             /* Save Request Pointer       */

    driver = which;              /* Move Value From Stack      */

    SS_reg = _SS;                /* Save Stack Segment         */
    SP_reg = _SP;                /* Save Stack Pointer         */

    disable ();                  /* Disable Interrupts         */
```

```
    _AX = _DS;                  /* Obtain Data Segment        */
    _SS = _AX;                  /* Setup New Stack            */
                                /* Set Stack Ptr Value        */
    _SP = (unsigned int) &local_stk [STK_SIZE];
    enable ();                  /* Enable Interrupts          */

    if (driver)
    {                           /* Interrupt Entry Point      */
        rc = 0x0000;            /* Clear Return Code          */
                                /* DOS Request Packet Ptr     */
        r_ptr = MK_FP (ES_reg, BX_reg);
        if (r_ptr->command >= DOS_CMDS)
        {
            rc = ERROR_BIT | UNKNOWN_CMD;
        }
        else
        {
            rc |= (*dos_cmd [r_ptr->command]) (r_ptr);
        }
                                /* Set Driver Complete Bit    */
        r_ptr->status = rc | DONE_BIT;
    }
    else
    {                           /* Strategy Entry Point       */
        /* Don't Save ES:BX Because It's Passed To Interrupt!! */
    }

    disable ();                 /* Disable Interrupts         */
    _SS = SS_reg;               /* Restore Entry Stack        */
    _SP = SP_reg;               /* Restore Entry Stack Ptr    */
    enable ();                  /* Enable Interrupts          */

    _DX = DX_reg;               /* Restore DX Register        */
    _CX = CX_reg;               /* Restore CX Register        */
    _BX = BX_reg;               /* Restore BX Register        */
    _AX = AX_reg;               /* Restore AX Register        */

    _ES = ES_tmp;               /* Restore ES Register        */
    _DS = DS_tmp;               /* Restore DS Register        */
}
```

```
/* - - - - - - - - - - - - - - - - - - - - - - - - - - - - - - - -*/
/*                                                                 */
/*  FUNCTION:    S t r a t e g y                                   */
/*                                                                 */
/*  REMARKS :    Strategy is the routine that is called by the     */
/*               Operating System when this device is requested to */
/*               perform some activity (typically READs and WRITEs). */
/*                                                                 */
/*  INPUTS  :    ES:BX   Pointer To Request Packet                 */
/*                                                                 */
/*  NOTES   :    Register manipulations require this routine to    */
/*               be compiled with the TURBO C Compiler.            */
/*                                                                 */
/* - - - - - - - - - - - - - - - - - - - - - - - - - - - - - - - -*/

void far Strategy (void)
{

#ifdef  DEBUG
    geninterrupt (0x03);
#endif

    DOS_Setup (0x00, _ES, _DS, _AX);
}
```

```
/* - - - - - - - - - - - - - - - - - - - - - - - - - - - - - - -*/
/*                                                               */
/*  FUNCTION:    I n t e r r u p t                               */
/*                                                               */
/*  REMARKS :    Interrupt is the routine that is called by the  */
/*               Operating System immediately after the Strategy */
/*               routine has been called.  Interrupt is responsible */
/*               for performing the work required to accomplish the */
/*               requested operation.                            */
/*                                                               */
/*  INPUTS  :    ES:BX   Pointer To Request Packet               */
/*                                                               */
/*  OUTPUTS :    Status  Must Be Set In The Request Packet       */
/*               RETF    Must Be Used To Return From Interrupt   */
/*                                                               */
/*  NOTES   :    Register manipulations require this routine to  */
/*               be compiled with the TURBO C Compiler.          */
/*                                                               */
/* - - - - - - - - - - - - - - - - - - - - - - - - - - - - - - -*/

void far Interrupt (void)
{

#ifdef   DEBUG
    geninterrupt (0x03);
#endif

    DOS_Setup (0x01, _ES, _DS, _AX);
}
```

Here is the source listing for **dos_drvr.c**.

```
/* - - - - - - - - - - - - - - - - - - - - - - - - - - - - - -*/
/*                                                             */
/*  PROGRAM :       D O S   D e v i c e   D r i v e r          */
/*                                                             */
/*  REMARKS :       This file contains the set of command      */
/*          routines specified by the DOS Technical Reference  */
/*          Manual.                                            */
/*                                                             */
/*          The following include files are required to        */
/*          compile this file :                                */
/*          DOS_DD.H                                           */
/*          WORM.H                                             */
/*                                                             */
/* - - - - - - - - - - - - - - - - - - - - - - - - - - - - - -*/


/* - - - - - - - - - - - - - - - - - - - - - - - - - - - - - -*/
/*                                                             */
/*      DOS  Device Driver Required Includes / Constants       */
/*                                                             */
/* - - - - - - - - - - - - - - - - - - - - - - - - - - - - - -*/


#include    "dos_dd.h"          /* DOS  Command Structures     */
#include    <dos.h>             /* DOS Specific Definitions    */
#include    <string.h>          /* C String Library Prototypes */
#include    "worm.h"            /* WORM Header File            */
```

```
/* - - - - - - - - - - - - - - - - - - - - - - - - - - - - - -*/
/*                                                             */
/*  FUNCTION:    I n i t _ c m d                               */
/*                                                             */
/*  REMARKS :                                                  */
/*                                                             */
/*  INPUTS  :   r_ptr    Pointer To Request Packet             */
/*                                                             */
/*  OUTPUTS :   Status  Returned In Function Return Value      */
/*                                                             */
/* - - - - - - - - - - - - - - - - - - - - - - - - - - - - - -*/

unsigned int Init_cmd (struct REQ_struct far *r_ptr)
{
    r_ptr->req_type.init_req.num_of_units = 1;

    bpb_ary [0] = (unsigned int) &bpb;
    r_ptr->req_type.init_req.BPB_ptr =
                        MK_FP (_DS, (unsigned int) bpb_ary);

    r_ptr->req_type.init_req.end_ptr =
                        MK_FP (_DS, (unsigned int) End_code);

    Disk_BIOS (GET_PARAMS, 0x00, 0x00, 0x00, 0x00, 0x00,
               &disk_info);

    return OP_COMPLETE;
}
```

```
/* - - - - - - - - - - - - - - - - - - - - - - - - - - - - - -*/
/*                                                             */
/*  FUNCTION:    M e d i a _ c h e c k _ c m d                 */
/*                                                             */
/*  REMARKS :                                                  */
/*                                                             */
/*  INPUTS   :   r_ptr    Pointer To Request Packet            */
/*                                                             */
/*  OUTPUTS  :   Status   Returned In Function Return Value    */
/*                                                             */
/* - - - - - - - - - - - - - - - - - - - - - - - - - - - - - -*/

unsigned int Media_check_cmd (struct REQ_struct far *r_ptr)
{
    unsigned int    rc;

    rc = Send_command (MK_FP (0x0000, 0x0000), 0, 0, READ_SENSE);

    if (rc != STATUS_NO_ERROR)
    {
        rc = (STATUS_ERROR | UNKNOWN_MEDIA);
        r_ptr->req_type.media_check_req.return_info =
                                            UNSURE_MEDIA;
    }
    else
    {
        rc = STATUS_NO_ERROR;
        r_ptr->req_type.media_check_req.return_info =
                                            MEDIA_UNCHANGED;
    }
    r_ptr->req_type.media_check_req.return_ptr = "NO NAME ";

    return rc;
}
```

```
/* - - - - - - - - - - - - - - - - - - - - - - - - - - - - -*/
/*                                                          */
/*  FUNCTION:    B u i l d _ b p b _ c m d                  */
/*                                                          */
/*  REMARKS :                                               */
/*                                                          */
/*  INPUTS  :    r_ptr    Pointer To Request Packet         */
/*                                                          */
/*  OUTPUTS :    Status  Returned In Function Return Value  */
/*                                                          */
/* - - - - - - - - - - - - - - - - - - - - - - - - - - - -*/

unsigned int Build_bpb_cmd (struct REQ_struct far *r_ptr)
{
    r_ptr->req_type.build_bpb_req.BPB_table = &bpb;

    return OP_COMPLETE;
}
```

```
/* - - - - - - - - - - - - - - - - - - - - - - - - - - - - - - - - - -*/
/*                                                                     */
/*  FUNCTION:    I n p u t _ c m d                                     */
/*                                                                     */
/*  REMARKS :                                                          */
/*                                                                     */
/*  INPUTS  :   r_ptr    Pointer To Request Packet                     */
/*                                                                     */
/*  OUTPUTS :   Status  Returned In Function Return Value              */
/*                                                                     */
/* - - - - - - - - - - - - - - - - - - - - - - - - - - - - - - - - - -*/

unsigned int Input_cmd (struct REQ_struct far *r_ptr)
{
    unsigned int    i;
    unsigned int    rc;
    unsigned int    cnt;
    unsigned long   sec;

    cnt = r_ptr->req_type.i_o_req.count;
    if (cnt > 127)                          /* > 64 Kbytes        */
    {
        r_ptr->req_type.i_o_req.count = 127;
        cnt = 127;
    }

    sec = r_ptr->req_type.i_o_req.start_sector + bpb.hidden;

    if ((sec > bpb.num_sectors) ||
        ((sec + cnt) > bpb.num_sectors))
    {
        r_ptr->req_type.i_o_req.count = 0x0000;
        return (STATUS_SNF);
    }

    for (i = 0, rc = 0; i < cnt; i++, sec++)
    {
        rc |= Send_command (r_ptr->req_type.i_o_req.buffer_ptr,
                Which_sector (sec), 1, READ_3363);
    }

    if (rc != STATUS_NO_ERROR)
```

```
    {
        rc = Xlate_error (rc);
        r_ptr->req_type.i_o_req.count = 0x0000;
    }

    return rc;
}
```

```
/* - - - - - - - - - - - - - - - - - - - - - - - - - - - - - - - - -*/
/*                                                                   */
/*  FUNCTION:    O u t p u t _ c m d                                 */
/*                                                                   */
/*  REMARKS :                                                        */
/*                                                                   */
/*  INPUTS  :   r_ptr    Pointer To Request Packet                   */
/*                                                                   */
/*  OUTPUTS :   Status  Returned In Function Return Value            */
/*                                                                   */
/* - - - - - - - - - - - - - - - - - - - - - - - - - - - - - - - - -*/

unsigned int Output_cmd (struct REQ_struct far *r_ptr)
{
    unsigned int    i;
    unsigned int    rc;
    unsigned int    cnt;
    unsigned long   sec;

    cnt = r_ptr->req_type.i_o_req.count;
    if (cnt > 127)                              /* > 64 Kbytes       */
    {
        r_ptr->req_type.i_o_req.count = 127;
        cnt = 127;
    }

    sec = r_ptr->req_type.i_o_req.start_sector + bpb.hidden;

    if ((sec > bpb.num_sectors) ||
        ((sec + cnt) > bpb.num_sectors))
    {
        r_ptr->req_type.i_o_req.count = 0x0000;
        return (STATUS_SNF);
    }

    for (i = 0, rc = 0; i < cnt; i++, sec++)
    {
        rc |= Send_command (r_ptr->req_type.i_o_req.buffer_ptr,
                Check_sector (sec), 1, WRITE_3363);
    }

    if (rc != STATUS_NO_ERROR)
```

```
    {
        rc = Xlate_error (rc);
        r_ptr->req_type.i_o_req.count = 0x0000;
    }

    return rc;
}




/* - - - - - - - - - - - - - - - - - - - - - - - - - - - - - -*/
/*                                                             */
/*  FUNCTION:   U n k n o w n _ c m d                          */
/*                                                             */
/*  REMARKS :                                                  */
/*                                                             */
/*  INPUTS :   r_ptr    Pointer To Request Packet              */
/*                                                             */
/*  OUTPUTS :   Status  Returned In Function Return Value      */
/*                                                             */
/* - - - - - - - - - - - - - - - - - - - - - - - - - - - - - -*/

unsigned int Unknown_cmd (struct REQ_struct far *r_ptr)
{
    return UNKNOWN_CMD;
}
```

```
/* - - - - - - - - - - - - - - - - - - - - - - - - - - - - - - -*/
/*                                                               */
/*  FUNCTION:   S e n d _ c o m m a n d                          */
/*                                                               */
/*  REMARKS :   Send_command initiates the command specified     */
/*          by the input parameters through the IBM 3363         */
/*          adapter BIOS.                                        */
/*                                                               */
/*  INPUTS  :   b_ptr   Pointer To The Buffer                    */
/*              sec     The Specified Sector Number              */
/*              cnt     The Number Of Sectors To Transfer        */
/*              cmd     The Specified Command                    */
/*                                                               */
/*  OUTPUTS :   Status  Returned In Function Return Value        */
/*                                                               */
/* - - - - - - - - - - - - - - - - - - - - - - - - - - - - - - -*/

unsigned int    Send_command (unsigned char far *b_ptr,
                              unsigned long sec,
                              unsigned int  cnt,
                              unsigned char cmd)
{
    unsigned int    trk;           /* Track Number              */
    unsigned int    far *i_ptr;    /* Far Pointer To Integer    */
    void    (far *bios_ptr) (void); /* 3363 BIOS Entry Pointer  */

    i_ptr = MK_FP (0x0040, 0x00B0);
    reg_bx = *i_ptr++;
    reg_es = *i_ptr;
    bios_ptr = MK_FP (reg_es, reg_bx);

    reg_ah = cmd;                   /* CDB Command               */
    reg_dl = DEVICE_ID;             /* Initialize ID In CDB      */
    trk = (sec / SEC_PER_TRK);      /* Track Number              */
    reg_cx = trk;
    reg_dh = (unsigned char) (sec % SEC_PER_TRK);
    reg_al = cnt;                   /* Number Of Blocks          */

    reg_es = FP_SEG (b_ptr);
    reg_bx = FP_OFF (b_ptr);

    _ES = reg_es;
```

```
        _BX = reg_bx;
        _CX = reg_cx;
        _DH = reg_dh;
        _DL = reg_dl;
        _AH = reg_ah;
        _AL = reg_al;

        bios_ptr ();

        reg_ah = _AH;
        reg_al = _AL;
        reg_dh = _DH;
        reg_dl = _DL;
        reg_cx = _CX;
        reg_bx = _BX;

        return reg_ah;
}
```

```
/* - - - - - - - - - - - - - - - - - - - - - - - - - - - - - -*/
/*                                                             */
/*  FUNCTION:    W h i c h _ s e c t o r                       */
/*                                                             */
/*  REMARKS :    Which_sector reads the diskette drive and     */
/*               returns the actual sector number required for the */
/*               IBM 3363 operation.                           */
/*                                                             */
/*  INPUTS  :    sec     The Logical Sector Number Requested   */
/*                                                             */
/*  OUTPUTS :    sec     The Actual Sector Number Required     */
/*                                                             */
/* - - - - - - - - - - - - - - - - - - - - - - - - - - - - - -*/

unsigned long Which_sector (unsigned long sec)
{
    unsigned int    cyl;
    unsigned int    head;
    unsigned int    sector;
    unsigned int    mag_sec;
    unsigned int    mag_byte;

    mag_sec = (FP_OFF (sec) >> 7) + 1;
    mag_byte = (FP_OFF (sec) && 0x7F) << 2;

    cyl = ((mag_sec / disk_info.max_secs) / disk_info.max_heads);
    head = ((mag_sec / disk_info.max_secs) %
            disk_info.max_heads);
    sector = ((mag_sec % disk_info.max_secs) + 1);

    Disk_BIOS (READ_DISK, 0x00, head, cyl, sector, 1, mag_buf);

    return *((unsigned long *)(&mag_buf [mag_byte]));
}
```

```
/* - - - - - - - - - - - - - - - - - - - - - - - - - - - - - - - - -*/
/*                                                                   */
/*  FUNCTION:    C h e c k _ s e c t o r                             */
/*                                                                   */
/*  REMARKS :    Check_sector checks whether the specified           */
/*            sector has already been written to.                    */
/*            If so, it allocates a new sector and returns it.       */
/*            Otherwise, it returns the specified sector number.     */
/*                                                                   */
/*  INPUTS  :    sec      The Logical Sector Number Requested        */
/*                                                                   */
/*  OUTPUTS :    sec      The Actual Sector Number Required          */
/*                                                                   */
/* - - - - - - - - - - - - - - - - - - - - - - - - - - - - - - - - -*/

unsigned long Check_sector (unsigned long sec)
{
    unsigned long    i;
    unsigned char    found;
    unsigned int     cyl;
    unsigned int     head;
    unsigned int     sector;
    unsigned long    actual;
    unsigned int     mag_sec;
    unsigned int     mag_byte;

    actual = Which_sector (sec);

    Send_command (MK_FP (0, 0), actual, 1, READ_SCAN);
    if (!((reg_ah == 0x0B) && ((reg_cx & 0xFF) == 0)))
    {
        for (i = actual, found = 0;
            ((i < MAX_SECTORS) && (!found));
            i += 128)
        {
            Send_command (MK_FP (0, 0), actual, 128, READ_SCAN);
            if (reg_ah == 0x0B)
            {
                found++;
                actual = (actual + (reg_cx & 0xFF));
            }
        }
```

```
        mag_sec = (FP_OFF (actual) >> 7) + 1;
        mag_byte = (FP_OFF (actual) && 0x7F) << 2;

        cyl = ((mag_sec / disk_info.max_secs) /
                                      disk_info.max_heads);
        head = ((mag_sec / disk_info.max_secs) %
                                      disk_info.max_heads);
        sector = ((mag_sec % disk_info.max_secs) + 1);

        Disk_BIOS (READ_DISK, 0x00, head, cyl, sector, 1,
                   mag_buf);
        *((unsigned long *) (&mag_buf [mag_byte])) = actual;
        Disk_BIOS (WRITE_DISK, 0x00, head, cyl, sector, 1,
                   mag_buf);
    }

    return actual;
}
```

```
/* - - - - - - - - - - - - - - - - - - - - - - - - - - - - - - -*/
/*                                                                */
/*  FUNCTION:    X l a t e _ e r r o r                            */
/*                                                                */
/*  REMARKS :                                                     */
/*                                                                */
/*  INPUTS  :    r_ptr    Pointer To Request Packet               */
/*               u_ptr    Pointer To Units Array Element          */
/*               a_ptr    Pointer To Adapters Array Element        */
/*               d_ptr    Pointer To DevHlp Entry Point           */
/*                                                                */
/*  OUTPUTS :    Status   Returned In Function Return Value       */
/*                                                                */
/* - - - - - - - - - - - - - - - - - - - - - - - - - - - - - - -*/

unsigned int Xlate_error (unsigned int error_num)
{
    switch (error_num)
    {
        case IBM_SUCCESS :
            return STATUS_NO_ERROR;

        case IBM_ADAPTER_BSY :
            return STATUS_BUSY;

        case IBM_INVALID_CNT :
        case IBM_INVALID_SEC :
        case IBM_INVALID_TRK :
        case IBM_INVALID_DRV :
        case IBM_TRK_OVERFLW :
            return STATUS_SNF;

        case IBM_INVALID_CMD :
            return STATUS_BAD_CMD;

        case IBM_INT_TIMEOUT :
            return STATUS_NOT_READY;

        case IBM_CMD_FAILED :
        case IBM_SENSE_FAIL :
        case IBM_DMA_CROSSED :
            return STATUS_GENERAL;
```

```
        default:
            return STATUS_GENERAL;
    }
}
```

```
/* - - - - - - - - - - - - - - - - - - - - - - - - - - - - - - - -*/
/*                                                                 */
/*  FUNCTION:    D i s k _ B I O S                                 */
/*                                                                 */
/*  REMARKS:    Disk_BIOS allows the C function to directly        */
/*          call the disk BIOS (INT 0x13) that exists in ROM.      */
/*                                                                 */
/*  INPUTS  :    cmd          Disk Command                         */
/*               drive        Disk Driver Number                   */
/*               head         Disk Head Number                     */
/*               track        Disk Track Number                    */
/*               sector       Disk Sector                          */
/*               count        Number Of Sectors                    */
/*               b_ptr        Buffer Pointer                       */
/*                                                                 */
/*  OUTPUTS :    status       Return Status Defined As Follows     */
/*                            0x00 Operation Successful            */
/*                            0x01 Bad Command                     */
/*                            0x02 Address Mark Not Found          */
/*                            0x04 Record Not Found                */
/*                            0x05 Reset Failed                    */
/*                            0x07 Driver Parameter Activity Fail  */
/*                            0x09 Attempt DMA Across 64Kb         */
/*                            0x0B Bad Track Flag Detected         */
/*                            0x10 Bad ECC On Disk Read            */
/*                            0x11 ECC Corrected Data Error        */
/*                            0x20 Controller has Failed           */
/*                            0x40 Seek Operation Failed           */
/*                            0x80 Attachment Failed To Respond    */
/*                            0xBB Undefined Error Occurred        */
/*                            0xFF Sense Operation Failed          */
/*                                                                 */
/* - - - - - - - - - - - - - - - - - - - - - - - - - - - - - - - -*/

unsigned int Disk_BIOS (unsigned int    cmd,
                        unsigned int    drive,
                        unsigned int    head,
                        unsigned int    track,
                        unsigned int    sector,
                        unsigned int    count,
                        void            far *b_ptr)
   {
```

```
    unsigned int    rc;
    unsigned char   CL_reg;
    unsigned char   CH_reg;
    unsigned char   DL_reg;
    unsigned char   DH_reg;
    unsigned char   far *c_ptr;

    if (cmd != 0x08)
    {
        sector = ((sector & 0x003F) | ((track & 0x0300) >> 2));
        track = (track & 0x00FF);
        _AX = FP_SEG (b_ptr);
        _ES = _AX;
        _BX = FP_OFF (b_ptr);
        _DL = drive;
        _DH = head;
        _CL = sector;
        _CH = track;
        _AL = count;
        _AH = cmd;
        geninterrupt (0x13);
        rc = _AX;
    }
    else
    {
        _DL = drive;
        _AH = cmd;
        geninterrupt (0x13);
        rc = _AX;
        DL_reg = _DL;
        DH_reg = _DH;
        CL_reg = _CL;
        CH_reg = _CH;
        c_ptr = b_ptr;
        *c_ptr++ = DL_reg;
        *c_ptr++ = DH_reg;
        *c_ptr++ = CL_reg;
        *c_ptr = CH_reg;
    }
    return rc >> 8;
}
```

Here is the source listing for worm.h.

```
/* - - - - - - - - - - - - - - - - - - - - - - - - - - - - - - -*/
/*                                                              */
/*  PROGRAM :  W O R M   D D   H e a d e r                      */
/*                                                              */
/*  REMARKS :   This file contains the structures and manifests */
/*          required by a DOS Device Driver.                    */
/*                                                              */
/* - - - - - - - - - - - - - - - - - - - - - - - - - - - - - - -*/

extern  void    far Strategy ();        /* Strategy Routine      */
extern  void    far Interrupt ();       /* Interrupt Routine     */

extern  void    End_code ();
extern  struct  BPB_struct  bpb;
extern  struct  BPB_struct  *bpb_ary [DEVICES];

extern  unsigned char    reg_ah; /* AH Register - Command        */
extern  unsigned char    reg_al; /* AL Register - Block Count     */
extern  unsigned char    reg_dh; /* DH Register - Sector Number   */
extern  unsigned char    reg_dl; /* DL Register - Drive Number    */

extern  unsigned int     reg_cx; /* CX Register - Track Number    */
extern  unsigned int     reg_es; /* ES Register - Buffer Segment  */
extern  unsigned int     reg_bx; /* BX Register - Buffer Offset   */

extern  unsigned char    mag_buf [512];   /* Temp. Sector Buffer  */
extern  struct  INFO_struct disk_info;  /* Disk Params Struct     */
```

```
/* - - - - - - - - - - - - - - - - - - - - - - - - - - - - -*/
/*                                                            */
/*      IBM 3363 Device Driver Support Function Prototypes    */
/*                                                            */
/* - - - - - - - - - - - - - - - - - - - - - - - - - - - - -*/

extern  unsigned long    Which_sector (unsigned long sec);
extern  unsigned long    Check_sector (unsigned long sec);
extern  unsigned int     Xlate_error  (unsigned int  error_num);

extern  unsigned int     Send_command (unsigned char far *b_ptr,
                                       unsigned long sec,
                                       unsigned int  cnt,
                                       unsigned char cmd);

extern  unsigned int     Disk_BIOS (unsigned int   cmd,
                                    unsigned int   drive,
                                    unsigned int   head,
                                    unsigned int   track,
                                    unsigned int   sector,
                                    unsigned int   count,
                                    void           far *b_ptr);
```

```
/* - - - - - - - - - - - - - - - - - - - - - - - - - - - - - - - -*/
/*                                                                 */
/*        Disk Parameter Information Structure                     */
/*                                                                 */
/* - - - - - - - - - - - - - - - - - - - - - - - - - - - - - - - -*/

struct  INFO_struct
{
    unsigned char    num_drives;
    unsigned char    max_heads;
    unsigned char    max_secs;
    unsigned char    max_tracks;
};


/* - - - - - - - - - - - - - - - - - - - - - - - - - - - - - - - -*/
/*                                                                 */
/*        Request Packet Return Status Definitions                */
/*                                                                 */
/* - - - - - - - - - - - - - - - - - - - - - - - - - - - - - - - -*/

#define        STATUS_DONE          DONE_BIT
#define        STATUS_BUSY          BUSY_BIT
#define        STATUS_NO_ERROR      OP_COMPLETE
#define        STATUS_ERROR         ERROR_BIT
#define        STATUS_W_PROT        (STATUS_ERROR | WRITE_PROTECT)
#define        STATUS_BAD_UNIT      (STATUS_ERROR | UNKNOWN_UNIT)
#define        STATUS_NOT_READY     (STATUS_ERROR | NOT_READY)
#define        STATUS_BAD_CMD       (STATUS_ERROR | UNKNOWN_CMD)
#define        STATUS_DATA          (STATUS_ERROR | CRC_ERROR)
#define        STATUS_SNF           (STATUS_ERROR | NOT_FOUND)
#define        STATUS_GENERAL       (STATUS_ERROR | GENERAL_FAIL)
#define        STATUS_UNCERTAIN     (STATUS_ERROR | UNCERTAIN)

#define        RESET_3363      0x20    /* 3363 Selective Reset    */
#define        READ_SENSE      0x21    /* 3363 Read Sense Command */
#define        READ_VERIFY     0x23    /* 3363 Read Verify Command */
#define        READ_3363       0x29    /* 3363 Read Block Command */
#define        WRITE_3363      0x32    /* 3363 Write Block Command */
#define        READ_SCAN       0x42    /* 3363 Read Scan Command  */

#define        MAX_SECTORS 393300L     /* Maximum # Of Sectors    */
#define        BLOCK_SIZE      512     /* Number Of Bytes/Block   */
```

```
#define      SEC_PER_TRK      23         /* Sectors Per Track         */

#define      DEVICE_ID        0x00       /* Logical Unit Of WORM      */
#define      READ_DISK        0x02       /* Read Disk Command         */
#define      WRITE_DISK       0x03       /* Write Disk Command        */
#define      GET_PARAMS       0x08       /* Get Disk Parameters Cmd   */
#define      UNSURE_MEDIA     0x00       /* Unsure About Media        */
#define      MEDIA_UNCHANGED  0x01       /* Sure About Media          */

#define      IBM_SUCCESS      0x00       /* Successful Command        */
#define      IBM_INVALID_CMD  0x01       /* Invalid Command           */
#define      IBM_INVALID_DRV  0x02       /* Invalid Drive             */
#define      IBM_INVALID_TRK  0x03       /* Invalid Track             */
#define      IBM_INVALID_SEC  0x04       /* Invalid Sector            */
#define      IBM_INVALID_CNT  0x05       /* Invalid Block Count       */
#define      IBM_ADAPTER_BSY  0x07       /* Adapter Busy              */
#define      IBM_INT_TIMEOUT  0x08       /* Interrupt Timeout         */
#define      IBM_DMA_CROSSED  0x09       /* DMA Crosses 64K Boundary  */
#define      IBM_SENSE_FAIL   0x0A       /* Sense Failed              */
#define      IBM_CMD_FAILED   0x0B       /* Command Failed            */
#define      IBM_TRK_OVERFLW  0x0C       /* Maximum Track Overflow    */
```

Index